TO ANSWER
DUTY'S CALL

Remembering the Old Crosbeians who fell
in World War I

TREVOR W. HILDREY

First published in Great Britain in 2015 by Osprey Publishing,
PO Box 883, Oxford, OX1 9PL, UK
PO Box 3985, New York, NY 10185-3985, USA
E-mail: info@ospreypublishing.com

Osprey Publishing, part of Bloomsbury Publishing Plc

A CIP catalogue record for this book is available from the British Library

Trevor W. Hildrey has asserted his right under the Copyright, Designs and Patents Act, 1988, to be identified as the Author of this Work.

Image acknowledgements
Edgar Golding image, p.80: By Courtesy of the University of Liverpool Library: Faculty of Veterinary Science – S2957/7.

ISBN: 978 1 78442 128 1
Epub ISBN: 978 1 78442 129 8
PDF ISBN: 978 1 78442 130 4

Editor Ruth Sheppard
Index by Zoe Ross
Typeset in Adobe Garamond Pro
Design and Layout by Stewart Larking
Originated by PDQ media, Bungay, UK
Printed in China through Worldprint Ltd

15 16 17 18 19   10 9 8 7 6 5 4 3 2 1

Osprey Publishing supports the Woodland Trust, the UK's leading woodland conservation charity. Between 2014 and 2018 our donations will be spent on their Centenary Woods project in the UK.

www.ospreypublishing.com

CONTENTS

FOREWORD

It is a great honour for me to write the foreword to this book. As an historian, I have visited the battlefields of World War I on many occasions, and with hundreds of schoolchildren. Place names such as Ypres or 'Wipers', Loos, the Somme and Messines Ridge have entered British military history, and evoke memories and images of human tragedy on a massive scale. The names of the villages and towns of Belgium and northern France have been stitched onto the regimental colours of every unit of the British and Commonwealth armies as battle honours; they are also carved on countless war memorials across the UK, and are to be found in the history books, diaries, letters home and memoirs of individuals, businesses and schools.

A visit to the imposing Lutyens Memorial at Thiepval, Northern France, dedicated to the missing of the Somme, those with no known resting place, shows the scale of the loss on just one part of the Western Front. Carved into the white stone are some 72,195 names. What are we to make of such casualty figures? The name of at least one Old Crosbeian is found on the walls at Thiepval: Second Lieutenant Francis Zacharias, from 3rd Battalion South Wales Borderers. His story is found in this book along with all his fellow school mates who did not return from the war.

To commemorate the centenary of the start of World War I, in 2014 the Master of Wellington College, Dr Anthony Seldon, co-wrote a book called *The Generation Lost, Public Schools and The Great War*. The book laid bare the contribution and sacrifice of public schools during World War I. Merchant Taylors' Crosby sent some 731 young men to war, and 155 never returned – a death rate of some 21.2 per cent and one of the highest mortality rates of any school in the war. The names of these 155 Old Crosbeians are found in this book, as are their stories. These accounts give us a moving and powerful insight into their lives, and help us personalise the loss of each individual, when casualty figures are usually expressed in the thousands.

The title of this book, *To Answer Duty's Call*, is taken from the school song, still much loved by current generations of Old Boys. It speaks of a bygone age where duty and honour were ideals to be lived out and celebrated. Perhaps one century later, these values have been too much neglected and the current generations should strive to emulate and articulate these ideals, so beloved by our forebears.

I am extremely grateful for the care and attention that Mr Trevor Hildrey, our school archivist and author of this book, has lavished on this publication and I trust it goes some way to honour the contibution and sacrifice of the 155, and of their loved ones.

Mr D. H. Cook
Headmaster
Merchant Taylors' Boys' School
April 2015

INTRODUCTION

The title of this volume should be familiar to all present and past pupils, staff and parents. To those to whom it is not familiar, it is a line from the second verse of the school song.

All the boys whose biographies are included here will have sung this song on speech days, at concerts and other gatherings.

Some of these biographies are quite short, as indeed were the lives they represent.

It is hoped that this volume will allow us to see more than just a list of names when we look at the war memorial in the school library; it is hoped that it will allow us to see the people behind the names. The biographies are, of necessity, factual in tone. It is difficult, 100 years after their deaths, to ascribe too much in the way of characteristics to the Old Boys. Were they cheerful, arrogant, cooperative? Who knows? Even those who knew them are long dead.

Some statistics should be pointed out. The youngest OC to die was 18 years old, the oldest 45. The average age of those who did not return was 26.

Several families lost two sons in the war: the Bings, Brodbelts, Fairbairns (on the same day), Le Rougetels, Millers, Radfords, Rowatts, Sheards, Stockdales, Singlehursts, Teagues, Watts and families like the Beardwoods who lost one son from Merchant Taylors' and one from elsewhere.

It is hoped that some semblance of their lives may be gleaned from these pages. For as George Eliot asserts in *Adam Bede*:

'Our dead are never dead to us until we have forgotten them'

Let us remember them.

T. W. Hildrey
January 2015

ACKNOWLEDGEMENTS

The help and cooperation of the following is acknowledged:

Dix, Noonan & Webb (DNW) Ltd – for permission to use the photograph of Charles Norman Innes Dunman.

Ellesmere College – for supplying the photograph of Rodney Richard Johnson.

Northeast Medals – for permission to use images of cap badges from their website.

Preston Historical Society – for permission to use the photograph of Croston almshouses. In particular, Beth Hayes who took the original photograph.

Liverpool Record Office, Liverpool Libraries for permission to use images from *Liverpool's Scroll of Fame.*

Reverend Janet Roberts, vicar of St Nicholas's church, Blundellsands, and Carol Tarr for permission to use the photograph of Harry Kinder Liversidge which appeared on St Nicholas's website.

Debbie Bridges for permission to use the photograph of the Hamm family.

Jane Gage for permission to use the image of Eric Coulthard Hughes.

Alma Semotiuk for permission to use the images of William Somerville Limrick and his family.

Britishbattles.com for permission to use the image of the officers of HMS *Good Hope.*

Liverpool University for permission to use the image of Edgar Golding.

In addition to the above, I would extend my thanks to the Headmaster, David Cook, who quickly and enthusiastically accepted the possibilities of this project when it was originally suggested to him and to David Blower who read and corrected the proofs.

I would particularly like to acknowledge the help of Ruth Sheppard in the editing of the material. Her knowledge and eye for detail have contributed enormously to the removal of errors and irrelevancies and any that remain are entirely down to me.

To my wife, Val, go my thanks for taking the time to carry out an initial proof-reading of the manuscript and for tolerating the monologues in which I tend to indulge.

GRAVE REFERENCES

Each of these biographies ends with a reference to the burial place of, or the memorial to, the Old Crosbeian concerned where these are known.

The grave references are those given by the Commonwealth War Graves Commission (CWGC) and include the name of the burial site which, in the case of CWGC cemeteries, is then divided into a plot, a row and a grave. These are detailed on the CWGC website, each cemetery being accompanied by a plan.

Those whose remains were never found were recorded on memorials such as the one at Thiepval, which records over 72,000 names of those who died on the Somme and have no known grave. The names on this memorial are listed as being recorded on a pier and face. The memorial has 16 piers (numbered 1–16) and each of these has 4 faces (lettered A–D). A soldier commemorated in pier and face 13A is obviously recorded on pier 13, face A. A soldier may be commemorated on more than one pier and face.

The memorials at Ypres etc, however, have reference only to panels.

OXFORD LOCAL AND SENIOR EXAMS

These exams were the GCSEs and A levels of their day (the end of the 19th and the beginning of the 20th century). The two main levels were Oxford Local Junior exams and Oxford Local Senior exams. Students taking either of these had first to take a preliminary exam. This last was intended for pupils under 14 years of age, the junior exam for those under 15 and at the time when these pupils were at school there was no age limit on the senior. The results would be expressed as a 1st Class, 2nd Class or 3rd Class.

THE 6TH BATTALION KING'S (LIVERPOOL REGIMENT) IN WORLD WAR I

TO THE GLORY OF GOD – AND IN MEMORY OF THE OFFICERS N·C·Oᶲ & MEN OF THE 1/6 & 2/6 RIFLE B ᴵᵀᴺˢ THE KINGS LIVERPOOL REGᵀ WHO SERVED AND FELL IN THE YPRES SALIENT·MAR·JULY 1915·OCT 1916·DEC 1917

When the school's cadet corps was officially recognised by the West Lancashire Association (Territorial Force) on 30 March 1915 its affiliation to the 6th (Rifle) Battalion King's (Liverpool Regiment) was also approved.

Of the 731 Old Crosbeians who served in World War I no fewer than 63 are recorded as joining the 6th Battalion King's (Liverpool Regiment). This must, surely, allow it to be viewed as the 'school's battalion'.

The 6th Battalion can trace its origins back to 1859, when it was set up as a rifle volunteer corps. Following the Childers Reforms of 1881 it became known as the 2nd Volunteer Battalion King's Regiment and as such fought in the Boer War. Further reforms by Lord Haldane in 1908 converted the Volunteer Force into the Territorial Force at which time it changed its name to the 6th Battalion (Rifles) King's Regiment (Liverpool).

On the outbreak of war in 1914, the 6th was based at Princes Park Barracks and it was here that it mobilised. Eventually, three battalions were formed: 1/6th, the first-line battalion which went to France in 1915, 2/6th, the second-line battalion which went overseas in 1917 and 3/6th which was home based and supplied reinforcements for the 1/6th and 2/6th.

Following training in Canterbury, the 1/6th sailed to Le Havre in February 1915 where they joined 15th Brigade, 5th Division with whom they fought at Ypres in April 1915. The following month they took part in the attack on Hill 60 (p.21) where they suffered severe casualties.

At the beginning of 1916, they transferred to 165th Brigade, 55th (West Lancashire) Division and participated in most of the major battles of the Western Front:

1916 Battle of the Somme
1917 Third battle of Ypres (Passchendaele)
    Battle of Cambrai
1918 Battle of Lys
    German retreat

The 2/6th joined the 57th Division in 1915 and went to Aldershot in July 1916, sailing to France on 14 February 1917. They participated in:

1917 Battle of Passchendaele
1918 Battle of Arras
    Battle of the Hindenburg Line

HILL 60
5 MAY 1915

Hill 60 does not really deserve the name 'Hill'. In reality it is no more than a mound of spoil which was produced when French workers excavated a cutting for the Ypres–Comines railway in the mid-19th century. Named by the army after its height above sea level (60m) it was a mere 50m above the surrounding area which, nonetheless, made it a useful observation point for artillery spotters and which, consequently, meant it was repeatedly fought over by both sides in the war.

Initially captured by the Germans in December 1914 it was retrieved by the British on 17 April 1915, taken back by the Germans on 18 April and regained by the British later that day. In early May, the Germans counter-attacked and retook the Hill. The reoccupation followed a series of attacks between 1 May and 5 May.

On 5 May 1915 the 6th Battalion took part in its first major action. The men from the battalion were ordered to march off at 10.15 a.m., their destination, 15th Brigade Headquarters. On arrival the companies were then ordered to various places. C Company was sent to Zillebeke village from which it was to attack the enemy trenches. By late afternoon, no communication having been received from C Company, patrols from D Company moved out to discover what had happened to them.

C Company was in the thick of the fighting and suffered 60 casualties over the period 5–6 May, 15 of whom were killed in action. The 6th Battalion as a whole suffered almost 100 casualties, 22 being killed. Four of the 22 were Old Crosbeians: Allan Stanley Haynes, Thomas Every Teague and the two Fairbairn brothers, Arthur and William, killed on the same day in the same attack. Not only did the two Fairbairns die within minutes of each other, they had enlisted at the same time as well; Arthur was given the number 1329 and William 1330.

In the July 1915 issue of the school magazine there are detailed accounts of the exploits of 6th Battalion at Hill 60 by four Old Boys who were present. These contributors are not identified by name, only by numbers: 2, 5, 6 and 7. No 5 commented:

... then the order came 'Get ready to double', down went all impediments, great coats, valise and haversack (I have lost everything). We started to double up a turnip field for about ten yards, then the Germans started with machine guns and rifle fire – the boys fell – it was just murder – no use getting up to run, the machine gun was too ready – we had to go on, no stopping to look after the wounded ...

While No 6 reported:

My old Company lost captain and one lieutenant killed and the other lieutenant wounded, Sergeants Royle and Milton wounded, two Fairbairns and Tommy Teague killed, Ridge, Geo Batcheldor, Eastwood, Hutchinson, Lindsay, Taylor, Miller, Whinyates, Le Rougetel [all Old Boys of the school] and heaps of others wounded.

Hill 60.

TIMELINE

1914

4 August	Great Britain declares war on Germany
7 August	British Expeditionary Force arrives in France
23 August	Battle of Mons begins
10 September	**Liversidge, Harry Kinder**
23 September	**Kyrke-Smith, Arthur**
18 October	First battle of Ypres begins
29 October	Turkey enters the war
1 November	Battle of Coronel
1 November	**Dowding, Geoffrey Marischal**
8 December	Battle of the Falklands

1915

17 January	**Clark, Harold Wolfenden**
28 February	**Teague, Basil Every**
1 March	**Vaughan, Alfred Francis Campbell**
22 April	Second battle of Ypres begins
23 March	**Chappell, Colin**
25 April	Allied troops land in Gallipoli
5 May	Attack on Hill 60
5 May	**Fairbairn, Arthur West**
	Fairbairn, William Ritchie
	Haynes, Allan Stanley

5 May	**Teague, Thomas Every**
10 May	**Acton, Reginald**
12 May	**Radford, Amyas Leigh**
15 May	Battle of Festubert begins
17 May	**Millington, Herbert Hugh**
27 May	**Dean, Josiah Stanley**
16 June	Battle of Hooge
16 June	**Banister, Charles Wilfred**
	Hawksley-Hill, Geoffrey
	Speers, John Gregg
7 July	**Pearson, Frederick Phillips**
10 August	**Williams, John Heber**
25 September	Battle of Loos begins
25/26 September	**Collinson, Arthur Amery**
	Milner, Lawrence Frank
	Watts, Thomas William
30 September	**Harris, Phillip**
10 October	**Barnes, George**
14 October	**Grant, George Campbell**
27 December	**Carson, Thomas Wright**

1916

27 January	Conscription introduced
4 February	**Whitehead, William Frederick**
5 April	**Wakeford, Harold**
9 April	**Daniels, Thomas Harold Rayner**
14 April	**Brodbelt, Guy**
23 April	**Bousfield, Eustace**
29 April	British forces surrendered to Turks at Kut
30 April	**Singlehurst, Robert Bruce**
31 May	Battle of Jutland begins
10 June	**Fox, Donald Pearson**
18 June	**Dykes, Tom Gray**
28 June	**Stephenson, Arthur Theodore**
1 July	Battle of the Somme begins
1 July	**Allen, Sydney Raymond**
	Brockbank, Charles Norman
	Kelsall, Alfred Joseph
	Rowatt, David

3 July	**Grieve, Allan Edward**
	Hivey, Charles Henry
4 July	**Miller, Wilfrid Heard**
16 July	**Cooban, Adrian Deighton**
30 July	Attack on Guillemont
30 July	**Rowatt, Edmund**
	Standring, William Shuttleworth
	Turner, Richard
	Vaughan, John
7 August	**McDiarmid, David**
10 August	**Harding, Norman Ernest Jasper**
12 August	**Hughes, Eric Coulthard**
13 August	**Ferguson, Charles Henry**
15 August	**Irwin, Innes Elden**
18 August	**White, Bernard**
21 August	**Baines, Francis Slater**
4 September	**Bice, William Francis**
8 September	**May, Adrian Robson**
10 September	**Kemp, Charles Kenneth Nuthall**
12 September	**Hedley, Joseph Walton**
15 September	Battle of Flers-Courcelette begins
15 September	**Grensted, Alfred**
	Roberts, Arthur
16 September	**Le Rougetel, Bertram**
25 September	**Watts, Norman Luther**
	Zacharias, Francis Herbert
1 October	Battle of Le Transloy begins
10 October	**Dunlop, Thomas Hume**
	Haigh, Gerald Rayner
12 October	**Haworth, Randolph Singleton**
	Kennedy, Hugh
28 October	**Murdoch, Ronald Hamilton William**
12 November	**Mansergh, Harry Reid**
13 November	Battle of the Ancre begins
14 November	**Morrison, Vernon MacDonald**
22 November	**Radford, Walter Cyril Leigh**
20 November	**Watt, Robert Stapleton**

1917

13 January	**Bell, Francis Howard**
25 January	**Trampleasure, William**
16 January	**Mellor, Francis Rigby**
4 February	**Le Rougetel, Guy**
26 March	First battle of Gaza
6 April	USA declares war on Germany
9 April	Second battle of Arras
9 April	**Stewart, John Nelson**
10 April	**Wright, John Crosby**
1 May	**Johnson, Rodney Richard**
2 May	**Hamm, William George**
3 May	**Beardwood, Harold Bennett**
	Turnbull, James William
6 May	**Stott, Gilbert**
7 May	**Owen, Iorwerth ap Rowland**
10 May	**Fry, Percival Norman**
3 June	**Conby, Henry Brodie**
26 June	**Sheard, Geoffrey Senior**
20 July	**Johnson, Arthur Ellis**
25 July	**Horsfall, John Brown**
31 July	Third battle of Ypres (Passchendaele) begins
31 July	**Brock, Eric George**
	Dunman, Charles Norman Innes
	Ford, Clement William
	Nickel, George Gaston
	Wray, Francis Alan
2 August	**Hume, William Walter Kenneth**
14 August	**Whinyates, Harold Bennett**
18 August	**Hoyer, Beauchamp Hassing**
7 September	**Edwards, John Llewelyn**
15 September	**Jackson, Godfrey**
19 September	**Cobham, Elijah**
	Golding, Edgar
20 September	**Lunt, Harold George**
24 September	**Deane, Wellesley Venables**
4 October	**Rees, Leofric**
19 October	**Harley, Robert Alexander**
5 November	**Mountfield, Robert Noel**
11 November	**Evans, Eric Ben**

14 November	**Dean, Kenneth Johnson**
19 November	**Stowell, Thomas Brown**
20 November	Battle of Cambrai
23 November	**Mercer, Thomas Milbourn**
30 November	**Grant, Douglas**
13 December	**Winslow, Thomas Maitland**
unknown	**Williams, Herbert**

1918

29 January	**Mayer, John Stuart**
18 March	**Smith, Allan Wenman**
21 March	Start of the German Spring Offensive
21 March	**Singlehurst, Reginald**
22 March	**Allen, Arthur Laugharne**
	Sheard, Fraser Morton
23 March	**Knight, Allan**
	Limrick, William Somerville
1 April	Royal Air Force founded
8 April	**Ross, Harold**
10 April	**Stockdale, Clifford**
18 April	**Brodbelt, Arthur Dell**
27 April	**Fell, Robert Ernest**
31 May	**Jack, James Charles**
12 June	**Bing, Edward Charles Cameron**
5 July	**Howson, James Charles**
26 July	**Bing, Eric St Loy**
30 July	**Veevers, Edgar Samuel**
9 August	**Whitehead, Herbert John**
21 August	Second battle of the Somme begins
21 August	**Bird, Frederic Valentine**
22 August	**Pugh, Clarence**
25 August	**Jones, Herbert Leonard**
29 August	**Miller, Allan Mackenzie**
31 August	**Shaw, Charles Conway**
1 September	**Pringle, Walter Leslie**
9 September	**Hansom, Oswin**
18 September	Battle of Épehy begins
18 September	**Fryer, Charles Herbert**
19 September	**Williams, John Rayner**

1 October	**Bark, Norman**
8 October	**Lever, Francis Kirkpatrick**
30 October	**Wrathall, Reginald John**
4 November	**Evans, Norman Edward**
11 November	Armistice signed
26 November	**Neale, Francis Ernest**
2 December	**Pugh, Edward Rhodes**
19 December	**Duncan, Walter**
unknown	**Brown, John**

1919

3 January	**Parkes, Douglas Kenneth**
13 January	**Yorke, Frederick**
25 January	**McFarlane, Duncan Keith**
12 February	**Mein, William Edwin Gordon**
6 March	**Turner, Edwin Syers**
November	**Stephenson, Arnold Bracey**

Reginald Acton

Second Lieutenant
5th Battalion South Lancashire Regiment
MTS 1905–10

Reginald Acton was born on 8 June 1894 in Waterloo, Liverpool and was the son of James Dunn Acton and his wife Elizabeth (formerly Edwards).

James and Elizabeth were married on 23 April 1892 at St Mary's church, Walton on the Hill. They had four children but only two survived to adulthood: Reginald and his younger sister, Alice, born in 1900. Reginald's father worked as a 'Corn Merchant' and by 1891 he and his wife were already living in Crosby at 3 Queen's Road.

It was probably from here that Reginald set out for his first day at Merchant Taylors' on 1 May 1905. He had previously been educated at Ballure House Preparatory School, Blundellsands, and on being accepted by his new school he was awarded a Harrison Scholarship. He does not seem to have made any sporting contribution to the school during his time but he successfully sat his Oxford Local Junior exams in 1909 gaining a 3rd Class Honours and repeated this performance in the Seniors in 1910. This was the year in which, on 29 July, he left the school and, according to the school's register, went to work in a bank. However, other records show him working in 1911 as a corn broker's apprentice, which is not surprising as his father was a senior man in J. Montgomery & Co, Merchants and Millers.

Shortly after war broke out, Reginald was granted a commission, being gazetted second lieutenant in 5th Battalion South Lancashire Regiment with effect from 19 October 1914. He embarked, with the battalion, on the SS *King Edward* and landed at Le Havre on 13 February 1915 where they became part of 4th Division and took part in the second battle of Ypres in April and May 1915. On 28 April, the battalion moved to Vlamertinghe in preparation for their part in the battle and at the beginning of May moved into the front line occupying trenches in front of Wieltje.

There is some doubt about the actual date of Reginald's death. *The School Review* records:

On Sunday morning, May 9th, before dawn, he went forward, accompanied by one man, Private Pye, towards the enemy's right. Finding no one, he returned and went forward again to the left. When crossing a brook they were fired on by a trench mortar, and both were wounded, Acton fatally. After a considerable interval they were rescued and brought back to our lines. Death occurred on May 10th 1915.

The battalion's war diary, however, records that he was a casualty of 8 March with death occurring on the 9th which is in agreement with the Commonwealth War Graves Commission records. He was 20 years old.

He was buried in plot I grave 4 at Bailleul Communal Cemetery Nord.

ARTHUR LAUGHARNE ALLEN

Private
291399
15th Battalion Welsh Regiment
MTS 1908–15

In the baptism register of St Thomas's church, Seaforth, Arthur Laugharne Allen is recorded as having been baptised on 11 September 1898. His father was William Arthur Allen, a bank accountant, of 10 Cecil Road. His mother's name is given as Lily, the same name which appears in the records of the Commonwealth War Graves Commission. However, other records, including two census returns, show quite convincingly that Arthur Laugharne Allen was born in Seaforth on 11 August 1898, the son of William Arthur Allen and his wife Ellen Mary Julia Allen (formerly Laugharne) who had married in 1888 in Rhayader, Radnorshire where her father was the vicar.

Arthur was the fifth of six children. The two oldest, Noel (born 1890) and Ruth (born 1891) were born in Welshpool, Montgomeryshire but the last four children, Barbara (born 1894), Cyril (1897), Arthur (1898) and Gladys (1900) were born in Seaforth, indicating a move into the area between 1891 and 1894. In 1901 they were living at 58 Rawson Road, Seaforth; Arthur's father was working as a banker's clerk. In 1906, Arthur's older brother Noel died, aged 16.

On 16 September 1908, after having been tutored at home, Arthur entered Merchant Taylors' – the same year as his brother Cyril and nine years after his brother Noel, who joined in 1899. His father seems to have been promoted as the admissions register records his occupation as 'Bank Manager'.

By 1911, the family had moved to 100 South Road, Waterloo (this was actually the address of the North & South Wales Branch of the London City and Midland Bank for which his father worked, so they were probably living in the flat above). Arthur left school on 31 March 1915 and, according to the school register he 'entered a bank', no doubt his father's.

Joining the army, probably in November 1916, Arthur initially enlisted in the Pembroke Yeomanry being later posted to the 7th Battalion Welsh Regiment and then the 15th Battalion (the Carmarthen Pals) probably joining them in the Armentières region.

Arthur was wounded in action near Armentières when his position came under German shellfire and he died on 22 or 23 March 1918 (sources differ) as a result of these wounds. He was 19 years old.

He is buried in plot VI row A grave 48 in Cite Bonjean Military Cemetery, Armentières.

SYDNEY RAYMOND ALLEN

Second Lieutenant
16th Battalion Manchester Regiment
MTS 1905–09

Sydney Raymond Allen was born at Seaforth, Liverpool on 10 March 1894. He was the third child and second son of George Thomas Allen and his wife Ada Eliza Allen (formerly Harris). He was baptised on 28 March at St Thomas church, Seaforth, the register giving the family's address as 15 Cecil Road and his father's occupation as cashier.

By 1901 the family had moved to 5 Alexandra Road, Waterloo and grown to five children: James George Allen (born 1890), Eileen Ada (1892), Sydney (1894), Kenneth Harris (1895) and Dudley (1899). Sydney's father was working as a provision broker's manager.

Sydney entered Merchant Taylors' School on 17 September 1905 after being privately educated at home and left the school on 29 July 1909 taking up an apprenticeship with Messrs Alfred Dobell & Co, Timber Merchants in Liverpool.

In 1911 the family was living in the same house at 5 Alexandra Road, Waterloo. One more child, Ronald (born 1901 in Waterloo), had been added to the family. Sydney, now 17, was working as a 'Timber Broker's Apprentice'.

His apprenticeship was due to be completed in 1915, but almost immediately war broke out, he joined the 6th Battalion King's (Liverpool Regiment) on 7 August 1914, and was given the regimental number 2003 with the rank of private. He arrived in France with the 6th in February 1915.

He was gazetted on 1 April 1915 as second lieutenant with 16th Battalion Manchester Regiment with effect from 20 March 1915 and joined his new regiment on Salisbury Plain where they were still undergoing training. He returned to France, with the Manchesters, on 6 November 1915 coming home in May of the following year for a period of leave. He arrived back in France and rejoined his battalion in time for the opening moves of the battle of the Somme.

Sydney was killed on 1 July 1916, the first day of the battle of the Somme. He was shot through the head while leading a bombing party during the attack on the fortified village of Montauban. He had, earlier in the campaign, been wounded while rescuing another officer from no man's land.

His body was not recovered and he is commemorated on pier and face 13A and 14C of the Thiepval Memorial.

FRANCIS SLATER BAINES

Lance Corporal
1869
1st/6th Battalion King's (Liverpool Regiment)
MTS 1902–11

Francis Slater Baines was born on 12 September 1891 at Walney, Lancashire, the son of John Baines and his wife, Elizabeth (formerly Slater). He had one brother, John Slater Baines (born 1890 in Greenwich) and a sister Elizabeth (born 1900 in Great Crosby). His father was a 'Commission Agent' who, if his absence from home at the time of several censuses is any indication, spent a good deal of time away from his family. At the time of the 1901 census, Elizabeth and the children were living at 22 Victoria Road, Crosby from which Francis attended Ballure House Preparatory School. On 1 May 1902 Francis began his career at Merchant Taylors', being elected to a Harrison Scholarship on entry.

While at the school, he played for the rugby 1st XV (1909–11) and the cricket XI (1909/10). His rugby playing was summarised as 'good in both attack and defence' and he was described as a 'strong runner'. His cricket performance was, it seems, less successful. Even as a middle order batsman, his batting average for 1910 of 4.45 was regarded as disappointing and he was not in the team list for 1911.

Academically, he gained a Pass in the Oxford Local Preliminary examination in 1904, 3rd Class Honours in the Junior exams in 1906 and 1st Class Honours in 1907 and then 2nd Class in the Senior exams in 1908 followed by 1st Class in 1909. He was also a monitor 1909–11. By 1911 the family had moved to 8 Coronation Road, Great Crosby. Francis left the school on 11 April 1911 and joined the Royal Insurance Co, Ltd.

Francis was another 'early joiner' when war broke out. He attested for four years' service with the Territorial Force – 6th Battalion King's (Liverpool Regiment) – on 8 August 1914, one month short of his 23rd birthday.

On 24 February 1915 he embarked on SS *City of Edinburgh* at Southampton and landed in France with the battalion the following day.

He was promoted to lance corporal on 19 May 1916. In July the 55th Division moved south to take up a position opposite the village of Guillemont. About 8 August, 55th Division entered the village and it was presumably during this advance that Francis received gunshot wounds to the left thigh and arm, which resulted in fractures to both, on 9 August 1916. On the same day he was admitted to No 21 Casualty Clearing Station and on the following day to No 1 South African General Hospital at Abbeville. On 11 August he was transferred to the Hospital Ship *Marama* and was shipped home to England on 13 August 1916. Arriving back in this country he was admitted to Netley Hospital where his wounds became gangrenous. He died at Netley at 5.30 a.m. on 21 August 1916, three weeks before his 25th birthday.

Francis is buried in grave C636 in St Luke's churchyard, Great Crosby.

CHARLES WILFRED BANISTER

Second Lieutenant
4th Battalion Royal Fusiliers
MTS 1904–10

Charles Wilfred Banister was the youngest of the four children born to Howard Cottrell Banister and his wife Blanch (formerly Bright) who married in 1879. Their first child, John Bright Banister, was born in 1880, their second, Howard, in 1881 and their third, Mary Vivien in 1887. By the time Charles was born on 9 March 1893, his oldest brother John was nearly 13 years old and by the time of the 1901 census John was at Jesus College, Cambridge, studying medicine. Charles, however, was still living at home at Elmshurst, Merrilocks Road, Blundellsands with his parents, his brother Howard and his sister Mary. His father was working as a 'Sales Manager for an Alkali Manufacturer'.

Charles had his early education at 'Marine', a private preparatory school in Blundellsands before entering Merchant Taylors' on 17 September 1904 by which time both his older brothers had completed their education at Merchant Taylors'. Howard had also gone up to Jesus College, Cambridge.

In 1907 Charles obtained a Pass in his Oxford Local Junior exams following this with 2nd Class Honours in 1908. In 1909 he obtained a Pass in the Senior exams and again followed this with a 2nd Class Honours in 1910. In his final year at school he was tennis champion winning both the Open Singles and the

Handicap Doubles. He left school on 21 December 1910 and was educated privately at home before going up to Jesus College, Cambridge to study law – the third brother to enter the college. In 1911 the family was still living at the same address in Merrilocks Road.

When war broke out in August 1914, Charles had not finished his law degree. Giving up his studies, he went through Royal Military College, Sandhurst and obtained a commission with the Royal Fusiliers, being gazetted second lieutenant in the infantry with effect from 16 November 1914. He was posted to the Royal Fusiliers (City of London Regiment) from 17 February 1915.

According to his records, he arrived in France on 9 June 1915 and on 16 June took part in the battalion's attack on Bellewaarde. During this battle, the battalion advanced too quickly and came under fire from both friendly and enemy artillery. The battalion withdrew to a communications trench where it was bombarded for the rest of the day by high-explosive, and later, gas shells. Twenty-two officers and 820 men of the battalion began the attack, 15 officers and 326 men were casualties. Banister was among those killed, a week after his arrival in France.

He has no known grave and is commemorated on panels 6 and 8 of the Ypres (Menin Gate) Memorial.

NORMAN BARK

Lieutenant
Royal Air Force
MTS 1908–13

Norman Bark was born in Waterloo on 13 January 1896. He was the only child of Arthur Septimus Bark and his wife Annie Louise Bark (formerly Gorst) of Litherland.

On 15 February 1896, he was baptised at the South Shore parish church (Holy Trinity) in Blackpool, the church in which his parents had been married in 1895. His father worked as an 'Estate Agent' and although Norman was baptised in Blackpool the family was, at the time, living at 24 Ferndale Road, Waterloo, Liverpool. By 1901 they had moved to 5 Alexandra Mount, Litherland, an area which has since been partially redeveloped but which, at the time, would have contained some rather large houses.

As a youngster Norman attended Oakes Institute in Walton, the forerunner of Alsop High School, and came to Merchant Taylors' on 16 September 1908 travelling in from Stanley Cottage, 101 Sefton Road, Litherland. They were still at the same address in 1911 in which year Norman obtained a Pass in the Oxford Local Junior exams and the following year repeated the performance in the Seniors.

While at the school, Norman proved himself an accomplished athlete playing for the rugby XV in the 1912/13 season and in his last year in the school winning the Open Mile and Open Hurdles Cups.

Leaving school on 30 July 1913 he became an articled pupil to Messrs Chalmers, Wade & Co, chartered accountants starting work in August and remaining with them until August 1914.

On the outbreak of war he enlisted with the 6th Battalion King's (Liverpool Regiment) and went with them to France in February 1915. On 15 August 1916 he received a commission and was gazetted to the King's Own Scottish Borderers, taking part in the fighting at Vimy Ridge and the Somme after which he was invalided home. His injuries were considered to be severe enough to ensure he did not go back into the infantry and he was given, in February 1917, a post as assistant to the colonel in charge of records at the Army Records Office, Lichfield remaining in that post until August 1917.

Norman then joined the Royal Flying Corps with effect from 4 October 1917. Following training he went back to France in February 1918 as an observer in a balloon section. Promoted to temporary lieutenant on 15 February 1918, he was killed while serving with 7 Kite Balloon Section on 1 October 1918.

He is buried in plot VI row D grave 14 at Dadizeele New British Cemetery.

GEORGE BARNES

Rifleman
2286
6th Battalion King's (Liverpool Regiment)
MTS 1904–09

George Barnes was born on 6 December 1893 in Bootle, Lancashire. He was the only child of James Barnes and his second wife, Emma Elizabeth (formerly Price), who had previously been his housekeeper. The couple had married in 1892 following the death of Jame's first wife, Margaret, who probably died in 1888.

As early as 1881, George's father seems to have been running a sizeable ship repair firm employing 30 men and 12 boys and in 1901 his business was continuing to thrive. He and his family were living at 46 Merton Road, Bootle, and the household consisted not only of his wife, Emma, and George but also his mother, aged 81 and three of his children from his first marriage, James, Maggie and Lucy.

As a small child, George attended a private preparatory school in Bootle, the name of which was not recorded in the Merchant Taylors' admissions register, before going on to Merchant Taylors' on 16 January 1904. He sat his Oxford Local Junior exams in 1908 and 1909, obtaining a 3rd Class Honours in the former and improving to a 2nd Class Honours in the latter.

The school records show he left Merchant Taylors' on 22 December 1909 with an accompanying note stating that he joined a corn merchant's office. However, other sources show that he took up an engineering apprenticeship with a Liverpool firm and, indeed, the 1911 census gives his occupation as 'Apprentice Marine Engineer'. He and his parents were still living at 46 Merton Road and it is not unreasonable to think that he was working for his father's firm.

George eventually moved to the north-east of England and finished his apprenticeship with the Northumbrian Engine Works in Wallsend where he was working when the war broke out.

On 2 September 1914 he enlisted in 6th Battalion King's (Liverpool Regiment) and on 24 February 1915 went to France with the battalion on the SS *City of Edinburgh* and moved into the Ypres area.

In October 1915, George was accidentally killed while on patrol at Vaux. The battalion's war diary records for 10 October 1915, 'All quiet. Casualties to noon 1 other rank accidentally killed and 1 other rank accidentally wounded' but does not say how.

He is buried in grave C8 in the Suzanne Communal Cemetery Extension.

HAROLD BENNETT BEARDWOOD

Private
53950
1st Battalion Royal Welsh Fusiliers
MTS 1903–04

Harold's father, John Edward Beardwood, was a native of Preston. His mother, Elizabeth (formerly Bennett) was a schoolteacher from Penwortham on the other side of the River Ribble. They married in the parish church at Penwortham on 15 January 1884. Although Elizabeth was still living in Penwortham at the time of their marriage, John had moved to Formby, Lancashire where he was working as a 'Railway Agent'. After the wedding, they returned to Formby and it was there that Harold was born on 23 May 1888 joining his brother Fredrick Charles who had been born there in 1886.

By 1891, John had become the stationmaster at Formby and he, and his family, were recorded as living at the railway station, presumably in the stationmaster's house. Brothers for Harold arrived in late 1891 (Sidney Edward) and early 1896 (Edgar Crompton) though none of his brothers attended Merchant Taylors'.

By 1901, Harold's father had changed career, becoming the postmaster of Formby. The family were living in Chapel Road according to the census but this should, perhaps, say Chapel Lane.

In 1903, Harold joined Merchant Taylors' but spent only a short time there, leaving in 1904.

Harold's father, John, was still the Formby postmaster in 1911 and was living in the accommodation provided by the post office. He was no doubt helped by Frederick who was a 'Sorting Clerk and Telegraphist' while Harold and Sidney were both employed as 'Insurance Clerks', Harold being employed by the Royal Insurance Company.

Initially, on enlisting, Harold seems to have served in the 15th Battalion King's (Liverpool Regiment). He was given the regimental number 36065. He later transferred to 1st Battalion Royal Welsh Fusiliers being given the number 4119, later renumbered as 53950. The fact that he is entitled only to a pair of World War I medals rather than a trio shows he did not go over to France until some time in 1916 at the earliest.

Harold Beardwood died of wounds on 6 May 1917. This seems to coincide with the battalion's attack on the village of Bullecourt, part of the Hindenburg Line, on 3 May 1917. He is buried in plot I row F grave 5 in Achiet-le-Grand Communal Cemetery Extension.

Harold's younger brother Sidney died of wounds less than six months later, on 17 September 1917.

FRANCIS HOWARD BELL

Lance Corporal
464686
47th Battalion Canadian Infantry
MTS 1905–09

Francis Howard Bell was born on 30 September 1894 in Blackburn, Lancashire. He was the third surviving son of

Thomas Penrice Bell, and his wife Elizabeth (formerly Howard). His father was a commercial traveller dealing in rice and spices.

His parents married on 8 April 1882 at St James's church, Walton on the Hill and in 1883 Elizabeth gave birth to twin girls, Margaret and Elizabeth. A year later in 1884, their first son, Thomas, was born but he died aged four. Another daughter, Annie, was born in 1886 but died very soon afterwards. 1890 saw the birth of another son who was also named Thomas. There then followed a move to Blackburn where the next two sons, John and Francis were born in 1892 and 1894 respectively. Finally Stuart was born in Waterloo in 1897 and Beatrice in 1901. All the children had the middle name 'Howard'.

Beatrice did not arrive in time for the 1901 census which shows Thomas and Elizabeth and their children: Margaret, Elizabeth, Thomas, John, Francis and Stuart living at 19 Norma Road, Waterloo along with a governess. Thomas (senior) continued to work as a commercial traveller dealing in spices.

Francis entered Merchant Taylors' on 16 January 1905 before which he had attended a private preparatory school in Waterloo. He left the school on 29 July 1909 and started an apprenticeship with Messrs Houghton Bros, fruit brokers.

In 1911 the family was still living at the same address. Thomas (senior) was still selling spices, Margaret was a piano teacher, John and Francis were both apprentices, John in timber, Francis in fruit and the two youngest were still at school. Wishing to follow a career in farming, Francis was released from his apprenticeship and, at some point before the outbreak of war, emigrated to Canada to become a farmer. He later moved to Vancouver, British Columbia and became a machinist.

On 12 January 1916, he enlisted into the 158th Battalion of the Canadian Expeditionary Force and was initially given regimental number 645264 (later changed to 464686). Later, on 3 November 1916, he transferred to the 62nd Battalion. He arrived in France and volunteered for service with A Company, 47th Battalion and was involved in the battles of the Somme and Ancre moving into the Carency sector in January 1917. While in this sector, he was killed in action by a German trench mortar during a heavy bombardment on 13 January 1917.

He is buried in plot VI row A grave 13 at Villers Station Cemetery, Villers-au-Bois.

WILLIAM FRANCIS BICE

Second Lieutenant
1st Battalion Norfolk Regiment
MTS 1907–08

William Francis Bice was born on 11 September 1896 in Roehampton. He was the son of William Archer Bice and Matilda Isabel Bice (formerly Hickman). His father worked as a 'Commercial Agent' and at the time of his marriage (1894) was living in Huelva, Spain though he married in Richmond.

After William's birth, the family moved back to Spain where four other children are known to have been born to William (senior) and Matilda: Margarita Isabel (born 1898), Ethel May (1900), Charles (1905) and Francis (1907). None of these births seems to have been registered in England and the 1911 census shows Margarita and Ethel to have been born in Huelva.

William attended Merchant Taylors' briefly in 1907 (possibly leaving in 1908) after which he seems to have transferred to Manchester Grammar School to complete his education, possibly at the time his family moved to Stockport.

Following school, he seems to have taken a job as a clerk. There is a record of a William Francis Bice, a 17-year-old clerk, embarking at Liverpool aboard the SS *Oropesa* on 11 December 1913 bound for Vigo, Spain and possibly returning on the same ship in March 1914 from Corunna. By 1914 the family was living at 23 Stanley Road, Heaton Moor.

William went on to Manchester University where he was a cadet in the Officers' Training Corps from January 1915 to January 1916 and applied for a commission on 10 December 1915. He was commissioned as a second lieutenant in the 10th (Reserve) Battalion of the Norfolk Regiment with effect from 20 January 1916. He was reassigned to the 1st Battalion in time to go overseas and they arrived in the Somme sector in the middle of July 1916. On 4 September, 1st Norfolks (including William in A Company) were in the first wave in the attack in Falfemont Farm, south of Guillemont where their advancing lines came under intense German machine-gun fire from Combles ravine, resulting in the failure of the attack. In the words of the battalion's war diary:

A & B Coys assaulted. Very heavy machine gun fire opened on them immediately. Captain Farmer and a few men of A Coy. succeeded in reaching the SW corner of the Farm but were bombed out and the remainder of the attack was held up by cross machine gun fire. The situation then became very involved as all the officers but two were either killed or wounded and the advance over a 600 yard front was very split up as the only way to go on was by crawling from shell-hole to shell-hole – any attempt at an advance was immediately stopped by the machine gun fire.

William was killed in action in this attack and although his body was recovered and buried, the location of the grave was lost and he is commemorated on pier and face 1C and 1D of the Thiepval Memorial.

EDWARD CHARLES CAMERON BING

Lieutenant
25th Battalion Canadian Regiment
MTS 1908–10

Edward's father, Edward Lewis Bing married Lois Greenwood Trahair in the registration district of Portsea in 1892. Shortly afterwards, on 20 April 1893 they travelled from Southampton to Pernambuco, Brazil, aboard SS *Tagus*. The first three of their four children were born in Pernambuco. Edward Charles Cameron was born on 19 January 1894, Lorna in 1898 and Eric St Loy (see p.41) in 1899.

In May 1900, the family is recorded as arriving in Southampton from Pernambuco aboard the SS *Elbe*. The father's occupation is given on the passenger manifest as company manager. By 1901 they seem to have settled in Mirtle (sic) Cottage in Newlyn, Cornwall.

Edward joined Merchant Taylors' on 16 January 1908 having previously attended Waterloo High School meaning that Edward (senior) must have brought his family north at some time between 1901 and 1908. The school admissions register gives Edward's father's occupation as 'Superintendent in a Cable Co'. Another son, Stuart Logan, was born to Edward and Lois in 1908 in Waterloo, Liverpool. In his short time at the school, Edward gained a Pass in his Oxford Local Junior exams in 1909. He left the school on 28 July 1910 and joined the Anglo South American Bank, London where he was probably still working in 1911 as the census return has him working as a 'Bank Clerk' and living in an apartment in Barnet, London. He was referred to as Cameron Bing, born in Brazil. The rest of the family was living at 7 Norma Road, Waterloo.

During the war he enlisted as a private (No 68357), rising to the rank of lance sergeant and being later commissioned as a lieutenant in 25th Battalion Canadian Infantry with effect from 20 January 1917.

The Commonwealth War Graves Commission gives his date of death as 11 June 1918. However, the battalion's war diary gives 12 June 1918. For this day it records:

NEUVILLE VITASSE

Situation quiet throughout the early part of the day. At 3.00 pm our front and support lines were heavily shelled for about 20 minutes, in retaliation to a barrage put down by the Division on our left flank. ... Casualties – killed in action, Lieut E C C Bing and 8 other ranks; wounded Capt W A Livingstone and 21 other ranks.

Edward Bing is buried in plot II row H grave 13 of Wailly Orchard Cemetery.

ERIC ST LOY BING

Private
313039
7th Battalion Gordon Highlanders
MTS 1908–13

Eric St Loy Bing was the younger brother of Edward Charles Cameron Bing (see p.40). The third child of Edward and Lois Bing, he was born in Pernambuco, Brazil, on 5 February 1899 and would have been just a toddler when the family travelled to Southampton aboard the SS *Elbe*.

By 1901 they were living in Mirtle (sic) Cottage in Newlyn, Cornwall though on the night of the census, 31 March, Edward (senior) seems to be away from home. Between 1901 and 1908, the family moved north and was living in Waterloo in 1908 when another son, Stuart Logan, was born.

Eric attended a private preparatory school in Waterloo before arriving at Merchant Taylors' on 17 September 1908, a few months after his brother. His father's occupation is given as 'Superintendent in a Cable Co'.

In 1911, the family had moved to 7 Norma Road, Waterloo. Eric's father was again away from home on the night of the census but his mother was living at this address with her daughter Lorna and youngest son Stuart.

Eric left the school on 30 July 1913 and, according to the register, left England, probably to return to Brazil.

During the war he initially served in the 14th Battalion London Regiment as Private 515037, enlisting at Wood Green. He later transferred to the 7th Battalion Gordon Highlanders and was killed in action on 26 July 1918, aged 19. This date would indicate that he died in the battle of Tardenois when the 1/7th Battalion was serving as part of the 51st (Highland) Division and was ordered to bolster an over-stretched section held by the French who were facing a large enemy attack.

Eric Bing was buried in plot VI row D grave 6 of the Marfaux British Cemetery.

FREDERIC VALENTINE BIRD
BSC

Lieutenant
Royal Air Force
MTS 1905–09

Frederic Valentine Bird was the first of two children born to Frederic Joseph Bird and his wife Mary Elizabeth Bird (formerly Botterill). He was born in Liverpool on 9 May 1892 and baptised at St Bride's church on 30 October. The family home at the time was 49 Upper Parliament Street. Four years later, in 1896, Frederic's younger sister was born and named Mary Gertrude. By 1901, the family had moved to 29 Church Road, Waterloo and his father's occupation in the census of that year was given as 'Manager, Rice and Spice Mills'.

Frederic entered Merchant Taylors' on 17 September 1905 having previously attended the Grammar School, Blackburn. While at the school he obtained a 3rd Class in the Oxford Junior Local exam in 1907. The following year he obtained a Pass in the Senior exam and in 1909 improved this to a 2nd Class before leaving on 29 July 1909 to study chemistry at Liverpool University. Frederic graduated BSc in chemistry and physics from Liverpool and then worked as an assistant demonstrator in biochemistry at the Liverpool University Medical School from January to June 1915.

Wishing to make a contribution to the war effort he initially enlisted in the Royal Engineers. He went to France on 17 July 1915 and was eventually promoted to corporal. Later he transferred to the Royal Flying Corps and on 16 June 1917 he began a course at the School of Military Aeronautics. Following this he moved, on 21 July 1917, to 41 Training Squadron at Doncaster for elementary instruction and flying training. He received further instruction at

46 Training Squadron starting on 8 August 1917 and was gazetted temporary second lieutenant on the same day with effect from 19 July 1917, being confirmed in his rank of second lieutenant on 30 August 1917. In September he continued with his training attending courses at the Artillery and Infantry Cooperation School at Winchester and the School of Aerial Gunnery at Turnberry. Promotion to lieutenant followed on 1 April 1918, the day the Royal Air Force came into existence, and he was posted to No 12 Squadron, a reconnaissance squadron, on 24 April 1918. On 1 July 1918 while piloting an RE8 aircraft he struck a ridge when landing from a photographic flight; he was not harmed. On 8 August he and his observer Second Lieutenant W. Holmes were injured when they were forced to land in a cornfield between Givenchy and Manin following engine failure.

On 21 August 1918, Frederic was flying an RE8 aircraft on patrol. He and his observer, Second Lieutenant Leslie Millar Stubley, were both killed when the aircraft collided with the cable of a balloon on the Bienvillers–Monchy road.

He is buried in plot XVIII row E grave 15 in Bienvillers Military Cemetery. Leslie Stubley is buried in grave 14.

EUSTACE BOUSFIELD

Private
2314
Worcester Yeomanry
MTS 1895–96

The Bousfields were a wealthy family who had at one time owned and lived in the Mulberries, the house later bought by the Merchant Taylors' Company which would become part of Merchant Taylors' Girls' School.

Eustace Bousfield was born on 8 November 1885 in Bromborough, the second child and eldest son of Henry Michael Bousfield and his wife, Annie Wilkinson Bousfield (formerly Tetley). A sister, Katie Constance had preceded him into the world in 1882 and he was followed by two brothers: Reginald Michael in 1888 and Henry Hugh (later to become Rear Admiral Bousfield) in 1889. Katie was born in Waterloo and the two brothers in Hooton, Wirral. Tragedy struck in 1890 when their father, a member of the Liverpool Stock Exchange, died aged only 34, struck down by the Russian flu pandemic of the time. He died in the Wirral. By 1891, Annie and the family had moved to Crosby and were living at 28 College Road where she was described as 'Living on her own means'. A further indication of their relative wealth comes from the fact that she employed a governess and two servants.

Eustace attended Merchant Taylors' for a short time only, seemingly arriving in 1895 and leaving in 1896 to attend Bedford County School, a private school formerly known as the Bedford Middle Class Public School, at which he was boarding at the time of the 1901 census.

On leaving school Eustace started his working life in an insurance office in Liverpool, before deciding to try his hand at farming in New Zealand. After a short time he gave this up and moved to the Malay States to try rubber planting but ill health forced him back to England where he took up fruit and poultry farming in Evesham, Worcestershire.

When war broke out Eustace joined the Worcester Yeomanry, which, as part of the 1st South Midland Mounted Brigade, was ordered to Egypt where they were camped close to Alexandria in April 1915. The brigade was dismounted in August and sent, as infantry, to Suvla Bay to take part in the infamous campaign on the Gallipoli peninsula. When this campaign failed and Gallipoli was evacuated in January 1916, the regiment was sent back to Egypt where they acted as guard on the Suez Canal being based on Katia or possibly Oghratine. On 23 April 1916, both of these places were overrun by a Turkish attack in which Eustace was killed.

He is commemorated on panels 3 and 5 of the Jerusalem Memorial.

ERIC GEORGE BROCK
MC, BA

Captain
7th Battalion King's (Liverpool Regiment)
MTS 1902–11

Eric George Brock was born in Liverpool on 19 March 1893. His father was George Albert Brock BA, a Congregational minister. His mother was Minnie Constance Brock (formerly Winzar). The couple had four children. Eric George was born in 1893, Enid Agnes in 1894 and Raymond Sidney in 1899. Eric's youngest sister, Pearl Constance did not arrive until 1905. All of the children were born in Waterloo.

From the private preparatory school that Eric attended in Waterloo, he entered Merchant Taylors' in January 1902 having gained an entrance scholarship. In 1904 he made his first attempt at the Oxford Local Junior exam and gained a Pass. In 1905 he gained a 3rd Class Honours and in 1906 and 1907, a 1st Class. In 1909 he obtained a 1st Class in the Senior exam with distinctions in Latin, Greek, Mathematics, Higher Mathematics and French. He took first place in England in Mathematics and Higher Mathematics. In 1911 he won several prizes: the Tyler Prize for Ancient History, the Montefiore Prize for Latin and the Windermere Prize for English as well as winning the Oxford Local exam award for the boy taking first place in the Senior exams in England. He was also awarded the Great Crosby Scholarship. On 27 November 1911, Eric left the school and then went up to St John's College, Cambridge as a mathematical scholar and eventually graduated BA in 1914.

Though his intention had been to join the Civil Service, he enlisted on the outbreak of war and applied for a commission being gazetted second lieutenant with effect from 16 October 1914 and being posted to the 1st/7th Battalion King's (Liverpool Regiment). He landed in France on 27 May 1915 and took part in the battle of Loos (27 September–18 October 1915). Eric was promoted to temporary lieutenant with effect from 28 April 1916.

The award of his Military Cross was gazetted on 20 October 1916 possibly for the attack on Guillemont. The citation reads:

> For conspicuous gallantry during operations. When patrolling he found a company without senior officers and at once took command, organised the defences and, though cut off for two days, finally managed to join up on both flanks.

He was gazetted lieutenant from 5 June 1917. This was quickly followed on 21 June by promotion to the rank of acting captain. Within ten days of his promotion, Eric Brock was killed in action in the opening hours of the battle of Pilckem Ridge on 31 July 1917.

Eric George Brock's body was not recovered for burial and he is commemorated on panels 4 and 6 of the Ypres (Menin Gate) Memorial.

CHARLES NORMAN BROCKBANK

Captain
18th Battalion King's (Liverpool Regiment)
MTS 1894–98

Charles Norman Brockbank was born on 14 September 1884. He was the only child of Robert Henry Brockbank and his wife Marion Annie Brockbank (formerly Johnson) who had married in the registration district of Leicester, Marion's place of birth, in 1883.

Charles entered Merchant Taylors' on 13 September 1894, the day before his tenth birthday. The family address was given as Mersey Road, Blundellsands and his father's occupation was given as 'General Broker'. He stayed at Merchant Taylors' for four years leaving at the end of the Christmas term 1898, aged 14, to attend Malvern College. After leaving Malvern College, he travelled extensively on the continent, in Canada and the United States and eventually went to work for Messrs Forbes, Forbes Campbell & Co in Karachi. He spent five years in commerce in India. Returning from India he became a partner in his father's firm of William Porter & Co.

He volunteered for service immediately upon the outbreak of hostilities, joining the second of the Liverpool Pals battalions, the 18th, and before the end of September was raised to the rank of lieutenant, later becoming captain. The battalion was allocated to 89th Brigade, 30th Division, which left for France in November 1915 and landed at Boulogne. There was a change of brigade on 25 December 1915 when the 18th moved from 30th Brigade to 21st Brigade. Shortly afterwards the battalion's war diary records that on 11 January 1916, 'Captain C N Brockbank and two privates were wounded by rifle grenades'.

The battalion went into action on the disastrous first day of the battle of the Somme, 1 July 1916. It was their task to attack the village of Montauban. Initially they suffered heavy casualties from machine-gun fire but eventually took their objective by 10 a.m.; heavy enemy shell fire followed in the afternoon.

It was on this day, 1 July 1916, that Charles Brockbank was killed in action. Leading his men into the attack he was wounded twice and died soon afterwards. Graham Maddocks in his book *Liverpool Pals* quotes a passage by Private Steele, 18 King's (Liverpool Regiment) who was sent by Lieutenant-Colonel Trotter to see how the attack was going. He reported that there was '... one mass of dead men as far as you could see, right and left! The first one I came across was a captain, Captain Brockbank, he'd been hit twice. One of the fellows told me afterwards he'd been hit and got up and then been hit again in the throat'. He was one of three Old Crosbeians who lost their lives in the attack on Montauban.

He is buried in plot V row U grave 8 of the Danzig Alley British Cemetery at Mametz.

Arthur Dell Brodbelt

Lieutenant
Royal Garrison Artillery
MTS 1898–1901

Thomas Bryde Brodbelt (a native of Liverpool) and Lucy Littlewood (a Londoner) were married on 17 July 1879 at Christ Church, Hornsey. At the time of their marriage, Thomas was living in Tattenhall, a village 8 miles south-east of Chester. He earned his living as an engineer. Thomas and Lucy presumably returned to Tattenhall after their wedding and their first child, Muriel Lucy, was born there in the first quarter of 1882. She was followed by three other children: Thomas Warbrick Bryde in 1884, Arthur Dell on 28 February 1886 and Guy (see p.48) in 1888, all born in Tattenhall.

By 1891, Thomas, now describing himself as 'Mechanical Engineer and Timber Merchant', and his family had moved to the impressive Brook Hall in Tattenhall.

At some time between 1891 and 1898, the family moved to the Crosby area. On 18 January 1898 Arthur entered Merchant Taylors' and in the admissions register the family's address was given as 6 Oxford Road, Waterloo, an address which must have offered much less space than Brook Hall! Not long after Arthur became part of the school, his father died (in the third quarter of 1898).

Arthur played rugby with the second XV as a forward where he was described as 'an energetic player who dribbles well'. Arthur spent four years at the school and left in July 1901 having achieved a Pass in his Oxford Local Junior exams. He went on to become an insurance inspector at Gosforth and at the Liverpool and London Globe Insurance Co Ltd.

On the outbreak of war he volunteered as a dispatch rider and in May 1915 he joined the Inns of Court Officers' Training Corps eventually being granted a commission as second lieutenant with the Royal Garrison Artillery with effect from 16 September 1915. He was posted to Malta in February 1916 and then volunteered for service in France. He was promoted to temporary lieutenant on 4 August 1916 and lieutenant with effect from 1 July 1917. On 27 September 1917, he went to France and joined his unit, 264 Siege Battery, Royal Garrison Artillery, which was armed with four 9.2-inch howitzers. In March 1918, the German army began its final major offensive of the war and Arthur's battery was moved to support the Amiens sector. On 18 April 1918, probably during the battle of Lys, he was mortally wounded.

He is buried in plot VI row A grave 7 of the Chocques Military Cemetery.

GUY BRODBELT

Lieutenant
9th Battalion King's (Liverpool Regiment)
MTS 1899–1900

Guy Brodbelt was the youngest child of Thomas Bryde Brodbelt and Lucy Littlewood. He was born in Tattenhall on 23 September 1888. By 1891, the family had moved to the impressive Brook Hall in Tattenhall. At some time between 1891 and 1898, the family moved to the Crosby area. In 1898 Guy's father, Thomas, died at the early age of 44.

A few months later, on 2 May 1899, Guy joined his older brother Arthur (see p.47) at Merchant Taylors'. Unlike his brother he left the school after just one year, at Easter 1900, having obtained an entrance scholarship for Christ's Hospital where, among other activities, he joined the Officers' Training Corps.

After leaving Christ's he trained as a chartered accountant and was articled to Mr E. J. Walker, Messrs Lloyd, Walker and Evans of Liverpool. He was secretary of the Liverpool Chartered Accountants Students' Association and by 1911 he was a member of the Association of Chartered Accountants though still listed as a 'Chartered Accountants Student'. He was still living at home at 6 Oxford Road, Waterloo. He founded his own firm just before the start of the war and in 1914 won the Liverpool Chartered Accountants Golf Competition and the Heal Challenge Cup at the Liverpool Banking and Insurance Golf Club. He was also a keen chess player.

Before war started, Guy had served in the ranks of the 6th (Rifle) Battalion of the King's (Liverpool Regiment) for a number of years. After the outbreak of hostilities, he re-enlisted as a private (No 1923) and soon, on 4 December 1914, he was commissioned as a second lieutenant in the 9th Battalion of the regiment. Later, as of 15 May 1915, he was promoted lieutenant. His records show he had no overseas service while serving in the ranks but first went to France on 14 April 1915.

He was involved in the battles at Festubert on 9 May and Loos on 25 September as well as in other engagements in October 1915. Exactly a year after arriving in France, on 14 April 1916, he was shot in the head by a sniper while commanding a company.

He is buried in plot III row B grave 19 of the Douchy-Les-Ayette British cemetery.

JOHN BROWN

Rank unknown
Number unknown
Royal Welsh Fusiliers
MTS 1899–1902

John Brown was born on 23 December 1887 in Farnborough and was the eldest son of Henry Brown and his wife Lucy. Within the family he seems to have been known as Jack. He was their first son, following six daughters: Hannah (born 1874 in India), Laura (born 1876 in Shorncliffe, Kent), Lucy (born 1877, Pembroke Dock), Dorothy (born 1882, Weedon, Northamptonshire), Ethel (born 1884 at Charlcote, Warwickshire) and Joyce (born 1886, Aldershot). He was followed by yet another girl, Sybil (born *c.* 1890 in Stoke, Devon).

By 1891 the family was living at 68 Hertford Road, Bootle and Henry was working as a 'Superintendent Steward' in a club.

Following their arrival in Liverpool, two more children arrived, William (born in Bootle in 1892) and May (born in Seaforth in 1896).

John entered Merchant Taylors' on 2 May 1899 at which time his father was still working as a 'Superintendent Steward' and he was living at 1 Elm Road Seaforth.

The 1901 census showed the whole family (other than Laura) still living at home, though 'home' had moved to Moss Lane in Orrell and Ford, Liverpool. John's father's occupation was listed as 'Army Pensioner' which certainly fits in with the varied birthplaces of his children.

John left the school at Christmas 1902 after which he disappears from the record other than a mention in the school register that he was killed in action serving with the Royal Welsh Fusiliers in 1918.

A Jack Brown enlisted in Waterloo, Liverpool, served with the Royal Welsh Fusiliers as Private 58220 and was killed in action on 27 August 1918 but there is no evidence to link him with 'our' John Brown.

Thomas Wright Carson

Second Lieutenant
6th Battalion Duke of Wellington's (West Riding)
Regiment
MTS 1894–98

Thomas Carson never knew his father, William, who died shortly before Thomas was born on 29 November 1884 at Sunnyside, Sutton-in-Craven, Yorkshire. William Carson had married Thomas's mother, Fanny Bairstow, at Skipton in 1879 and their first son, William Bairstow was born in Lytham, Lancashire in 1882 by which time William had been vicar of Girlington, Bradford for three years.

By 1891, Thomas, his mother and brother had moved to 146 Duke Street, Southport. They later moved to 3 Oakdale Road, Waterloo, the address from which Thomas set out for his first day at Merchant Taylors' on 13 September 1894.

He remained at the school for about four years, leaving in July 1898 to move to Lancaster Grammar School where he is recorded as a boarder in the 1901 census, by which date, his mother and brother had moved back to Skipton.

After leaving school, Thomas studied law and became a solicitor in Llanelli where he was practising in 1911.

Giving up his job with the law firm when war broke out, Thomas enlisted in the 2nd/6th Battalion West Riding Regiment in September 1914 and was soon commissioned as second lieutenant on 6 October 1914 reaching France on 3 November 1915. After about a month in France, he was transferred to 1st/6th Battalion of the regiment in the middle of December 1915.

On Monday 27 December, Thomas volunteered to go on patrol with two others into no man's land between the two front lines. While on patrol, a flare was sent up by the enemy and the three members of the patrol threw themselves flat on the ground in the usual way. When the flare had burnt out, Carson could not be found. A search was made but no trace of him found. It was thought he had been taken prisoner. Enquiries made in Germany produced a response from Countess E. Blucher von Wahlstatt who reported a conversation with a German officer who had found the body of a young British officer carrying papers in the name of Carson. The Germans had buried him and marked his grave.

He was later reburied in Sanctuary Wood Cemetery in plot V row J grave 6. He was 31 years old.

COLIN CHAPPELL

Rifleman
2238
1st/6th Battalion King's (Liverpool Regiment)
MTS 1899–1905

Colin Chappell was born on 5 August 1888 at Ashton on Mersey in the south of Manchester. His parents, George Chappell and his wife Emily (formerly Thompson) had married in 1883 and already had two children when Colin was born, Robert Kingsley (born 1885) and Dorothy (born 1886) both also born in Ashton. Sometime between 1888 and 1890, they moved to Southport as their fourth child, Lilian, was born there in the last quarter of that year.

In 1891, George, Emily and the family were living at 11 Cross Street, Southport and George was working as a secretary to an insurance company. Their youngest child, Lilian, did not live long, dying in the first half of that year when only a few months old.

In 1899, when he was about 11 years old, Colin entered Merchant Taylors' School. By 1901 the family had moved to 14 Adelaide Terrace, Waterloo, Liverpool, a large house overlooking the River Mersey. While at Merchant Taylors', Colin does not seem to have been a winner of prizes but he represented the school in the rugby XV in 1903, 1904 and 1905 playing at full-back where his performance was summed up in *The School Review* as 'slow of pace but a good kicker'. He left school in 1905 and took up a position with Messrs J. H. Townley & Sons in the Liverpool Stock Exchange.

On 7 May 1909 he was gazetted second lieutenant in the 5th Battalion King's (Liverpool Regiment), a Territorial battalion, with effect from 7 March 1909. Promotion to lieutenant in 5th King's was announced in the *London Gazette* on 15 August 1911, to date from 19 May of that year. He eventually resigned his commission on 29 May 1912.

By 1911, Colin was working as a 'Stockbroker's Clerk' while his brother, Robert, was described as a 'Barrister'. Indeed Robert went on to be KC then QC and was appointed a judge on the Isle of Man.

On the outbreak of war Colin enlisted as a private in 1st/6th Battalion of King's (Liverpool Regiment) on 1 September 1914 and was given the regimental number 2238. The battalion left for France on 25 February 1915, landed at Le Havre and became part of 15th Brigade, 5th Division operating in the Ypres area. Only a month after he arrived in France, Colin Chappell was killed in action on 23 March 1915.

He was buried in Sanctuary Wood Cemetery, plot IV row G grave 15. In St Vincent's church, Burton-by-Lincoln, the village in which his father was born, there is a plaque commemorating his death 'while helping a wounded comrade at Kleine Zillebeke'.

HAROLD WOLFENDEN CLARK

Sapper
638
Royal Engineers
MTS 1897–1902

Harold Wolfenden Clark was the son of Joseph Wilson Clark and the grandson of Joseph Clark, headmaster of Merchant Taylors', Crosby from 1829 to 1850.

He was born at Oxton in Cheshire on 28 November 1884 to Joseph and his wife Hannah (formerly Wolfenden). The middle child of three, he was preceded by Margaret Winifred in 1881 and followed by Dorothy in 1888, the former born in Waterloo, the latter in Oxton.

In 1891 they were living in Oxton at 6 Silverdale Road where Joseph was working as a stockbroker.

Harold joined Merchant Taylors' in June 1897 by which time the family had moved to 1 Hereford Road, Seaforth. His father gave his occupation as 'Formerly Stock & Share Broker'.

They were still living at the same address in 1901, Harold's father still enjoying his retirement, and in the following year, Harold left the school.

In 1910, Harold's father died aged 64. Harold and his mother were still living in Hereford Road in 1911. He was working as a clerk with Liverpool Corporation. His sister Margaret was nursing in a London hospital.

At the start of the war, Harold was another of the former pupils who enlisted quickly. He attested on 8 August 1914 and joined the Lancashire Fortress Company, Royal Engineers. While serving with this unit at Templebreedy, Cork he was accidentally killed (apparently by falling off a cliff) on 13 January 1915.

He is buried in the churchyard of St Luke's church, Great Crosby in grave C213.

ELIJAH COBHAM
MC MA

Chaplain 4th Class
Army Chaplains' Department
MTS 1890–93

Elijah's father, John, consistently described himself on census forms as a 'Licensed Victualler' which brings to mind an image of a man serving pints of beer in a pub. He was, in fact, the owner of the Bear's Paw Restaurant at 53 Lord Street, Liverpool; a restaurant widely regarded at the time as the best in the city and which operated until it was destroyed by a Luftwaffe bomb in 1941. The restaurant was a successful venture and, clearly, Elijah did not grow up in poverty. Indeed, when John died in 1889, he left an estate valued at the time at over £22,000 (several million pounds by today's standards).

John had married Martha Ann Matches in Cockermouth in 1863 and over the next twenty years the couple had eight children. Elijah had three older brothers: George Henry (born 1866), John Lawrence (1873) and Harold (1877) and three older sisters: Alice (1868), Elizabeth (1872) and Martha Hargreaves (1878). Elijah was born on 31 October 1880 in Waterloo. A younger sister, Ellen Mary, was born in 1882.

On 10 January 1889, when Elijah was only eight years old, his father died. He was buried in the grounds of St Helen's church, Sefton.

Elijah entered Merchant Taylors' on 10 September 1890. His older brothers John and Harold showed a certain amount of sporting flair, John being a member of the cricket and rugby teams and winning the Fives Challenge Cup and Harold playing in the rugby XV. The only sporting success ascribed to Elijah in *The School Review* was the winning of the Sack Race on Sports Day in 1891!

John went on to Corpus Christi College, Cambridge. Harold left Merchant Taylors' in 1892 to attend Glenalmond School, Perth and was followed there by Elijah in 1893. Sadly, Harold died at Glenalmond School in 1894.

Elijah went up to Emmanuel College, Cambridge on 3 October 1900. He graduated BA in 1903 and MA in 1907. After Cambridge, he entered the Church, was made deacon in 1906 and ordained priest in 1907.

On 4 August 1913 he sailed to Mombasa. His plan was to become a missionary at Nakura, East Africa. In August 1914, hostilities began in Africa. The British settlers were enrolled in a volunteer force in which Elijah became a corporal. This force was later disbanded and Elijah returned to his religious duties until the Expeditionary Force arrived when he offered his services as an orderly with the RAMC.

He later joined the Army Chaplains' Department and was attached to the King's African Rifles. While in action with them on one occasion several men were wounded. Cobham returned to the battlefield to recover them but was mortally wounded himself. For this action he was awarded a Military Cross which was gazetted on 8 March 1918. Although no citation appears in the *London Gazette* to accompany the award, a statement was issued to his next of kin on 13 January 1919 which reads:

> He met his death in attempting to bring in wounded under heavy fire. He had already rescued two men and was shot whilst bringing in a third. An officer who exercised a great power for good over all ranks and one who could ill be spared.

He died on 19 September 1917 aged 37. He is buried in Dar-es-Salaam War Cemetery in plot V row A grave 15.

ARTHUR AMERY COLLINSON

Captain
9th Battalion East Surrey Regiment
MTS 1892–1902

Arthur Amery Collinson was the fifth of six children born to Thomas Antwis Collinson and his wife Margaret Alice (formerly Carter). The eldest child was James Walter (born 1874) who was followed by William Leonard (born 1876), Nellie (born 1878), Frederick Baker (born 1881), Arthur Amery (born 7 August 1884) and finally Alice Mabel in 1890.

Arthur's father was a bootmaker who employed a sizable workforce and by 1891 had moved into the house, at 4 College Road, Crosby, in which he was to spend the rest of his life and raise his family.

The following year, Arthur and his brother Frederick entered Merchant Taylors' on 7 September 1892, joining their brother William who had arrived in 1885. The eldest brother, James, had attended the school from 1883 until 1890. William and Arthur were both granted Harrison Scholarships.

In 1901, all six children were still living at home in the same house in College Road. James and William were both helping their father in the family business and Frederick was working as an assistant in their shop.

Arthur, however, persevered with his studies and in July 1902 left the school having been awarded the Derby Prize for Modern Languages and the Stanley Prize for Natural Science. He also passed the London Matriculation with Honours being placed 9th out of 3,000 candidates.

Going on to study law, he obtained a first class in his final examinations and was awarded the Atkinson Conveyancing Gold Medal, the Law Society's Timpron Martin Gold Medal and the Enoch Harvey Prize for the best Liverpool candidate.

By 1911 he was working as a solicitor and living in a boarding house at 39 Shrubbery Road, Streatham.

Before the war he was a member of the 2nd Volunteer Battalion King's (Liverpool Regiment) and, with them, shot in competition at Bisley, the national shooting centre in Surrey, where he won the Clement Smith Gold Medal.

At the start of the war he was managing clerk with Messrs Waltons and Co of 101 Leadenhall Street, London and enlisted as a gunner (No 444) in the Honourable Artillery Company on the day war was declared. In September 1914 he was commissioned as a second lieutenant in the 9th Battalion East Surrey Regiment, was promoted lieutenant in December of the same year and eventually captain on 9 May 1915.

The battalion landed in France on 1 September 1915 and formed part of the 24th Division concentrated in the Étaples and St Pol area. Lengthy forced marches then took them into the battle of Loos where he was reported missing on 25/26 September 1915 afterwards being officially described as killed in action. He has no known grave and is commemorated on panels 65 to 67 of the Loos Memorial.

HENRY BRODIE CONBY
DSC

Lieutenant
Royal Naval Reserve
MTS 1902–03

Henry Brodie Conby was the youngest child of Henry Brodie Conby, a master mariner, and his wife Sophia Louisa Conby (formerly Blake). They had married in Dublin in October 1882 and their first child, Alice Jessie was born in Dublin in August 1883. Their second child, Robert Blake was born in 1885.

By 1888 they were living in England as Henry (junior) was born in Rock Ferry, Cheshire on 5 September 1888, being baptised there on 4 November 1888.

Henry joined Merchant Taylors' on 1 May 1902 when the family was living at 16 Brooke Road, Blundellsands. He left school at Christmas 1903 and went to sea, qualifying for his Second Mate's certificate on 9 July 1909.

Henry's older brother, Robert, had gone to study at HMS *Conway* between January 1900 and December 1901 but tragically died at sea on 5 October 1904.

By 1911, Henry's mother and father had moved back to Ireland and the census shows them living in Arklow, Wicklow. In the same year, on 7 July, Henry (junior) qualified for his First Mate's certificate and on 4 December 1914 he obtained his Master's certificate.

He was appointed to the Royal Naval Reserve in January 1915, being appointed temporary sub-lieutenant RNR, and was initially (from March) on the books of HMS *White Oak* for duty with net drifters working out of Poole, Dorset. Before long he was transferred to HMS *Attentive* for service with drifters of the auxiliary patrol based in Dover. Henry was promoted to acting lieutenant with seniority dating from 8 January 1915.

He took leave in 1915 and married Eleanor Hutchinson Armstrong at Enniscorthy, Ireland.

His services clearly impressed his superiors. He was Mentioned in Despatches for services with the auxiliary patrol and awarded the Distinguished Service Cross, the citation reading:

For the excellent services rendered by him at all times; he has been present with the Patrol in all the principal operations against the enemy.

In February 1917, Henry and Eleanor had a son whom they named Harry Brodie Conby.

Henry was working with net drifters out of Dover. These were requisitioned fishing vessels whose job was to tend to the anti-submarine nets laid across the Dover Strait. Connected to these nets were electrically triggered mines that exploded when they came into contact with metal objects. On Sunday 3 June 1917, one of the mines exploded and damaged the net. Henry Conby, aboard the 67-ton Lowestoft-registered drifter *George V*, was sent to investigate and make repairs. As repairs were under way there was an explosion which caused the drifter to roll over and sink within two minutes taking nine of the crew, including Conby, with her. There were two survivors.

Henry's body was not recovered for burial and he is commemorated on the Chatham Naval Memorial.

ADRIAN DEIGHTON COOBAN

Major
16th Battalion King's Royal Rifle Corps
MTS 1894–98

Adrian's parents, James Cooban and Jane (formerly Lowe) were married at St Mary's, Grassendale on 14 September 1881. James was described as a 'Corn Factor' and both the bride and groom's fathers were described as 'Gentleman'. James and Jane had three children, two of whom were still alive in 1911. Adrian Deighton, the eldest, was born on 4 August 1882 and his sister, Jane Lois was born in 1884. The third child has not been identified but it seems he/she had died by 1891 as had James.

The census return for 1891 shows Jane, a widow, and her two children living in the home of her mother, Jane Lowe, herself a 78-year-old widow, at 19 Adelaide Terrace, Waterloo.

Adrian joined Merchant Taylors' in 1894 and left the school in 1898 to join the London and Lancashire Fire Insurance Co Ltd.

He was an enthusiastic member of the Church Lads' Brigade (CLB) and had enrolled as a lieutenant in 1900. By 1901, the family had moved to 16 Kinross Road, Seaforth. Adrian was 18 and working as an 'Apprentice Agent in Cotton and General Services'. He was promoted to captain in the Church Lads' Brigade in 1905 and to major in 1908.

Sometime between 1901 and 1911, Jane and Adrian (still unmarried) moved across the Mersey where, in 1911, they were living at 114 Woodchurch Lane, Prenton. Adrian was working as a clerk in an insurance company. In 1912 he was appointed commanding officer of Emmanuel Company in CLB.

When war broke out he joined the 5th Battalion King's (Liverpool Regiment), enlisting as a rifleman and was soon commissioned captain on 15 September 1915 being appointed to the 16th Battalion King's Royal Rifle Corps (a Church Lads' Brigade battalion) and taking command of A Company. The battalion sailed from Southampton on 16 November 1915 and arrived in Le Havre on 17 November. Cooban had by this time been promoted major.

Early in January 1916 the battalion took over part of the line at Givenchy. In July they were moved into the Somme area where the battle – which had started on 1 July 1916 with enormous losses – was still raging. The battalion was eventually assigned the taking of High Wood, a strongly held German position. When they entered the wood on 16 July 1916 they came under heavy machine-gun fire resulting in many casualties. One of the casualties was Adrian Cooban.

He is buried in plot V row G grave 32 of Caterpillar Valley Cemetery, Longueval.

THOMAS HAROLD RAYNER DANIELS

Second Lieutenant
6th Battalion King's Own Royal Lancaster
Regiment
MTS 1905–14

In 1895, Thomas Charles Edward Daniels married Florence Hilda Rayner in Conway, North Wales. Their two children were both born in Conway, the elder, Thomas Harold Rayner was born on 23 July 1896, and the younger Audrey Isabel Daniels in 1897.

After barely six years of marriage, Florence was left a widow when Thomas Charles Edward, a schoolmaster, died on 9 February 1901 aged only 40.

When the census was taken at the end of March 1901 Florence was living with her mother-in-law, Fridiswid Charlotte Daniels, at Fern Lea, Allerton Road, Liverpool, no doubt still mourning the loss of her husband. Meanwhile, Thomas and his sister were still living in Wales being cared for by their aunt, Lucy Williams, Florence's sister, at Brynrhedyn, Conway and spending time with their cousin John Rayner Williams (see p.200).

On 17 September 1905, Thomas entered Merchant Taylors' as a Harrison Scholar, having previously been tutored privately at home. In 1910, he made his first attempt at the Oxford Local Junior exams and obtained a Pass.

By 1911 Florence had moved to 21 Alexandra Road, Great Crosby and was working as a domestic science teacher. She was sharing the house with her sister Lucy Helen Williams, also a widow, her two children, Thomas and Audrey (though her son seems to have been known as Harold), her sister's son John Rayner Williams and a niece, Lorna, who was born in Australia.

In 1911 Thomas repeated his Oxford Local Junior exams and gained a 3rd Class, improving this to a 2nd Class two years later in 1913.

He left the school on 30 July 1914 to go up to Sidney Sussex College, Cambridge. However, the war seems to have intervened as he was gazetted second lieutenant on 18 December 1914. According to his medal index card, he first entered a theatre of war on 30 January 1916 when he arrived at Port Said which means that he missed the battalion's sojourn in Gallipoli in 1915. After Gallipoli, the battalion moved to Egypt and then on to Mesopotamia in February 1916. As part of the 13th Division they were assigned to help in the relief of the siege of Kut. This attempted relief began on 6 April 1916 and resulted in the battle of Sanniyat on 9 April 1916. It was on this date and probably in this battle that Second Lieutenant Daniels was killed, aged 19. Initially he was thought to be a prisoner of the Turks but was later reported to have died.

He is commemorated on panel 7 of the Basra Memorial.

JOSIAH STANLEY DEAN

Captain
7th Battalion King's (Liverpool Regiment)
MTS 1897–1905

Of the 12 children born to Josiah Dean and his wife Elizabeth Emily Dean (formerly Berridge), 11 survived to be recorded in the 1911 census. Of these, seven were boys and all of them attended Merchant Taylors'.

Josiah Stanley Dean was the seventh surviving child and was born on 16 July 1888 at Aintree, Liverpool.

Josiah (senior) and Elizabeth were married in 1877. By 1891, when they were living at 91 Moss Lane, Walton, the family already included eight children: Gilbert Dean Dean (born 1878), Winifred Dean Dean (1880), Thomas Berridge Dean (1881), William Frederick Dean (1883), Arthur Devereux Dean (1884), Margaret Dean Dean (1886), Josiah Stanley Dean (1888) and Dorothy Dean Dean (1889). To help out with this large family they had a nurse, a cook and a maid.

In about 1892 or 1893, Josiah moved his family to The Dunes, a large house in Warren Road, Blundellsands.

Josiah began his career at Merchant Taylors' on 14 September 1897. His four older brothers had preceded him; Gilbert had already left in 1895.

The family was still living at The Dunes in 1901 where three new additions had increased the roll call to 11 children: John Athelstan Dean was born in 1891, Ernest Norman Dean in 1893 and Elsie Dean Dean in 1894. Of the older children, Gilbert was working as a solicitor's articled clerk, Thomas as a marine insurance clerk and William as a ship owner's apprentice.

Josiah left the school in 1905 and, judging by his later involvement, found employment in the cotton trade.

In 1909 he gained a commission in the 7th Battalion King's (Liverpool Regiment), a Territorial battalion, being appointed second lieutenant on 1 January 1909. After almost two years he was promoted to lieutenant on 1 December 1910.

1911 found Josiah (junior) still living at home at The Dunes along with six of the other children. Arthur was working as a solicitor, Margaret as a domestic science teacher, Josiah as a cotton salesman, John as an insurance clerk and Ernest as a cotton merchant's apprentice.

Josiah was the representative of Davies Benachi and Co, Cotton Merchants, Liverpool in Charleston, South Carolina until 1914 in which year he sailed home from Philadelphia to Liverpool aboard the SS *Haverford*, arriving on 11 April.

On the outbreak of war he presumably joined his battalion when they were mobilised at their headquarters in Bootle and then moved to Canterbury. They landed at Le Havre on 8 March 1915 and became part of 6th Brigade of the 2nd Division. The first major action to be faced by the battalion was at the battle of Festubert in May 1915. It was in this battle that Josiah Dean was fatally wounded, succumbing to his wounds on 27 May.

He is buried in plot II row A grave 22 of the Boulogne Eastern Cemetery.

KENNETH JOHNSON DEAN

Private
35991
1st Battalion Loyal North Lancashire Regiment
MTS 1910–14

When John Dean married Margaret Jane Johnson at St David's church, Wigan in 1889 he was a mining engineer living in Ince-in-Makerfield, part of Wigan, Lancashire. He was part of the coal mining industry and was later a colliery manager.

They had six children, two of whom had died by 1911. Their first child, William Johnson was born in 1892 but died in 1895 aged two. Kenneth was the third of those who survived and was born at Standish, Lancashire on 22 November 1897. He had an older sister, Hilda (born 1890) and brother, Eric Victor (born 1895).

In 1901, John and his family were living at 14 Grove Lane, Standish, Lancashire. The following year another son, Horace Spencer, was born at Standish.

Kenneth attended Wigan Grammar School from 1905 until 1910, then moved to Merchant Taylors' on 14 September 1910, aged 12. He boarded in Mr Milton's boarding house in College Avenue and passed his Oxford Local Junior exam in 1913. In the summer of 1914, he made the cricket XI. In *The School Review* he is described as: 'small but very keen. A good change bowler and very promising with the bat. Should make a good player as he grows in height and strength'.

He left the school on 30 July 1914 to become a surveyor.

Kenneth waited to attest until 25 May 1916 when he signed his attestation papers at Wigan, giving his address as The Grove, Standish, his occupation as an 'articled pupil at a surveyors' and his father as next-of-kin.

He had to wait until 17 October 1916 to be mobilised and four days later on 21 October was posted as gunner with the Royal Field Artillery. Having passed through his training with 76th Training Reserve Battalion, he seems to have been transferred to the 1st Battalion Loyal North Lancashire Regiment on 11 January 1917, the day he embarked at Folkestone for Boulogne.

Kenneth was severely wounded while returning from an attack on Passchendaele Ridge and was taken to No 4 Casualty Clearing Station at Lozinghem where he died from his wounds on 14 November 1917 aged 19.

He is buried in plot XIII row C grave 9 of the Dozinghem Military Cemetery.

WELLESLEY VENABLES DEANE

Second Lieutenant
Royal Field Artillery
MTS 1907–11

Wellesley Venables Deane was born on 13 September 1896 in Didsbury. He was the son of Thomas Deane and his wife Kate Sobain Deane (formerly Dux) who had married in 1889. He was the fifth of their seven children, all of whom were given the middle name Venables: Thomas was born in 1890, Eric in 1891, Kate in 1892, Nevill in 1895, Wellesley in 1896 and Noel in 1898. The final child, Mary, arrived later, in 1901, after the census.

In 1901, the family were living at 26 Kingston Road, Didsbury and Thomas was working as an insurance agent.

By the time Wellesley came to Merchant Taylors' on 17 September 1907, his father had retired. Given that Nevill and Noel arrived at the school in the same year, it seems likely that the family moved into the area in that year.

Wellesley's brother, Thomas, had moved out by 1911 but the other five children were still living at home, which was now 36 Oxford Drive, Waterloo.

In the year that he left school, Wellesley was only old enough to compete in the under-15 events on Sports Day but he acquitted himself well, winning the long jump (with his brother Noel in second place) and coming second in the 100 yards, 220 yards, hurdles and high jump. Wellesley was a member of the school's Debating Society and gave his maiden speech to the gathered membership on 18 March 1910 while still only 13.

Wellesley left school on 27 July 1911 to work in a general merchant's office and on the outbreak of war enlisted as a private (No 1880) in the King's (Liverpool Regiment) with whom he went to France on 24 February 1915. He was wounded while with the King's and returned home. His commission as second lieutenant in the East Lancashire Brigade of the Royal Field Artillery with precedence from 2 November 1915 was gazetted on 15 August 1916.

He served with D Battery 95th Brigade Royal Field Artillery and was killed in action on 24 September 1917, being buried in plot VII row A grave 4 of the Huts Cemetery near Ypres.

GEOFFREY MARISCHAL DOWDING

The officers of HMS *Good Hope*. Midshipman Dowding is second from the left in the front row.

Midshipman
Royal Naval Reserve
MTS 1907–10

Geoffrey Marischal Dowding's father, Reverend Charles Dowding, spent some years as a missionary in Dibrugarh, Assam and it was here that Geoffrey was born on 7 December 1894. His father and mother (Kathleen Dowding, formerly Sargent) must have moved to India shortly after their marriage in 1890 for their first three children were all born in Dibrugarh: John Charles Keith on 1 November 1891 and Eda Engayne in about 1893 and Geoffrey. They had moved back to England by the birth of their fourth child, Honor Margaret, in Keswick, in 1900.

In 1901, Charles was living in the vicarage at St John's in the Vale, Cockermouth with his wife and four children. It is possible that another son, Owen Herbert, was born in 1902 and another daughter, Rosamund, was born in 1904, both in Cumberland.

Between 1904 and 1907, the family moved to the Crosby area for in the latter year, Geoffrey started at Merchant Taylors' as a Harrison Scholar. In 1909, another sister, Kathleen Elinor was born and in the following year, Geoffrey left Merchant Taylors' and went on to be a student aboard HMS *Conway* until 1912.

HMS *Good Hope*.

On 9 January 1913 he was appointed a probationary midshipman, RNR and subsequently underwent training on HMS *Superb* from 9 May to July 1914. At the end of July he transferred to HMS *Good Hope*, possibly as part of the pre-war test mobilisation and was ordered to sea with her on the outbreak of war when she became flagship of Rear-Admiral Christopher Cradock's South Atlantic squadron.

At this time, the German East Asia squadron under Admiral von Spee was raiding commerce in the Pacific and Cradock, determined to destroy them, rounded Cape Horn at the end of October and sailed north while von Spee was sailing south. The two squadrons met off Chile on 1 November 1914 and after fierce fighting HMS *Good Hope* was sunk with all hands as was HMS *Monmouth*, another unit of Cradock's squadron.

Geoffrey Dowding has no known grave but the sea and is commemorated on panel 6 of the Portsmouth Naval Memorial.

WALTER DUNCAN
LLM

Lieutenant
8th Battalion King's (Liverpool Regiment)
MTS 1900–07

Walter's father, John Duncan, was a wholesale fish merchant in Liverpool. He and his wife, Emma, (formerly Farmer) had married in 1872. They had eight children altogether though one died before the 1911 census. Walter was the last of the surviving children to be born. The eldest child, John, was born in 1876. He was followed by James Alexander (1877), William Henry (1879), Elizabeth (1881), Emma (1883), Charles Frederick (1885) and finally Walter on 2 June 1889.

The first two children were baptised in St Silas's church and the register shows John and Emma were living at 17 Great Charlotte Street. Between the births of James in 1877 and William in 1879 they moved out of the city to the Waterloo area and by 1891 they were living in a large house at 15 Victoria Road, Waterloo. In 1897 Walter's eldest brother John, a scholar at Selwyn College, Cambridge, died after a short illness.

Walter entered Merchant Taylors' on 24 January 1900 as a Harrison Scholar and stayed at the school until July 1907, representing the school at cricket in 1907 and rugby in the 1906/07 season.

After school he attended Liverpool University where he read Law, qualifying LLB in 1910 and LLM in 1911 by which time John and Emma had moved to 20 Esplanade, Waterloo and Walter was still living at home and working as a solicitor's articled clerk with Edward Pickmere, Liverpool's town clerk. He qualified as a solicitor in 1912, the top candidate of the year and received several medals and prizes including the Timpron Martin Gold Medal, the Rupert Bremner Gold Medal, the Atkinson Gold Medal and the John Mackrell Prize. He then joined the firm of Alsop, Stevens, Crooks and Co.

Like a number of old boys, Walter had enlisted in the ranks of a Territorial battalion of King's (Liverpool Regiment) before the start of the war. In his case he became a private (No 1353) in the 6th Battalion and was immediately mobilised on the outbreak of hostilities but was soon commissioned as a second lieutenant in the 8th (Irish) Battalion. His commission was dated 9 January 1915. He crossed to France to join the battalion in July 1915 where they were fighting as part of the 51st (Highland) Division until January 1916 when they moved to the 55th (West Lancashire) Division concentrating in the Hallencourt area.

On 25 July 1916 the division moved to take up a position in the front line opposite the village of Guillemont. At 4.14 a.m. on the morning of 8 August the battalion moved to attack the village following an artillery barrage. Initially the advance went well. However, the battalions to their right and left could not sustain the attack. When the enemy counter-attacked, the men of 8 King's were left with Germans to their front, flank and rear. They were given the order to retire. According to the battalion's war diary, Duncan was reported to have been gassed and was taken prisoner and over the coming months and years was moved around from camp to camp in Germany. While a prisoner of war, his promotion to lieutenant was gazetted with seniority from 1 June 1916. On 3 February 1918 he escaped from Ludwigshafen. A detailed account of his imprisonment and escape was written by him and is held in the National Archives. This is an extract from that account:

> I escaped from Ludwigshafen on 3rd February 1918. The new exchange to Holland had begun, and three British had already left the camp. They were allowed to take 25 kilos of luggage, the remainder being sent to the Kommandantur 5 minutes' walk away, where the luggage was examined and sealed to be sent forward to Holland. The fourth British officer to leave was Major Shewan, of the Dublin Fusiliers, who had very little luggage, so I put labels with his name and regiment on a big packing case of mine, took off two padlocks and made an arrangement by which I could open the box from inside and no one could open it from outside as long as I was within. I got into this case, was wheeled round to the Kommandantur with the other luggage by two British orderlies under a German sentry, was put down on the pavement in a very solitary street while the other luggage was taken in, and when they were well into the building I came out of the box and walked away.

He travelled to Manheim and Frankfurt where:

> [I] killed an hour and a half in a cinema, and left the town when it began to grow dark, walking, and when it was quite dark I crawled. It took me eight hours to crawl to the frontier, and the sentries heard me once and got a lamp to search the ploughed field where I was, but fortunately they gave it up and I got into Holland.
>
> I had several narrow escapes of discovery, in particular on one occasion when I gave up my seat to a lady in a train! I ought, of course, to have offered it to her husband.

He returned home and was received by the King on 22 February 1918. He was granted three months' leave and appointed to the Home Intelligence Staff. In the autumn of 1918 he married Agnes S. Cameron of Glasgow. Their marriage was short-lived as he died on 19 December 1918, having developed pleurisy and then pneumonia. No doubt his ability to resist these was reduced by the privations of his captivity. He was Mentioned in Despatches for his 'gallant conduct and determination in escaping from captivity'.

Walter Duncan is buried in Anfield Cemetery in grave VII CE 1740.

THOMAS HUME DUNLOP

Private
36374
10th Battalion Cheshire Regiment
MTS 1893–97

Thomas Hume Dunlop was born on 17 September 1881, the son of Thomas Dunlop and his wife Charlotte Maria Dunlop (probably formerly Carlile). It seems likely that Charlotte was Thomas's second wife. Thomas (senior) was a minister of the United Presbyterian Church in Scotland and in 1875 he had tendered his resignation on the grounds that 'he desired to enjoy liberty as to marriage with a deceased wife's sister' and that he intended to emigrate to America where he would be free to contract such a marriage and also be a minister. However, before he could leave for America he accepted the pastorate of Emmanuel Congregational church in Bootle.

On 5 April 1891, Thomas, who was born in Kilmarnock, and Charlotte, who was born in Philadelphia but was a British subject, were living at 2 Fernhill Road, Bootle. Thomas's eldest daughter, Maggie C. Dunlop, was

22 years old and clearly from his first marriage. With his second wife he had had three children who were alive at the time of the 1891 census, Elizabeth Helen (born in around 1877) and Agnes (born in around 1887) as well as Thomas.

Thomas (junior) joined Merchant Taylors' on 12 September 1893, at which time the family was living at 6 St Alban's Square, Bootle. He remained at the school for almost four years and left at Easter 1897. During his time at the school, the final addition to the family was born in 1894 – a brother, Gavin Alexander. Thomas proved to be a musician of some promise and, after school, studied music. The census return of 1901 lists him as a music student living at 22 Balliol Road, Bootle. In 1905 he qualified as a piano teacher, having passed the exams set by the Royal Manchester College of Music, following which he moved to London. The 1911 census shows him living at 2 Cadogan Street, Chelsea, working as a musician (pianist, organist and theorist).

Thomas attested at Hoylake on 11 December 1915, giving his address as St Olave's, Mostyn Avenue, West Kirkby and his father as next of kin. However, he was not mobilised until 22 March 1916 when he was posted to the 14th Battalion Cheshire Regiment. At about this time his mother wrote to the Army Records Office to inform them of the death of her husband and that she was to replace him as next of kin. He embarked for France on 16 July 1916 and a week later, on 23 July, was posted to 10th Battalion Cheshire Regiment. On 9 October the battalion took part in the offensive which captured the northern face of 'Stuff Redoubt'. Thomas was wounded in this attack receiving several gunshot wounds. He was initially taken to No 49 Casualty Clearing Station at Contay before being transferred to No 1 Canadian General Hospital at Étaples where he died of his wounds on 10 October 1916.

Thomas is buried in plot VIII row B grave 1 of Étaples Military Cemetery.

CHARLES NORMAN INNES DUNMAN

Lieutenant
15th Battalion The Duke of Cambridge's Own
(Middlesex) Regiment
MTS 1887–94

Charles's father, Robert, a merchant in Shanghai, married twice. His first wife, Charlotte, was mother to his first three children: Gertrude Muriel (born

1873), Robert Leslie (born 1876) and Charles Norman Innes (born 10 January 1878). Robert married his second wife Harriet Edith Coates in 1881. They also had three children. All Robert's children were born in Shanghai but by April 1881, the three born to his first wife had returned to England and were boarding at 1 Atlantic Villas, Weston-super-Mare.

On 19 April 1887, Charles joined Merchant Taylors'. By 1891 Charles and his older brother Robert were boarding with a Mrs Lovegrove in Holden Street, Crosby, and they had been joined by their half-brother Thomas Newman Dunman. Robert attended the school from 1884 to 1892 and Thomas from 1891 to 1898. Charles left school in July 1894.

He seems to have enlisted in the 1st Volunteer Battalion Cheshire Regiment in 1899 and to have gone out to South Africa where, during the Boer War, he served with the 29th (Denbighshire) Company, 9th Battalion Imperial Yeomanry from which he was discharged on 3 March 1901. He then joined the South African Constabulary, being discharged on 25 January 1903.

While in South Africa, Charles met his future wife, Elsie Machan Thomas who had been born in Ahmadabad, India in 1885. They married in Pretoria on 10 December 1903. He gave his occupation as a theatrical professional.

Over the next few years they had three children. The first was Helen Margaret who was born in Pretoria in about 1907. They returned to England shortly afterwards, as their second child, Charles Cecil Morgan, was born in London in 1908 and their third, Sheila Gabrielle in about 1909.

At the time of the 1911 census the family was living at 5 Prince of Wales Road, Battersea when Charles was working for himself as a motor cab driver.

No doubt helped by his ability to drive, Charles attested for the Army Service Corps at London on 8 August 1914. Enlisting as a private he rose to be acting sergeant and arrived in France on 21 September 1914. He served there from September to November 1914 and from May to November 1915. As a company quartermaster sergeant with 32 Company, Army Service Corps he was discharged to a commission in 15th Battalion Middlesex Regiment being gazetted second lieutenant from 7 December 1915.

He was later gazetted to the Machine Gun Corps on 24 February 1917. Promotion to lieutenant followed on 1 July 1917. Part of the Machine Gun Corps eventually became the Tank Corps and Charles seems to have become part of this on its formation.

Charles was commanding a tank at the third battle of Ypres when his section of four tanks came under heavy machine-gun and artillery fire and three were hit and knocked out. Charles's tank was ditched just inside the new British front line and he was killed, according to his family, while climbing out of the tank.

He is buried in plot II row E grave 2 at Hooge Crater Cemetery.

THOMAS GRAY DYKES

Private
1188
Royal Army Medical Corps
MTS 1901–03

Thomas Dykes saw no active service during the war and, in fact served in wartime uniform for a short time only.

He was born on 21 July 1891, the only child of John Dykes and his wife Lilian (formerly Melville) who had married in Barrow-in-Furness in 1890 and both of whom hailed originally from Scotland.

By 1901 the family had moved to 19 Cecil Road, Seaforth from which John went to work as a ship surveyor for Lloyd's. This was the house that Thomas left for his first day at Merchant Taylors' on 10 September 1901 aged 10.

He stayed at the school for only two years, leaving in December 1903 when he was only 12 years old. It is possible the family moved out of the area as on 17 September 1909 he attested for four years' service in the Royal Army Medical Corps, Territorial Force, giving an address in Whitchurch, Glamorgan. He stated on his attestation form that he was a medical student at Cardiff University. He was enrolled as a private with number 229 into the 2nd Welsh Field Ambulance which had been set up in 1908 as a Territorial unit based in Cardiff. His number was changed over the years to 1188. His first annual training with the unit was at Aberystwyth in July and August 1910.

In 1911 he was living with his parents at St Margaret, Church Road, Whitchurch, and he was listed in the census as being a medical student. In this year he again underwent annual training with the Territorial Force in July and August, this time at Lamprey.

It seems possible that at around this time he moved to Liverpool University and to the Crosby area. On 26 February 1912 he transferred to 1st West Lancs Field Ambulance, another Territorial unit, and went to annual training at Kirkham Camp in August 1912. His original four-year attestation having expired in September 1913, he re-engaged for one year.

On 5 August 1914 he was appointed a second-class orderly but two months later on 16 October 1914 he was discharged as 'unfit for further military service'.

Thomas died in a sanatorium in Penmaenmawr, possibly suffering from tuberculosis, on 18 June 1916.

He is buried in the churchyard of St Luke's church, Crosby in grave C 575 where the memorial states he was a student at Liverpool University.

John Llewelyn Edwards

Lieutenant
Royal Field Artillery
MTS 1905–10

John Llewelyn Edwards was a late addition to his parents' family. He was born in Caerwys, Flintshire on 18 June 1894 to John Edwards and his wife Elizabeth, fourteen years after his sister Lilian Annie. John and Elizabeth seem to have had only two children.

In 1901 John Edwards, architect and builder, his wife Elizabeth and their six-year-old son, John Llewelyn, were living at Bodlondeb House in Caerwys; a house they had lived in since at least 1881.

It is possible that John's father died in 1903. He had certainly died by the time John's mother applied for him to attend Merchant Taylors', which he entered on 1 May 1905 having previously attended a national school in Caerwys.

In 1910 he sat and passed his Oxford Local Junior exams and left the school on 29 July in the same year and went on to Bangor Agricultural College.

Early in the war, on 30 September 1914, he was granted a commission from the Officers' Training Corps as a temporary second lieutenant and was posted to the Royal Field Artillery, arriving in France on 26 August of the following year.

He served with C Battery, 75th Brigade Royal Field Artillery which in September 1915 had joined the Guards Division as part of the Divisional Artillery. With this division he would have seen action at the battles of Loos, Flers-Courcelette, Morval and Pilckem Ridge. John Edwards was killed in action in the battle of Pilckem on 7 September 1917. An entry for 8 September 1917 in the notebook of Major H. Giffard, who was serving with 75th Brigade RFA at the time, indicates 'Quiet night, but heard that Waggon Lines had been bombed. Edwards (Lieut J L) and Jenkins (2/ Lieut G P) killed and we had four men killed and eight wounded. Shocking bad luck.'

He is buried in plot III row B grave 8 of the Canada Farm Cemetery.

Eric Ben Evans

Second Lieutenant
1st/2nd Battalion attached 2nd/8th Battalion
Lancashire Fusiliers
MTS 1907–10

John Evans and Phoebe Jane Smalley Wainwright were married in Ormskirk in 1893 and their eldest child, Eric Ben Evans was born on 3 February 1895. Enid Helen Mellor followed in 1897.

In 1901, the family was living at 8 Brook Lane, Ormskirk in a house called 'Brook Lea'. John was working as a draper's assistant. Phoebe's parents, Benjamin and Ellen (or Helen) Wainwright were living next door at No 10. A brother to Eric, Alan Wainwright Evans, was born in 1902.

Eric arrived at Merchant Taylors' on 17 September 1907, the application form giving his father's occupation as draper. He had previously attended a National School in Ormskirk.

While Eric was at Merchant Taylors', John and Phoebe's last child, John Leslie, was born, in 1908. Eric stayed at the school for about three years, leaving on 29 July 1910 aged 15 to join a bank according to the school records though in 1911 he was recorded as a student in the home of his 70-year-old uncle Josiah Wainwright at Heath House, Southmoor, Abingdon. In the same year, his parents and his three younger siblings moved to his grandparents' house at 10 Brook Lane with his grandmother, no doubt following Phoebe's father's death in 1908.

During the war he initially, in 1915, enlisted as a private with the 6th Battalion King's (Liverpool Regiment) with the regimental number 3683 (later 241545) and went to France on 24 December 1915. For his time with this unit he would have formed part of the 55th Division and would have seen action at Guillemont, Ginchy and Morval but was probably discharged to a commission before the battle of Pilckem Ridge took place.

He was commissioned as a second lieutenant in the Lancashire Fusiliers on 29 August 1917 being attached to the 2nd/8th Battalion which formed part of the 42nd Division in the Ypres area.

Eric Evans died on 11 November 1917 of wounds received in action and is buried in plot I row C grave 58 at Potijze Chateau Grounds Cemetery.

NORMAN EDWARD EVANS

Second Lieutenant
17th Battalion Royal Welsh Fusiliers
MTS 1910–15

Norman's parents were both from Yorkshire, his father, Albert Edward Evans, from Bradford and his mother, Florence (formerly Helliwell) from Sowerby Bridge. At some time in the 1890s, Albert moved to Liverpool, returning to marry Florence in Sowerby Bridge on 9 September 1897.

After their marriage, the couple returned to Liverpool where their first child, Norman Edward, was born on 4 December 1898. He was baptised at Christ Church, Kensington on 18 January 1899. Albert was working as a woollen warehouseman and living at 16 Hawkins Street, a small two-up-and-two-down terrace house in the centre of Liverpool.

By 1901, Albert had moved his family to the Fairfield district of Liverpool and occupied 23 Alford Street. He was still working as a woollen warehouseman and at the time of the census, Florence would have been pregnant with their second child, Frederick Percy, who was born on 17 April 1901.

Norman came into the school on 14 September 1910 on a free place having previously attended Christ Church School, Waterloo.

A third child, Alma, arrived in 1906. In 1911 the family was living at 37 Ferndale Road, Waterloo, with Albert having changed jobs to become a woollen salesman.

Norman obtained Passes in his Oxford Local Junior and Senior exams in 1913 and 1914 respectively. He represented the school at rugby for three seasons from 1913 to 1915 playing as a forward in the same team as S. B. McQueen who was later capped for Scotland, and left school on 31 March 1915. According to the school's records he worked in a bank after leaving school but his World War I service record lists him as an apprentice to a cotton broker from 1915 to 1917 though the latter date may be erroneous.

He seems to have started his war with the 63rd Training Reserve Battalion, a training battalion of the Royal Welsh Fusiliers, where he rose to the rank of lance corporal with regimental number 26662. On 13 August 1917 he joined 5 Officer Cadet Wing of the Royal Flying Corps at St Leonard's on Sea and moved to C Squadron of the Central Flying School at Uphaven on 8 September. On 8 November 1917 he was commissioned as temporary second lieutenant. He continued his training with 14 TS at Blandford and was posted to the Reserve depot on 9 April.

For some reason there is a note on his Royal Air Force record dated 4 May 1918 that states 'Recruit to cease receiving instruction in aviation'. He was later transferred to the 17th Battalion Royal Welsh Fusiliers as a temporary second lieutenant from 5 May 1918 and served with the 115th Brigade of the 38th Division. On 4 November 1918, the division attacked the village of Englefontaine. It was probably in this action that Norman Evans lost his life, though his loss is not recorded in the battalion's war diary.

He is buried in grave C 21 of Englefontaine British Cemetery.

ARTHUR WEST FAIRBAIRN

Rifleman
1329
1st/6th Battalion King's (Liverpool Regiment)
MTS 1905–12

Arthur West Fairbairn was born on 16 March 1895 into a wealthy middle-class family. His father, George Edward Fairbairn, a Scotsman, was an iron and brass founder who became director of Henry Wilson & Co Ltd, engineers, of Liverpool. This firm manufactured the cooking equipment for major transatlantic liners.

Arthur was the third child born to George and his wife, Jessie Fulton Fairbairn (formerly Ritchie), who had married in 1888. He was preceded by William Ritchie in 1889 and Ethel Fulton in 1892.

George Forrester was born in 1899 so that by 1901, living at 3 St Mary's Terrace (which seems to be the same as Park Terrace), Waterloo Park, the family had grown to three boys and one girl. William had already started at Merchant Taylors' having been admitted in 1900.

Shortly after the census return was taken, George and Jessie's last child, Harold Gibson, was born.

It was not until 17 September 1905 that Arthur entered Merchant Taylors', having previously attended a private preparatory school in Waterloo called 'Dunmore'. He was joined at Merchant Taylors' by George in 1909 and Harold in 1910.

Another move had taken them to a house called Sandown in Waterloo by 1911. That year Arthur gained a Pass in his Oxford Local Junior exam, and another Pass in the Senior in 1912 after which he left school on 31 July 1912 and went to work for the Royal Insurance Company.

Shortly after joining the Royal he attested for the Territorial Force on 4 November 1912 and was given regimental number 1329. Interestingly, the witness to his signature was Corporal T. E. Teague (see p.183). He enlisted in the 6th Battalion King's (Liverpool Regiment) for four years.

The battalion embarked on the SS *City of Edinburgh* at Southampton on 24 February 1915 and landed at Le Havre the following day joining the 5th Division. Arthur was admitted to 85 Field Ambulance and then to hospital suffering from influenza on 27 March but reported for duty on 2 April.

About a month later, on 5 May 1915, the battalion undertook an attack on Hill 60. It was during this attack that Arthur Fairbairn was killed in action with C Company. He has no known grave and is commemorated on the

Menin Gate on panels 4 and 6. His brother William Ritchie Fairbairn (see below) was killed in the same attack.

WILLIAM RITCHIE FAIRBAIRN

Rifleman
1330
1st/6th Battalion King's (Liverpool Regiment)
MTS 1900–06

William Ritchie Fairbairn was the eldest son of George Edward Fairbairn and his wife Jessie Fulton Fairbairn. He was born on 30 September 1889 and in 1891 was living with his parents at 6 Highfield Road, Walton-on-the-Hill. His father was working as an iron and brass founder's manager.

Three younger siblings arrived, Ethel in 1892, Arthur in 1895 and George in 1899. In 1900, at nearly 11 years of age, William arrived at Merchant Taylors' from his home at 3 Park Terrace, Waterloo.

In 1901, the whole family, complete with servant and nurse was living at 3 St Mary's Terrace, Waterloo Park which was possibly the same house as 3 Park Terrace above. George was still listed as an iron founder. William's final brother, Harold Gibson Fairbairn, was born just after the census of 1901.

He left the school in 1906 and went to work with Henry Wilson & Co Ltd, engineers, of Liverpool. This was the firm of which his father became director and which was responsible for supplying cooking and sterilising equipment to the major shipping lines such as White Star, Cunard and Blue Funnel. They would, eventually, supply and fit the kitchen equipment in the White Star Line's *Titanic*.

In 1911 the whole family was still at home, though 'home' had now become Sandown in Haigh Rd, Waterloo Park. William's occupation was listed in the census as 'engineer's draughtsman'.

On 4 November 1912, William attested into the 6th Battalion King's (Liverpool Regiment) for four years. He and his younger brother Arthur must have queued together to sign, as they were given consecutive regimental numbers – Arthur 1329, William 1330. William's and Arthur's signatures were both witnessed by another Old Crosbeian, Corporal T. E. Teague (see p.183).

As a reservist, William was probably mobilised soon after the beginning of the war. Not making a good start, he was confined to barracks for five days for carelessly discharging his rifle while at Gatwick on 19 September 1914.

The battalion embarked on the SS *City of Edinburgh* at Southampton on 24 February 1915 and landed at Le Havre the following day joining the 5th Division. About a month later, on 5 May 1915, the battalion undertook an attack on Hill 60. It was during this attack that William Fairbairn was killed in action. He has no known grave and is commemorated on the Menin Gate on panels 4 and 6. His brother Arthur West Fairbairn (see p.72) was killed in the same attack.

ROBERT ERNEST FELL

Private
47275
6th Battalion Leicestershire Regiment
MTS 1911–14

Robert's parents were both natives of Cumberland. His father, Joseph Tordiff Fell, was born in Workington and his mother, Sarah Ann (formerly Litt), in Crosthwaite (though in some returns she stated Portinscale). They married in 1887 and had four children, although one died in infancy.

Of the three surviving children, the eldest, Ann was born in Workington in 1889. The second, who was given his father's full name, Joseph Tordiff Fell, followed in 1897 and the third, Robert Ernest was born on 23 December 1898.

At some point between 1891 and 1897, Joseph moved his family to Liverpool, as his two sons were born in Kirkdale, Liverpool. In 1901, the family home was 21 Church Road, Seaforth where Sarah was living with her three children, one servant and two boarders.

By 1911 they had moved further out, to 14 Curzon Road, Waterloo. Robert's father was present on this occasion and gave his occupation as 'marine engineer', which could account for his not being home for the 1901 census. Robert's sister, Ann, now 22 years old, was working as a photographer, Joseph (junior) and Robert were still at school. Their mother, Sarah, seems to have been running the household as she no longer had a live-in servant.

Later that year, on 15 September 1911, Robert moved up from Christ Church School, Waterloo to begin his time at Merchant Taylors' joining his brother who had been at the school since 1909. The following year, 1912, Robert's father died at the early age of 49. Robert left the school on 8 April 1914 to go 'into farming' according to the school records.

Robert's army service record was lost during the bombing of World War II but he is known to have enlisted at Woolwich, originally into the Army Service Corps with regimental number 328760. He later seems to have been posted to the 6th Battalion of the Leicestershire Regiment and renumbered 47275. It is not known when he joined his new battalion but he was wounded in April 1918, possibly at the second battle of Kemmel. He died of his wounds on 27 April, at the age of 19.

He is buried in plot I row A grave 27 of the Esquelbecq Military Cemetery.

CHARLES HENRY FERGUSON

Corporal
240571
1st/6th Battalion King's (Liverpool Regiment)
MTS 1901–03

Charles's father, Charles Fawcett Ferguson, qualified as a master mariner in 1882 at the age of 25. Three years later, in 1885, he married Elizabeth Mark Jean Thompson. Both were natives of Workington, Cumberland. Charles was the oldest of the three children born to his parents. Born on 2 February 1888 he was also a native of Workington.

Being a master mariner, it seems his father was seldom home. Certainly he was away on the nights of the censuses of 1891, 1901 and 1911 and possibly his wife accompanied him on some of his voyages, for in 1891 Charles was staying with his aunts Mary Ann Thompson and Ella Thompson at 3 Portland Street, Workington.

Charles's sister, Dorothy, was born in the last quarter of 1891, also in Workington. A second sister, Elizabeth Mark Jean was born in 1893, and named after her mother, who seems to have died giving birth to her, aged only 36.

After six years of widowhood, Charles (senior) remarried in 1899, his new wife being Alice Heading Mitchell from Wallingford in Berkshire. Charles's father and stepmother had no children and in 1901, living at 30 Cavendish Road, Great Crosby, Alice was taking care of the three children from her husband's first marriage while Charles was again at sea.

Charles Henry Ferguson joined Merchant Taylors' on 23 April 1901 and stayed for only two and a half years leaving in December 1903 aged almost 16. As with a number of boys who left school at this time he joined an insurance firm as a clerk which was his occupation in 1911 when he was the only one of the children still living at home with his stepmother, though they had now moved to 6 St Alban's Square, Bootle. His sister

Dorothy was working as a governess teaching music and art in a private school in Porthcawl.

He joined the 6th Battalion King's (Liverpool Regiment) with regimental number 2189. This was later changed on renumbering to 240571. He crossed to France with the battalion, leaving on 24 February 1915 and landing at Le Havre the following day where they joined 5th Division. While so attached he would have taken part in the second battle of Ypres including the action at Hill 60 on 5 May 1915.

On 26 January 1916 the battalion was transferred to 55th Division and relieved the French in the Wailly-Bretencourt area. The battle of the Somme was launched on 1 July 1916. The 1st/6th did not suffer as badly on this day as many other battalions, their role being one of reinforcement. His final move came on 25 July 1916 when the battalion was relieved by 11th Division and moved south to the front line opposite the German-occupied village of Guillemont. It was here that Charles was killed in action on 13 August 1916, one of nine Old Crosbeians who were killed in the protracted taking of this village.

He has no known grave and is commemorated on pier and face 1D, 8B and 8C of the Thiepval Memorial.

CLEMENT WILLIAM FORD

Second Lieutenant
5th Battalion King's Own (Royal Lancaster) Regiment
MTS 1906–10

During the late 1870s or early 1880s Clement's father, Clement Thomas Ford, left his Islington birthplace and travelled north to Lancaster to take up a position as a bookkeeper/reporter with a newspaper. It was while in the north that he met Ellen Ford, a farmer's daughter from Aughton whom he married on 19 January 1885 at St Michael's church, Aughton.

At the end of 1885 their first child Florence Cropper was born. Four years later, in 1889, their first son, Herbert Reginald, was born only to die in 1890 aged one. The following year Frederick Taylor was born, also to die aged one.

Finally, Clement William was born on 29 January 1893 and was baptised, in Lancaster, on 8 March of the same year. His parents were living at the time at 42 Regent Street, Lancaster. His father gave his occupation as 'clerk'.

Clement (senior), his wife and two children were still living at 42 Regent Street in 1901 and had been joined by Clement's widowed 77-year-old mother.

Clement Thomas Ford died aged 49 in 1905 and the following year, on 17 September 1906, his son joined Merchant Taylors' from The Friends School in Lancaster. Clement's widowed mother remarried in 1907. Her new husband was Dodgson Kennedy, an accountant and the father of Hugh Kennedy (see p.114), who had joined the school on the same day as Clement. Clement left the school on 29 July 1910 and started work in a shipping office. Shortly afterwards, his stepfather Dodgson Kennedy died on 27 October 1910.

April 1911 found Clement still working as a shipping clerk and living with his mother and sister at Elmside, St Helens Road, Ormskirk.

During the war, Clement enlisted in the 28th Battalion London Regiment, the Artists' Rifles, as Private 5441. This had been established at the beginning of the war as an Officers' Training Corps at Bailleul which, from April 1915, had moved to St Omer. Cadet Ford was commissioned from Artists' Rifles Officers' Training Corps as second lieutenant on probation on 5 September 1916. He was posted to the 5th Battalion Royal Lancaster Regiment. By this date, the battalion was operating as part of 55th Division and he might well have arrived in time for the attack on Guillemont and the battle of Morval. He would certainly have been with them when the 55th moved to 29th Division at Ypres in October 1916.

On 31 July 1917 Clement was killed in action, probably in the attack on Pilckem Ridge. He is buried in plot XXXIV row F grave 12 of the Tyne Cot Cemetery.

DONALD PEARSON FOX

Lance Corporal
24347
Royal Army Medical Corps
MTS 1901–07

Donald's father Stuart Macdonald Fox was born on the Chincha Islands off the coast of Peru and was married three times. He married his first wife, Mary Catherine Frances Harnden in 1881 at St Nicholas, Brighton-le-Sands and with her had one child, Mary Dorothy, who was born in 1882. The following year his wife died aged 25. Stuart was remarried two years later, in 1885, to Blanche Pearson and with her had three children. Their first child, Donald Pearson was born on Christmas Eve 1887 in Waterloo. He was followed by Cyril Russell in 1889, born in Seaforth.

In 1891 Stuart and his family were living at 4 Hereford Road, Litherland. He was working as a commercial traveller. He and his wife, Blanche, had only two children at this stage but they had the help of a nurse and a servant.

Stuart and Blanche's third child arrived in 1895 but the birth cost Blanche her life and, no doubt in her memory, the new arrival was named Blanche. Stuart married his third wife, Margaret Ellen Evans, in 1898 and two more children soon arrived, George in 1899 and Florence Macdonald in 1900.

By 1901, the family had moved to 19 Litherland Road, Litherland from which Stuart was still working as a commercial traveller.

Donald entered Merchant Taylors' on 24 October 1901, giving his address as 11 Kinross Road, Waterloo. Towards the end of this year, his final sibling, Charles Ernest Macdonald, was born. Donald stayed at the school for nearly six years, leaving in April 1907.

Having moved yet again, in 1911 the family was living at 10 Walmer Road, Waterloo, Mary and Cyril had left home but all the other children were still living with their parents. Donald was working as a clerk.

He enlisted into the Royal Army Medical Corps as a private with number 24247 and arrived in the Balkans on 11 July 1915 and served with 41st Field Ambulance, which was with the 13th (Western) Division. The infantry landed on Cape Helles on the Gallipoli peninsula in July to relieve the 29th Division who had been fighting in the area since April. The 13th returned to Mudros at the end of the month landing at ANZAC Cove in August then moving to Suvla Bay. They were eventually evacuated from Helles in January 1916. On 12 February 1916 they moved to Mesopotamia to take part in the relief of Kut al Amara to which the Turks had laid siege in December 1915. On 26 April 1916, General Townsend surrendered his forces, and the town of Kut, to the Turkish army. Further attempts were made to recapture Kut using the 13th Division, among others, but these did not begin until December 1916. Donald Fox died on 10 June 1916, clearly between the fall of Kut and the beginning of attempts to recapture it. The nature of his death has not been traced. Though it could have been from enemy action, it is at least equally likely that he succumbed to one of the diseases which commonly struck the army in Mesopotamia: dysentery, malaria and heat-stroke in temperatures regularly in excess of 50°C.

He was buried in plot XV row E grave 10 of the Amara War Cemetery. Unfortunately, in 1933 the salts in the ground were found to have caused the material of the headstones to deteriorate and these were later removed. The cemetery was reported as largely destroyed in the recent fighting in Iraq.

PERCIVAL NORMAN FRY

Private
204443
1st/5th Battalion King's (Liverpool Regiment)
MTS 1908–12

Percival's father Alfred George Fry was a very experienced and highly qualified mariner. In 1890 he had qualified for his Extra Master's certificate, the pinnacle of qualifications for those in the Merchant Marine. This was undoubtedly why he seems never to have been at home at census time.

Percival was the first child born to Alfred and Ada Beatrice Mary Fry (formerly Thomas), about a year after their marriage in 1894. He was born in Bristol on 25 August 1895. He was followed by Marjorie Winifred in 1897 and Constance Julia in 1899, also born in Bristol.

In 1901, he, his mother and two sisters were living at 12 St Ronan's Avenue, Bristol. His father appears to have been at sea. While still in Bristol, Percival attended a private preparatory school called 'Mill House' in Redland, Bristol. Percival's brother, Kenneth George William, was born in Bristol in 1906.

Between 1906 and 1908 Alfred George Fry moved his family to the north-west and Percival joined Merchant Taylors' on 16 September 1908.

April 1911 found them living at 10 Kingsway, Waterloo. Again, Alfred was away at sea at the time of the census. In the same year Percival gained a Pass in his Oxford Local Junior exam and followed that in the next year with a Pass in the Senior exam.

Now 17, he decided he had had enough of school and left on 31 July 1912, going to work in an insurance office. He probably continued to work there after the war started for in 1915 he joined the Lancashire Hussar Yeomanry and was given the number 1821. After a while he was drafted to the King's (Liverpool Regiment) and joined the 1st/5th Battalion in France in December 1916.

At the beginning of 1917 the battalion was in the Ypres salient being shelled from three sides. Percival was wounded on 2 May 1917 and died on 10 May.

He is buried in plot XII row B grave 2A of the Lijssenthoek Military Cemetery.

CHARLES HERBERT FRYER

Private
83079
2nd/2nd Battalion London Regiment (Royal Fusiliers)
MTS 1912–16

Charles Fryer was born on 22 June 1900. He was, according to some records, born at sea and his full name seems to have been Charles Herbert Fryer. His father, Herbert Fryer, is listed in the school's admissions register as a 'Banker' and in the records of the Commonwealth War Graves Commission as 'Herbert Fryer of Salvador, Central America'.

Charles may have spent the early part of his life in Central America as he has not been traced in either the 1901 or 1911 census returns.

He joined Merchant Taylors' on 25 April 1912, having previously attended Blundellsands House School, a private preparatory school in Blundellsands. He left on 27 July 1916 intending to become a motor engineer.

During the war he enlisted at Seaforth and was posted to the South Lancashire Regiment as Private 44718. He later transferred to 3rd Battalion London Regiment with number GS/83079 and finally to the 2nd/2nd Royal Fusiliers with the same number.

It was while serving with the last battalion that 18-year-old Charles was killed in action on 18 September 1918. He is buried in plot III row C grave 3 of the Épehy Wood Farm Cemetery. The date and the burial place suggest he was killed in the battle of Épehy, an attack on an outpost of the Hindenburg Line.

EDGAR GOLDING

Lieutenant
Royal Flying Corps
MTS 1906–12

Edgar's father, Alfred Dickson Golding, married twice. He married his first wife Agnes Turner in 1871 and with her had at least four children: Richard Turner, born 1872, Herbert Dickson in 1873, Agnes Winifred in 1876 and Albert Edward in 1883. Agnes died in 1886 and was buried in Anfield Cemetery to be followed less than a year later, on New Year's Day 1887, by the couple's youngest child Albert, who was also interred at Anfield.

Alfred married his second wife, Lillian Alice Edwards, in 1887. Together they had six children of whom Edgar was the fifth. Eleanor Dorothy arrived in 1889, Alfred John in 1890, Frank Edwards in 1891 and George in 1893. Edgar was born on 1 October 1895 and was followed by Lillian Mary in 1899.

In 1901, Edgar was living with his parents and eight of his surviving brothers and sisters at 53 Litherland Park, Litherland, Richard having moved out. Brother Herbert, who had described himself in 1891 as an analytical chemist, now described himself as a manager to a curled hair factory.

On 1 May 1906, Edgar became part of Merchant Taylors', having entered from 'Summerhill School', a private school in Litherland.

By 1911, the family was still living at 53 Litherland Park. All the children of the 'first family' had moved out while all six of the 'second family' were still at home.

Edgar obtained a 3rd Class in his Oxford Local Junior exams in 1911, left the school on 31 July 1912 and went on to Liverpool University to study veterinary science.

He had completed just two years of his studies when war broke out and in 1914 he was mobilised into the Royal Army Medical Corps, which he had joined before the war. He was a driver with the 1st West Lancashire Field Ambulance, being promoted from private to honorary lieutenant on 1 January 1915. He was gazetted as transport officer to the 3rd West Lancashire Field Ambulance transferring afterwards to the Army Service Corps then to the Royal Flying Corps when foreign service eluded him. He spent some time training in Reading and Egypt. In May 1916 he joined No 3 Squadron in France. In September 1917 he was part of a group of planes on a training flight which spotted a lone German plane. The training flight followed it behind enemy lines where the flight was attacked by a number of German planes. Edgar was shot down and he became a prisoner of war. He died of wounds while a prisoner on 19 September 1917.

He is buried in plot IV row C grave 12 of Caudry British Cemetery.

DOUGLAS GRANT

Lieutenant
1st Battalion King's Own Scottish Borderers
MTS 1906–12

Douglas's father, George, married twice and produced six sons, four with his first wife and two with his second. All six attended Merchant Taylors'. He also had a daughter by his second marriage.

Douglas was the youngest of the sons of George's first wife, Jessie Ann. He was born in Formby on 29 July 1895 having been preceded by George in 1888, Alexander Henry in 1890 and John Leslie in 1893.

George Grant was the manager of an insurance and marine insurance broker and in 1901 was living in Milnthorpe House, Formby with his wife and four sons.

Douglas attended a private school in Formby before joining Merchant Taylors' on 16 January 1906. It must have been a sad start to his school career for shortly afterwards, sometime in the first quarter of 1906, his mother died.

Not long afterwards, in about 1909, his father remarried. His new wife, Isabella McKandy Simpson (ten years his junior) bore him two further sons and a daughter. William Simpson was fifteen years younger than Douglas and was born just in time for the 1911 census. At this time the family was living at Rowanlea in Formby. The oldest three sons of his first marriage had followed George into the insurance business. George (junior) was a clerk to an insurance broker, Alexander was an apprentice to an average adjuster and John was an apprentice in an insurance company. Douglas was still at school. That year he passed his Oxford Local Junior exams and represented the school as a member of the rugby XV.

The following year, 1912, saw the birth of Douglas's sister, Margaret and his departure from the school. He left on 31 July to enter, according to the register a 'general produce office'.

On the outbreak of war he joined up almost immediately becoming Private 3181 in the 1st/10th Battalion King's (Liverpool Regiment), the Liverpool Scottish, and travelled with them to France on 1 November 1914.

He received his commission on 25 June 1915 being gazetted second lieutenant on probation in the 3rd Battalion King's Own Scottish Borderers, a training unit based in Edinburgh. He was confirmed in the rank on 22 March 1916. When exactly he joined the 1st Battalion is uncertain but they had returned to France from Gallipoli and Egypt on 18 March and it may be that he joined around this time. Douglas's youngest brother, Alistair Donaldson Grant, was born in March 1916, at which time Douglas was probably fighting in the trenches. On their return to the Western Front the battalion fought on the Somme and *The School Review* records that he was twice wounded there but the war diary has no mention of it. It does, however, record his death in action in an attack on the village of Marcoing in the battle of Cambrai on 30 November 1917.

His body seems not to have been found as he is commemorated on panel 5 of the Cambrai Memorial at Louverval.

George Campbell Grant

Lieutenant
Royal Engineers
MTS 1899–1905

George Grant and Elizabeth Martin McHarg married in St Michael's church, Toxteth on 6 January 1885. They had three children: Elsie M. (1886), George Campbell (1 September 1888) and Frank Mortimer (1890). Both boys attended Merchant Taylors'. George (senior) was a cashier and in 1891 the family was living at 2 Willoughby Road, Waterloo.

Aged 11, George joined Merchant Taylors' on 13 September 1899, his father describing himself on the application form as 'Cashier' of 2 Willoughby Road, Waterloo.

George stayed at Merchant Taylors' for just over five years. Leaving in July 1905, he started an engineering apprenticeship under Lieutenant-Colonel Cecil Q. Henriques who was a civil engineer and chairman of John H. Wilson & Co of Liverpool.

By 1907, the family had moved to the Wirral, for here George's father died on 22 June at 152 Sea View Road, Liscard, Cheshire. He was 59.

They were still living at this address in 1911 when the census was taken. Elizabeth Martin Grant, now 61, was living on 'Private Means' with her two sons. George was working as a 'mechanical engineer's draughtsman' and Frank as a 'bank clerk'.

Having finished his apprenticeship in 1910 George worked under Lieutenant-Colonel Henriques from 1910 to 1912, in which year he was admitted as a student of the Institution of Civil Engineers. He was proposed for associate membership of the institution on 24 March 1914 while working as an assistant draughtsman. The applications book shows that he worked as an assistant under Lieutenant-Colonel Henriques in the design of locomotive steam cranes, steam and electric excavators, derrick cranes, steam capstans and a range of other devices. He took first place in the exam for AMInstCE and was awarded the Bayliss prize for 1914 based on this performance. He was elected an associate member by ballot on 7 December 1914.

The war having broken out, he volunteered early and was gazetted with a commission as second lieutenant in the Royal Engineers on 24 October 1914.

When he was wounded, he was serving with 96 Field Company RE. According to their war diary, Lieutenant Grant was wounded on the night of 13 October 1915 near Laventie, possibly while repairing the revetment of a trench. He was taken to 2nd London Casualty Clearing Station, at that time in Bailleul, where he died of his wounds the following day.

He is buried in Merville Communal Cemetery plot V row A grave 20.

Alfred Grensted

Private
G/19877
26th Battalion Royal Fusiliers
MTS 1896–1903

Born in Maidstone, Alfred's father, Fredric Finnis Grensted moved to Blundellsands, when in 1883 he became curate of St Nicholas's church, Blundellsands and second master of Merchant Taylors' School. He travelled to Croydon where he married Gertrude Ellen Plimpton on 3 January 1884 and their first son Lawrence William was born 6 December 1884. Just over two years later their second son Alfred was born, on 17 May 1887.

The 1891 census finds them living at 27 Cavendish Road, Crosby. The family was still living at that address when Alfred entered Merchant Taylors' on 22 January 1896, by which date his father had left MTS and become diocesan inspector of Religious Education for the Diocese of Liverpool.

In 1891 a sister, Theresa Charlotte, was born and in 1901 Alfred and his parents and sister were still living in the same house in Cavendish Road.

In 1902, Alfred was elected to a Harrison Scholarship and represented the school in the cricket XI. He also represented the school as a member of the rugby XV in the 1902/03 season when he was described as being 'an excellent half back'.

In 1903 he left the school to take up a position with Martin's Bank and continued his rugby involvement by playing for Waterloo Rugby Club and Lancashire County.

In 1911, the entire family, parents, two sons and a daughter were again living under one roof, though they had moved to Brooke Road.

Alfred stayed with the bank until 1915 at which time he joined the 26th (Service) Battalion of the Royal Fusiliers. Known as the Bankers' Battalion it was formed on 17 July 1915 by the Lord Mayor and City of London and was composed, mostly, of former bank clerks and accountants. The CWGC gives Alfred's number as G/19877 but his medal index card has B/19877. The battalion landed in France on 4 May 1916 and formed part of 124th Brigade, 41st Division, the latter being concentrated between Hazebrouck and Bailleul. In September 1916 the battalion took part in the battle of Flers-Courcelette and it was during this battle that Alfred was killed in action.

He is buried in plot II row G grave 5 of the Guards Cemetery at Lesboeufs.

ALLAN EDWARD GRIEVE

Second Lieutenant
2nd Battalion South Lancashire Regiment
MTS 1910–14

Allan Edward Grieve was born on 20 May 1897 in Dundee. He was the third of four children born to Allan McGregor Grieve and his wife Mary McKenzie Grieve (formerly Petrie), both natives of Scotland. They seem to have married in Scotland and moved to England about 1890. Their eldest child, Grace Milne was born in 1892 to be followed in 1895 by James, both born in Bootle. Mary returned to Scotland for the birth of Allan while their final child Walter Petrie was also born in Bootle, in 1900.

In 1901 the family was living at 50 Sidney Road, Bootle; a small terrace house from which Allan Grieve (senior) went to work as a commercial clerk.

At some time before Allan (junior) arrived at Merchant Taylors' on 4 September 1910 they had probably moved house as he had previously attended Christ Church School in Waterloo and the 1911 census shows them living at 82 Cambridge Road, Seaforth. Allan (senior) now described himself as a mercantile clerk.

Allan progressed well through school sitting his Oxford Local Junior exam in 1912 and gaining a 3rd Class. This he followed with a 2nd Class in the Senior exam in 1913 and a 1st Class in 1914. In this, his final year, he was appointed a monitor, represented the school at cricket and won the Windermere Prize for English.

He left the school on 30 July 1914 and joined the Bank of England in Liverpool where he remained until his eighteenth birthday when he applied for a commission. Having been gazetted second lieutenant, he crossed to France on 27 May 1916 and joined the 2nd Battalion South Lancashire Regiment on 29 May. Shortly afterwards, on 3 July, an attack was made on the enemy positions at Thiepval. The attack failed and 19-year-old Second Lieutenant Grieve was reported missing. The War Office later confirmed his death though his body was not recovered.

He is commemorated on pier and face 7A and 7B of the Thiepval Memorial.

GERALD RAYNER HAIGH

Sergeant
R/14158
18th Battalion King's Royal Rifle Corps
MTS 1889–94

Gerald Rayner Haigh was the only child of Frank Bramhall Haigh and his wife Ellen (formerly Rayner), who were married at St Peter's church in Birkdale on 4 April 1878. Gerald was born in Birkdale on 26 December 1878.

In 1881 Frank and his family were living at 1 Spa Street, Preston; Frank described himself as an 'Oil Merchant'. At about two and a half years of age, Gerald was baptised at St Nicholas's church, Liverpool.

On 27 November 1882, according to the divorce papers, Frank deserted his wife and son 'without cause' and seems not to have been seen again. In 1890 Ellen was granted a divorce on the grounds of adultery and desertion and her father John James Rayner took on the role of guardian and entered Gerald for Merchant Taylors', which he joined on 19 September 1889.

In 1891, Ellen and Gerald were living with her father, Gerald's guardian, at 16 Courtenay Road, Waterloo and three years later, at Easter 1894, Gerald left school, his education completed.

The following year, 1895, Gerald's mother, Ellen, remarried. She and her new husband, Edward Thornton Tuck moved into the Metropole Hotel in Wind Street, Swansea where he held the post of hotel manager. In 1901 Gerald was living with them at the hotel where he was working as 'Assistant Hotel Manager'.

By 1911, Ellen and Edward were still running the Metropole Hotel while Gerald had two census entries. One said he was visiting his mother and stepfather in Swansea and gives his occupation as 'Farmer' while the other gives his occupation as 'Market Gardener' living at The Croft, Bishopston, Glamorgan.

In 1912, Gerald married Alice Louise Watkins in Swansea.

Gerald was still working as a market gardener when he enlisted at Swansea on 7 June 1915, 'for the duration of the war'. He was actually called up a few days later on 19 June and joined the King's Royal Rifle Corps. He was promoted fairly rapidly – to corporal on 12 August 1915 and to sergeant in 23rd Battalion on 30 December being confirmed in this rank on 3 May 1916. A month before his confirmation in rank, his son Edward Rayner Gerald Haigh was born on 4 April 1916.

On 25 May 1916 he embarked on the SS *Golden Eagle* at Folkestone, arriving in France the following day and joining the 18th Battalion on 15 June.

He was killed in action on 10 October 1916, possibly in the battle of the Transloy Ridges, a late part of the battle of the Somme. Clearly his body was not recovered as he is commemorated on pier and face 13A and 13B of the Thiepval Memorial.

WILLIAM GEORGE HAMM
MC

Second Lieutenant
13th Battalion East Yorkshire Regiment
MTS 1911–13

William George Hamm's father, also William, was German by birth. He came to England sometime in the 1880s and appears to have settled in Liverpool where he married Pauline Happold in 1890. He became a naturalised British citizen in 1897, the year after William George Hamm was born on 28 August 1896.

William George was the fourth child to be born to his parents. Elizabeth Margaret was born in 1891, Bertha Pauline in 1893 and Frances Sophia in 1894. After William George, Pauline arrived in 1898 and Elsie Louisa in 1901. In 1901, William, Pauline and their six children were living at 209, Kensington, Liverpool with three servants. William was working as a master pork butcher.

By 1911 they had moved to Rose Dene, Liverpool Road, Maghull. Three more children had been added to the family: Albert Edward in 1902, Mabel Eugenie in 1905 and Ernest Lemuel in 1909.

William George entered Merchant Taylors' in 1911 aged about 15. He left the school two years later in 1913 to attend Trinity College, Dublin. He then became an assistant master at Eton House School in Hull.

William Hamm and his family in 1910. William George is the boy in the back row.

He enlisted in November 1915, initially with the 4th Battalion East Yorkshire Regiment and was given the regimental number 201799 rising to the rank of lance corporal. He was commissioned as second lieutenant on 25 October 1916 and was eventually posted to the 13th Battalion East Yorkshire Regiment serving with the Expeditionary Force from 13 December 1916. While serving with this battalion he was awarded the Military Cross on 21 March 1917. The citation reads:

> For conspicuous gallantry and devotion to duty. He showed great initiative in organising parties of bombers and patrols and succeeded in securing many strong positions which proved of the utmost value. He set a splendid example throughout the operations.

He was killed in action at Arras on 2 May 1917 while acting as bombing officer. He was originally buried in the Sunken Road at Bailleul-Sire-Berthoult and later reburied in Orchard Dump Cemetery, Arleux-en-Gohelle, section V row D grave 30.

OSWIN HANSOM

Private
77556
14th Battalion Welsh Regiment
MTS 1914–17

Oswin Hansom was 19 years old when he was killed in action. He was born at Fleetwood on 27 July 1899 the son of George Edward Oswin Hansom and his wife Clara Mary (formerly Gibbs). He was the eldest of four children.

In 1901, the family was still living in Fleetwood, at 3 Milton Terrace. George Edward Oswin Hansom was working as 'Manager in an Electrical Lighting Works'. At the time of the census, Oswin was the only child; his brother Edward, was born in Fleetwood in late 1901. In 1908, still living in Fleetwood, twin sisters were born, Christina Mary and Laura Mary M. (seemingly known as Monica).

Between 1908 and 1911 George moved his family to Merseyside and by 1911 was living at 37 Oxford Drive, Waterloo. He was still working as an engineer manager in an electricity supply company.

In 1914 Oswin began his career at Merchant Taylors'. He clearly had academic ability, being elected a Harrison Scholar and, in 1916, gaining 1st

Class Honours in his Oxford Local Senior exams with a distinction in French, being placed third in England. He made a contribution in other areas of school life as well. He was a member of the Debating Society and towards the end of his school career he proposed motions on 'the worthlessness of life' and 'the superiority of the sportsman to the scholar' though *The School Review*, while describing him as 'fluent' did suggest that he 'should treat subjects to more careful preparation'. He was elected as a monitor in 1916–17 and was part of the school's relatively new cadet force in which he was advanced from lance corporal to corporal on 3 May 1917, shortly before he left school that summer.

Exactly when he enlisted has not been determined but eventually he was posted to the 14th Battalion Welsh Regiment (CWGC actually has 4th Battalion but as they fought in Egypt and Gallipoli, it seems likely that this is a misprint and that the 14th, as recorded by *Soldiers Died*, is correct). As he joined the battalion late in the war, it would by that time have become part of the 38th (Welsh) Division and on 18 September took part in the battle of Épehy in which the forward outposts of the Hindenburg Line were attacked.

It was during this action that Oswin was killed by a shell splinter on 19 September 1918 and was buried in Grevillers British Cemetery, plot XIII row D grave 12.

NORMAN ERNEST JASPER HARDING
MB CHB

Lieutenant-Colonel
Royal Army Medical Corps
MTS 1890–92

Norman's father, Jesse Ham Harding, married Maria Kingston in 1873. Norman was the eldest of three children, being born on 3 February 1875 at Frome in Somerset. Between 1875 and 1878 Jesse brought his family to the north-west where a second son was born in 1878. A third child, a daughter, Dorothy, was born at sea (the North Atlantic) in 1880.

In 1881 the family was living at 59 Townsend Lane, West Derby with Jesse, at this time, working as a ship's master and Maria's sister Ellen living with them. Ellen was to marry Frederick Pasmore in 1883 and in 1891 was providing a home for Norman and his brother at Park Lodge, Waterloo Park, both boys having started at Merchant Taylors' in 1890.

Norman proved to be a more than capable sportsman while at Merchant Taylors', representing the school at rugby in 1890–92 and captaining the swimming team. He left the school in 1892 to attend Cambridge House School in Cambridge Road in Seaforth. He was clearly good academically as well as on the sports field progressing from Cambridge House to Edinburgh University in 1895 to study medicine. He completed his medical studies in 1900 graduating MB.

The country was at war with the Boers and Norman set sail from Tilbury Dock on 23 August 1900 for South Africa where he served as a civil surgeon and was wounded at Trigaardsfontein.

He clearly liked the service life and on his return from South Africa obtained a commission in the Royal Army Medical Corps, being gazetted lieutenant (on probation) with effect from 1 September 1902 and confirmed in that rank on 10 March 1903.

Norman's father died on 21 June 1904 at Basseterre on the island of St Christopher.

Norman was promoted to captain on 1 March 1906 and the following year married Dorothy Elizabeth Julia Wetton, who had served as a nursing sister in South Africa.

On 8 November 1912 he set sail from Liverpool on the SS *Mandingo* bound for a tour of duty in Sierra Leone and returned in 1913 being appointed medical officer at the Tower of London on 31 October. On 1 June 1914 he was promoted to major and on the outbreak of war was part of the British Expeditionary Force landing in France on 26 August.

Norman rose to be lieutenant-colonel while he was in charge of No 12 Stationary Hospital. This he did for two periods: 17 to 21 November 1914 and 28 April to 10 August 1916. At some point it seems he was seriously wounded and ended his war in India where he contracted cholera and died on 10 August 1916.

He is commemorated on the Kirkee 1914–18 Memorial. This is a memorial in Poona, India dedicated to those servicemen and women who are buried in civil cemeteries in India and whose graves can no longer be properly maintained.

ROBERT ALEXANDER HARLEY

Major
24th (Denbighshire Yeomanry) Battalion Royal Welsh Fusiliers
MTS 1895–96

Robert Alexander Harley was born into a family that became successful fish merchants who not only traded in fish but owned several Liverpool registered trawlers.

Born on 19 February 1882 he was the third child of Robert Harley and his wife Matilda (formerly Powell). Shortly afterwards, on 12 March, he was baptised in St Andrew's church. The church's register of baptisms records their address as Rocky Mount, Belmont Drive, Newsham Park and the father's occupation as 'Fish Salesman'.

Robert had two older sisters, Margaret Matilda (born in 1877) and Ann Elizabeth (1880). Two other siblings followed him: Ada in 1884 and Alfred James in 1886.

In 1881 the family was living at 88 Bedford Street South, Liverpool with Robert describing himself as a 'Fish Salesman' and his wife, Matilda, as a 'Fishmonger'.

Robert Alexander Harley entered Merchant Taylors' on 1 May 1895 giving his address as 88 Bedford Street, Liverpool. Probably because the travel between Bedford Street and Crosby was more involved in those days, he boarded with Mr J. H. Milton of College Avenue who is listed as his guardian. (John Herbert Milton was a member of staff at Merchant Taylors' who, with his wife, Harriet, ran a boarding house in College Avenue for a number of boys at the school.)

Robert stayed at the school for just over a year, leaving in July 1896. He seems to have gone into the family business of Harley & Miller, Fish Merchants of Liverpool. In 1901 he was living at 74 Bedford Street and gave his occupation as 'Fish Salesman'.

Robert (junior) married Frances Cecilia Wilton Bartholomew from Fairfield, Liverpool at the church of St John the Divine on 3 April 1906. By 1911 Robert and Frances had moved to 3 Langdale Road, Liverpool having moved on from 74 Bedford Street where Robert had been living at the time of his marriage.

During the war Robert gained a commission in the Denbighshire Yeomanry. He was promoted to temporary lieutenant on 1 June 1915 and in February 1916 he was advanced to temporary captain when he was seconded as assistant embarkation officer. On 9 April 1917 he was further advanced, while in the role of assistant embarkation staff officer, to temporary major. The Denbighshire Yeomanry had, by this time been dismounted and given a new role as infantry, changing their name to 24th (Denbighshire Yeomanry) Battalion Royal Welsh Fusiliers.

Robert died on 19 October 1917 at the London and South Western Hotel, Southampton. He was buried on 25 October 1917 in the Church of England Section of Allerton Cemetery, Liverpool, grave VIII 173.

Philip Harris

Rifleman
1890
6th Battalion King's (Liverpool Regiment)
MTS 1904–07

Philip Harris was the third and final child of Edward Harris and his wife Emily Maud who as Emily Maud McVitie married Edward in 1889. A daughter, Marjorie, was born to them in 1891. Two sons followed, Colin Edward in 1892 and Philip on 14 November 1893. All were born in Liverpool. Philip's father, Edward was a spice merchant and in 1901 was living in Maghull at Old Quarry Brook with his wife and three children.

They had moved into Crosby by the time Philip joined Merchant Taylors' on 28 April 1904, giving their new address as Moor Lodge, Moor Lane, Crosby and Edward giving his occupation as 'Colonial Produce Broker'. Philip's brother, Colin, came to Merchant Taylors' at the same time. Both boys stayed at Merchant Taylors' for three years, leaving in 1907.

The family stayed in Crosby but had moved to Moorside, Elton Avenue, Crosby by 1911 and both boys seem to have entered the family business; Colin as a clerk to a spice merchant and Philip as a clerk to a seed crusher.

On the outbreak of war, Philip must have been one of the first to enlist. His attestation papers, which he signed on 7 August 1914, gave his address as 41 York Avenue, Crosby, his occupation as 'Clerk' and his height as 5 feet 8 inches. He joined the 6th Battalion King's (Liverpool Regiment) as a private and was given the number 1890.

After training at Canterbury, the battalion sailed from Southampton to Le Havre aboard the SS *City of Edinburgh* on 24 February 1915, becoming part of 15th Brigade, 5th Division on arrival.

In the seven months between his arrival in France and his death, Philip and the battalion spent time at Bailleul, Vlamertinghe, Ypres and eventually ended up at Vaux Wood near the village of Suzanne.

Philip was killed in action on 30 September 1915. The battalion's war diary records that on this day the battalion was operating near Vaux and that 'at 2 p.m. a patrol of 30 men under Lieut Blackledge went out into the marsh and about 4 p.m. encountered an enemy patrol in 4th wood, brisk fighting ensued in which we lost one OR [other rank] killed and one OR wounded ...'

Philip is buried in Suzanne Communal Cemetery Extension in grave C 10.

GEOFFREY HAWKSLEY-HILL

Private
3299
1st/10th Battalion King's (Liverpool Regiment)
MTS 1907–12

There is some disagreement in documents as to whether this name is hyphenated or not. The school's register and the baptism register of Holy Trinity in Formby both have the hyphenated form so this has been adopted here.

William Frederick Hawksley-Hill and his wife Mary Alice (formerly Bew) had two children. The first, Geoffrey, was born at Formby on 23 April 1896 and after two months was baptised at Holy Trinity church, Formby on 20 June 1896. The family was probably quite affluent as the 1901 census records them as living in a house named 'Landsdowne' in Freshfield Road, Freshfield with William working as an 'assistant manager for an East India merchant'.

The couple's second son, Ronald Lynn, was born on 15 August 1902. Both boys attended Merchant Taylors' but Geoffrey left three years before Ronald arrived.

Geoffrey first came to Merchant Taylors' on 17 September 1907 having previously attended a private preparatory school in Formby. In 1911, with the family still living in the same house and his father still working for the East India Merchant, Geoffrey gained a Pass in his Oxford Local Junior exams and on 4 April of the following year he left school to join an insurance office.

On 29 August 1914, Geoffrey signed his attestation papers and was eventually posted to 1st/10th Battalion King's (Liverpool Regiment). This Territorial battalion, the Liverpool Scottish, was formed in August 1914 in Bootle though he seems not to have embarked for France until 23 January 1915. He no doubt suffered the rigours of trench warfare until the battalion was involved in its first major fight at Hooge on 16 June 1915 as part of 9th Brigade, 3rd Division. The Liverpool Scottish formed the second wave of a three-wave attack. However, the battle degenerated quickly into chaos and at the end, Geoffrey Hawksley-Hill was reported missing. He was later declared to have been killed in action though his body was never found.

He is commemorated on panels 4 and 6 of the Ypres (Menin Gate) Memorial.

RANDOLPH SINGLETON HAWORTH

Lance Corporal
15870
17th Battalion King's (Liverpool Regiment)
MTS 1901–02

Randolph Singleton Haworth was born on 23 February 1886 in Blackburn where his father, Moses, lived next to the Leeds–Liverpool canal and worked as canal agent. Moses and his wife, Margaret (formerly Singleton) had married in 1879 and by the time Randolph was born already had three sons: George Herbert (born 1880), James Cecil (born 1882) and Charles Singleton (born 1884). After Randolph came Reginald (1888) and Sydney (1890). By 1891, the family was living in Canal Cottage, Eanam, Blackburn where Moses still worked as canal agent.

At some time between 1891 and 1901, Moses moved his family out of Blackburn to Waterloo as they were living at 54 Ferndale Road when Randolph started at Merchant Taylors' on 22 January 1901. Reginald and Sydney started at the school in the same year, which might indicate that the move was recent. The three older boys were probably past school age when they arrived in Waterloo. Randolph stayed at the school only a short time, leaving in July 1902 and judging by later documentation probably went to work in a bank.

The 1911 census records Randolph as working as a bank clerk while Reginald was an accountant's clerk and Sydney had become a farmer. Only the three younger boys were living at home at Freshfield Farm, Freshfield.

Randolph was another Old Crosbeian who enlisted early in the war. His attestation papers (which show him still working as a clerk) are dated 31 August 1914 and he was posted initially to a city battalion, Liverpool Regiment.

On 4 August 1915 Randolph was transferred to 30th Division Cyclist Company with whom he remained until he was transferred to 17th Battalion King's (Liverpool Regiment), one of the Pals battalions, on 18 September.

The battalion moved to France on 7 November 1915 and formed part of 30th Division, which initially concentrated around Amiens. In July 1916, he was promoted to corporal and the following month was awarded a good conduct badge.

The division eventually took part in the battle of Albert and the battle of the Transloy Ridges. It was during the latter of these, which took place from 1 to 20 October that he was killed in action on 12 October 1916.

He is buried in Warlencourt British Cemetery in plot II row B grave 26.

Allan Stanley Haynes

Rifleman
1731
6th Battalion King's (Liverpool Regiment)
MTS 1901–07

Allan Allen Haynes married Harriet Ann Hughes in 1890. In April 1891 she was expecting their first child and, with her husband, was living with her parents at 3 St Edmond's Road, Bootle. Allan was a bookkeeper in the shipping trade.

Their son, Allan Stanley Haynes, was born on 30 September 1891 and was followed three years later in 1894 by a daughter, Frances Muriel Haynes. Allan's father died in 1899 at the young age of 39.

In March 1901 Allan and his sister, Frances were, on the night of the census, listed as living at 3 St Edmond's Road in the care of their uncle and aunt Frederick and Elizabeth Hughes.

Aged about ten, Allan first came to Merchant Taylors' in 1901. He stayed six years and left in 1907.

At some point, Allan volunteered as a Territorial for foreign service and was posted to 1/6th Battalion King's (Liverpool Regiment). He would have found himself at the beginning of 1915 training with the battalion at Canterbury. On 24 February 1915 they boarded the SS *City of Edinburgh* and sailed for France arriving in Le Havre the following day and the battalion became part of 30th Division. Leaving Le Havre they passed through Bailleul, Vlamertinghe and arrived at Ypres.

In April 1915, the British had taken a nearby strategic vantage point – Hill 60. Not really a hill but a spoil heap produced by the material excavated during the production of a cutting for a railway line, the hill was later retaken by the Germans and then again by the British. On 5 May the Germans again attacked and retook the hill. It was probably during this attack that Allan was wounded. Later the same day he died from his wounds.

He is buried in Bailleul Communal Cemetery extension Nord in plot I row E grave 175.

JOSEPH WALTON HEDLEY
BA

Captain
2nd/5th Battalion Lancashire Fusiliers
MTS 1898–99

Joseph's father, Matthew Hedley, became vicar of St Leonard's, Langho, Lancashire in 1868, the year before he married Jane Alice Ward. Matthew and Jane had seven children, all born at Langho. Joseph was their penultimate child and last son.

Their first child, George Ward Hedley, was born at Langho in 1871, followed by Mabel Elizabeth in 1872, Harold Thomas in 1874, Alice Gertrude in 1876 and Constance in 1877. Joseph Walton Hedley was born on 20 February 1880 and was baptised at St Leonard's church, Langho by his father nine days later. Matthew and Jane's final child, Bertha, was born in 1881.

In 1891 the family, including Joseph, was still living in the vicarage in Langho.

In January 1895, Matthew Hedley died after a rheumatic illness that affected his heart, He was 55 and still vicar of the parish he had entered in 1868. As a result of his death the family probably had to move out of the vicarage; the admissions register of the school shows that they were living at 1 St Paul's Square, Southport when Joseph entered the school on 19 January 1898. He had previously attended Clitheroe School.

Joseph only stayed at the school for a year and a half, leaving in July 1899. Nonetheless in that time he clearly entered into the spirit of the school and played for the rugby XV in the 1898/09 season and for the cricket XI in 1899. He also succeeded academically, leaving the school to go up to Brasenose College, Oxford where he continued with his rugby career, representing the college 1899–1901.

He graduated BA in 1903 and decided to follow a career as a schoolmaster, moving to Copthorne School in Crawley.

He was granted a commission when war broke out and was gazetted second lieutenant with 5th Battalion Lancashire Fusiliers on 15 December 1914. He was stationed at Bedford when he was promoted from second lieutenant to temporary captain on 25 April.

The battalion sailed for France on 3 May 1915, landing at Boulogne the following day. Shortly after landing, the battalion took part in the battle of Festubert.

The battalion moved to 164th Brigade of 55th Division on 7 January 1916 with whom it took part in the battle of Ginchy on 9 September 1916. It was during this action that Joseph was wounded. He died from his wounds on 12 September.

He is buried in Heilly Station Cemetery, Mericourt-L'Abbe in plot IV row F grave 6.

CHARLES HENRY HIVEY

Private
16085
17th Battalion King's (Liverpool Regiment)
MTS 1903–06

After their marriage in 1879, William Henry Hivey and Jane Frances Osborn had seven children, six of whom survived to adulthood.

The eldest of these, William, was born in 1880 and went on to become manager of the family sack merchant's company. Isabel followed in 1882. She went on to become an elementary school teacher. Gladys, born in 1886 became a domestic science teacher. Agnes, born in 1888, also became an elementary school teacher.

Charles Henry Hivey was born on 4 January 1891 in Toxteth Park. The census of 5 April 1891 shows the family living at 75 Berkley Street, Toxteth Park. In addition to the immediate family of William Henry (a sack and paper stock merchant), Jane and five children, the house was shared with Jane's father Joseph Osborn, aged 67 (a retired master mariner who kept an account of his voyages between 1853 and 1875 which are now held by the National Maritime Museum), and her two brothers Wilson and Ernest Osborn.

William and Jane's final child, Doris was born in 1894. By 1901 they had moved to 65 Sandy Road, Seaforth. All six children were living at home along with their parents and grandfather Joseph.

Charles was the only one of William and Jane's offspring to attend Merchant Taylors'. He arrived on 16 September 1903 and left in 1906 and seems not to have made a great impact on the sporting or academic scene.

By 2 April 1911 William (junior) had married and moved out but the other five children were still living at home. Charles was working as a 'Commercial Clerk'.

Charles enlisted on 31 August 1914 and was eventually posted to 17th Battalion King's (Liverpool Regiment), the first of the Liverpool Pals battalions to be formed. On 30 April 1915 the battalion was assigned to 89th Brigade in 30th Division and sailed for France on 7 November 1915.

The four Liverpool Pals battalions faced their first serious battle at the beginning of July 1916 – the battle of the Somme. On the first day of the battle, 1 July, 30th Division attacked towards the village on Montauban and the 17th Battalion was on the far right of the English force, with the French to their right.

Compared with the carnage on the rest of the front, the battalion suffered relatively few casualties during the opening of the attack on 1 and 2 July. 3 July was reported as a 'quiet day' but with German shelling continuing. It was on this day, perhaps as a result of this shelling, that Charles was killed in action.

His body was not recovered as he is commemorated in pier and face 1D, 8B and 8C of the Thiepval Memorial and has no known grave.

JOHN BROWN HORSFALL

Second Lieutenant
Machine Gun Corps
MTS 1903–05

John was the son of the wonderfully named Tom Brown Wheelhouse Horsfall and Elizabeth Jane Horsfall (formerly Place). Their first child, Thomas Place Brown was born in Bootle in 1884. Around 1884/85, T. B. W. Horsfall moved his family to Formby where their next child, Edith, was born in 1886. She was followed by May in 1888 and then by John Brown on 4 October 1889.

In 1891 they were living in Elson Road, Formby – Elizabeth Jane would live on this road until her death in 1936 and Edith until her death in 1964. Tom and Elizabeth's son, Percy, was born shortly after the census. The couple's final child, Douglas Beckwith, was born in 1893.

When John was only eight years old, his father died. He was about 45 years old and died on 10 May 1898 probably leaving his widow quite wealthy. Their house in Elson Road, Formby was quite large and Tom left her shares in several Castletown-registered sailing vessels, including the *Imberhorne, Venus, Progress, Manx King*.

In 1901 John's widow, Elizabeth, was living at Albion Villas, Elson Road, Formby with her six children.

On 28 April 1903, aged 13, John joined Merchant Taylors'. He stayed only two years leaving in 1905. On leaving school he seems to have gone to work as a clerk with the Mersey Docks and Harbour Board. He was certainly employed as such in 1911 when he was still living in the Elson Road house along with his mother, Edith, May, Percy and Douglas.

John was another of those Old Crosbeians who enlisted shortly after the outbreak of war. Posted to the 6th Battalion King's (Liverpool Regiment) he became Private Horsfall, regimental number 1429. He eventually rose to lance corporal within the regiment.

Going to France with the battalion on 24 February 1915, he would have found himself with a number of other Old Boys. Unlike several of these OCs he survived the battle of Ypres and the attack on Hill 60 and was recommended for a commission.

There are indications that he underwent training for his commission with D Company, 9th (Scottish) Officers' Cadet Battalion from which he was commissioned as a second lieutenant in October 1916 into the Machine Gun Corps, specifically 124 Company, which fought with 41st Division. By the time Second Lieutenant Horsfall joined his unit, the battle of the Somme was mostly over but the third battle of Ypres, Passchendaele, was still to come.

The 41st Division took part in the battle of Messine in June 1917. Between this confrontation and the battle of Pilckem Ridge which started on 31 July, Horsfall was killed in action. The official date is given as 25 July 1917 though his body was never recovered for burial. He is commemorated on panel 56 of the Ypres (Menin Gate) Memorial.

CHARLES JAMES HOWSON

Lieutenant
Royal Air Force
MTS 1901–08

Charles James Howson was the only surviving child of Alfred James Howson and Harriet Buckley Howson (née Callwood). He was born in Waterloo on 11 January 1892.

In 1901 the family was living at 'Parkside', Fir Road, Waterloo with Charles's father working as a 'Secretary to a Public Co'. Later the same year, on 10 September, Charles was admitted to Merchant Taylors'. He left the school in 1908.

By 1911, Charles was working as a clerk in a fire insurance office and was living with his parents at 77 Milton Road, Waterloo.

Before the war started, Charles seems to have been involved with the Territorial Force; the November 1912 edition of *The School Review* records that he won the half-mile race at the Liverpool Territorial Sports. He was probably a member of the 7th Battalion King's (Liverpool Regiment) as his medal index card records him as Sergeant Howson, regimental number 939 in this battalion at the beginning of the war. He went to France with this battalion, landing at Le Havre on 8 March 1915 where it joined 6th Brigade, 2nd Division and no doubt took part in the battle of Festubert from 15 to 25 May 1915 and the battle of Loos from 25 September to 19 October 1915.

Charles applied for and was granted a commission in the Royal Flying Corps being gazetted temporary second lieutenant (on probation) on 5 August 1916, a rank that was confirmed in July 1917. Posted to 32 Squadron he was flying DH5 aircraft and on 9 October 1917 was flying aircraft No A9173 when he suffered an engine failure that forced him to land south-east of St Julien. The enemy shelled his aircraft but Howson was uninjured.

Howson was flying another DH5 (No A9233) on 29 January 1918 when he was in combat with an enemy Albatros DV aircraft which was shot down over Staden, supposedly his third victory. A short time later, on 5 February 1918 he was promoted to temporary lieutenant and on 7 April claimed another victory, this time over a Fokker triplane.

At some point after this last victory he transferred to 95 Squadron, which was based at RAF Shotwick near Chester. On 5 July 1918, Charles Howson was 'swinging the propeller' of an Avro 504 when he was struck by the propeller suffering injuries from which he later died at Chester War Hospital.

He is buried in Liverpool (Anfield) Cemetery.

BEAUCHAMP HASSING HOYER

Gunner
1204
South African Heavy Artillery
MTS 1892–97

Beauchamp Hassing Hoyer was the son of Frederick Hoyer and Zoe Magdalen Hoyer (formerly Humphreys). His parents were married on 12 September 1872 at Holy Trinity church in Paddington and by the time their eldest child, Magdalen Zoe, was born in the middle of 1873 they had moved to the Liverpool area. After Magdalen three more girls were born: Christian Margaret in 1875, Susan Grahame in 1877 and Honor Noel in 1878. In 1880 their first son Humphreys Noel Hoyer was born.

Beauchamp was born on 25 June 1881, becoming the sixth child in the family. He was followed by Enge Gladys in 1885 and Russell Rosenkilde in 1888.

By 1891 the family had moved to 19 Harlech Road. In the 1881 census, Frederick had described himself as a 'Manufacturing Machinist' but in 1891 he claimed to be a 'Forwarding Agent'.

When Beauchamp applied to attend Merchant Taylors', his father's occupation was given as 'Engineer'. His first day at the school was 25 January 1892. He stayed for five years, leaving in July 1897.

When he left the school he became a bank clerk and in 1901 was still living at 19 Harlech Road with his parents and five of his brothers and sisters, Christian and Humphreys having moved out. In 1901, Russell followed his brother into the school but stayed for only two years, leaving in 1903.

Beauchamp served in the South African War as a trooper in the South African Constabulary.

His father, Frederick, died on 5 September 1909, while still living at 19 Harlech Road. His mother is recorded as dying on 31 July 1915 at Worthing.

Beauchamp married Gladys Janet Reynolds at an unknown date, possibly in South Africa.

He embarked at Cape Town aboard the *Walmer Castle* on 24 February 1917 presumably for England, from where he joined 73rd Siege Battery on 11 August as part of a draft. The battery had moved to Ypres in June and had been subjected to German shelling and bombing. The casualty records show that Beauchamp Hassing Hoyer was killed in action on 18 August 1917, very shortly after his arrival. The exact cause is unknown.

He is buried in Poelcapelle British Cemetery in plot LVI row C grave 8.

ERIC COULTHARD HUGHES

The Hughes family. Eric is on the right of the group.

Private
356104
1st/10th Battalion King's (Liverpool Regiment)
MTS 1909–12

Edward Morgan Hughes and Lizzie Coulthard both had connections with and lived in North Wales. It was there that they married in 1896. Shortly after their wedding they must have moved to Crosby where they settled in 8 Fairholme Road, which would be home for Lizzie and Edward for many years; they were still living there at the time of her death, in 1937.

Eric Coulthard was born to Edward and Lizzie on 18 November 1897, followed by Frederick Max in 1899, both boys eventually attended Merchant Taylors'.

Edward worked as a civil engineer and in the census of 1901 he also described himself as a 'Ship's Draughtsman'.

The final addition to the family, Edward Alan, was born in 1908. He seems not to have gone to Merchant Taylors'.

Eric started his career at Merchant Taylors' on 26 January 1909, having previously attended a private preparatory school in Waterloo called 'Dunmore' and then Merchant Taylors' Girls' School. His brother followed in 1910.

In 1911, Edward had 'reclassified' himself as 'Engineer Assistant to Superintendent Engineer'.

The following year, on 16 April 1912, Eric left Merchant Taylors' to become a boarder at Birkenhead School. He stayed there for two years, leaving in 1914 to take up an apprenticeship as an auditor with the Mersey Docks and Harbour Board.

Eric joined 1/10th Battalion King's (Liverpool Regiment) (The Liverpool Scottish) in April 1915 as a private and was given the regimental number 4483. He first went to France in July 1916 at which time the battalion was with the 55th (West Lancashire Division). At the end of that month the division moved to a new part of the front line opposite the village of Guillemont. In August he volunteered to join a draft of men attached to the 9th Battalion which attacked Guillemont on 12 August. He was wounded early in the attack and was seen lying in a shell hole about 50 yards from the British trenches when the next wave of attackers passed. It is believed he was later killed by a shell which fell on the advanced dressing station to which he is thought to have been taken. The battalion suffered over 200 casualties in this attack.

He was initially posted as missing in action and remained 'on the books' which accounts for his being given a new regimental number, 356104, when the Territorial Force was renumbered in 1917.

He was eventually buried in Guillemont Road Cemetery, Guillemont in plot VIII row F grave 4.

WILLIAM WALTER KENNETH HUME

Corporal
240034
1st/6th Battalion King's (Liverpool Regiment)
MTS 1899–1904

On 28 December 1875, William's parents James Hume and Margaret Knox were married in Edinburgh. He was a native Scot, being Edinburgh born, she had been born in Georgetown, Demerara, British Guiana but was a British citizen. Their first child, James Edgar, was born in 1877 in Liverpool to be followed, in Birkenhead, by Christina May in 1879 and Isabella Margaret in 1881. Christina died in 1886 when only six years old. Two years later on 24 August 1888, William Walter Kenneth was born in Hoylake.

Margaret's sister, Jane, who had been living with them in 1881 was still with them in 1891 in Cable Road, Little Meols, Hoylake with James (who was working as an iron merchant), his wife and three children.

The family moved to 12 Oakdale Road, Waterloo between 1891 and 1899 as this was the address given on William's application for Merchant Taylors'. He joined the school on 24 January 1899.

Margaret's sister seems to have become a fixture in the family home as she was still living with them in 1901 at the same address. James (senior) was now working as a 'Commission Agent', the same occupation he had given when William applied for entry to the school. The eldest son, James, had moved away and was working as a furniture salesman in Willesden.

William's father died in 1904. Whether as a result of this or not, William left the school in the same year and went to work for the London and Lancashire Fire Insurance Company. Two years later, in 1906, he joined the 2nd Volunteer Battalion King's Liverpool Rifles where he was an enthusiastic signaller and member of the shooting club.

By 1911, William, or Kenneth as his mother referred to him in the census return, was still working as an insurance clerk. He was now living at 9 Neville Road, Waterloo with his mother, sister and, of course, his aunt, Jane!

William's army service record has not survived but it seems that on the outbreak of war he was part of the 6th Battalion King's (Liverpool Regiment). He eventually rose to the rank of corporal.

The battalion shipped to France on 24 February 1915 and landed at Le Havre the following day. He then seems to have spent two and a half years in France during which the 5th and 55th Divisions, to which the battalion was attached at various times, took part in some of the worst fighting on the Western Front. In 1915 he would have seen the second battle of Ypres including the attack on Hill 60. In 1916 the battalion was moved south of Arras and he would have been present at the battles of Guillemont, Ginchy, Flers-Courcelette and Morval until they were withdrawn from this area and sent to the Ypres salient where he was killed on 2 August 1917, probably at the end of the battle of Pilckem Ridge.

He is commemorated on panels 4 and 6 of the Ypres (Menin Gate) Memorial.

INNES ELDEN IRWIN

Lance Corporal
3468
1st/6th Battalion King's (Liverpool Regiment)
MTS 1894–98

Innes's father was an engineer who, following his apprenticeship in Sunderland, largely remained in the north-east until 1877 at which time he became superintendent engineer of the Inman Steamship Company in Liverpool where he oversaw the building of a number of ships.

Having married Charlotte Wall in 1878, in 1883 he went into business as a consulting engineer and naval architect.

Innes Elden Irwin was born in Bootle on 22 October 1883, the second of the couple's three children. Their first, Thomas Cuthbert, was born in 1879 and the last, Noel Spencer in 1885.

His father's business clearly prospered for in 1889 he became a partner in the firm of Irwin, Atkinson and Young. In 1891, he styled himself as 'Consulting Engineer (Marine)' in the census return when he was living with his family at 1 St Alban's Road, Bootle, an area which has now completely disappeared and been replaced by office blocks.

On 1 May 1894, Innes first set foot inside Merchant Taylors', following his brother, Thomas, who had arrived in 1890 and preceding his brother, Noel, who would arrive two years later in 1896.

On 11 June 1897 Innes's father died aged 49 after a period of poor health.

Innes left the school at the end of the Christmas term in 1898 and became a cashier in the timber trade. His brother Thomas had left in 1895 and Noel would continue at the school until 1900.

By 1901, Charlotte and her two youngest sons had moved a few streets from St Alban's Road to 58 Trinity Street, Bootle and by 1911 had moved yet again, this time to 19 Fernhill Road, Bootle.

In 1913, Charlotte died and soon afterwards, or maybe even before her death, Innes moved in with his brother Thomas at 345 Old Chester Road, Rock Ferry.

Innes signed his attestation papers on 29 May 1915 giving his trade as 'Cashier' and stating that he had previously served with 1st Cheshire Engineers (Volunteers). He was posted to the 6th Battalion King's (Liverpool Regiment). They were already in France and he set sail from Southampton on 12 October 1915 to join them.

He was promoted to corporal on 12 August 1916 and two days later on 14 August (or more likely the early hours of 15 August) he received a shell wound and was admitted to No 1 (NZ) Stationary Hospital at Amiens, about 15 miles behind the front line where it acted as a casualty clearing station. It was in this hospital that Innes Irwin died of his wounds on 15 August 1916.

He is buried in St Pierre Cemetery, Amiens in plot III row A grave 2.

St Helen's church, Sefton (below) and St Luke's church, Crosby (above), the graveyards of which contain the graves of, or memorials to, a number of Old Crosbeians.

Henry Cradock-Watson was headmaster from 1903 until 1929. He corresponded with many of the old boys, and with their parents after they received news of their son's death.

Mrs Cradock-Watson also received letters from the boys at the front including this one from Fraser Sheard explaining that he had 'been very busy since 1st July' – the first day of the battle of the Somme.

Merchant Taylors' School Football XV., 1911-12.

H. Bottomley.   Rev. E. Hartley.   H. Thompson.   F. M. Sheard.   A. J. Burley.   A. G. Spedding.   W. M. Fitton.   G. Jackson.   D. Gore.   B. Wright, Esq.
A. S. Dod.   P. V. Alexander   E. L. Millard   J. P. Barron.   F. Yorke
(Vice-Capt.)   (Capt.)   (Hon. Sec.)
D. Grant.   J. S. Mayer.   C. Peacock.

The 1st XV of 1911/12. Five of the team – F. M. Sheard, G. Jackson, F. Yorke, D. Grant and J. S. Mayer – died as a result of the war.

Lynwood,
Harboro Road,
Waterloo,
Nr. Liverpool.

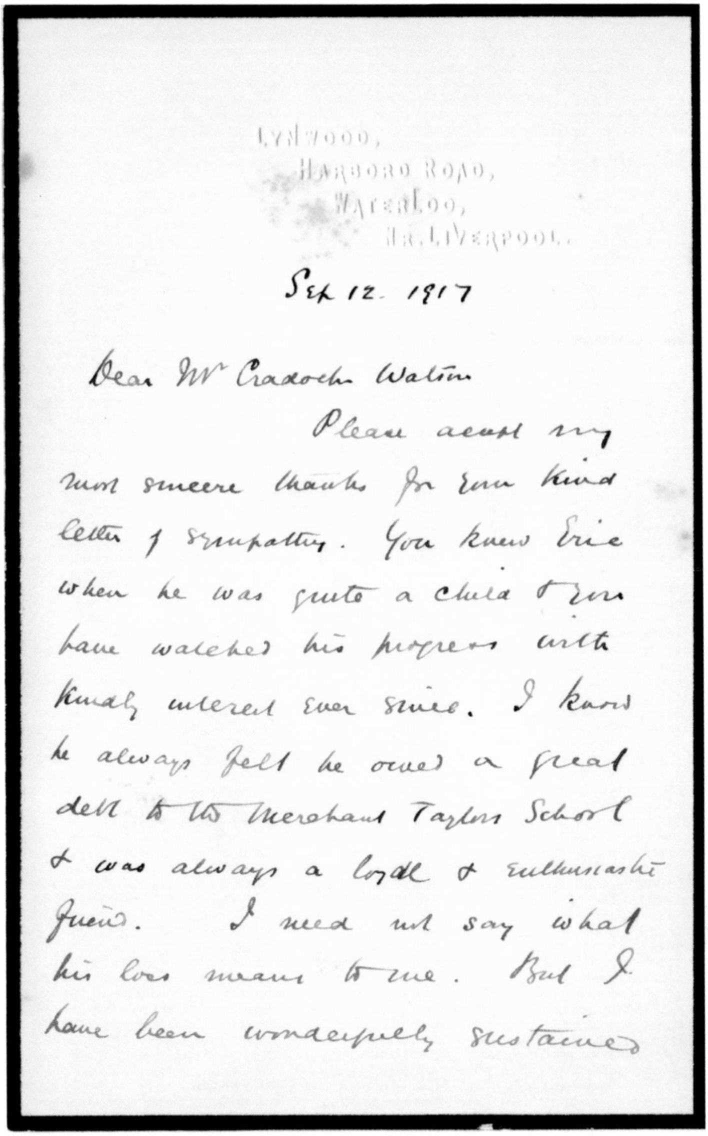

Sep 12. 1917

Dear Mr Cradock Watson

Please accept my most sincere thanks for your kind letter of sympathy. You knew Eric when he was quite a child & you have watched his progress with kindly interest ever since. I know he always felt he owed a great debt to the Merchant Taylors School & was always a loyal & enthusiastic friend. I need not say what his loss means to me. But I have been wonderfully sustained

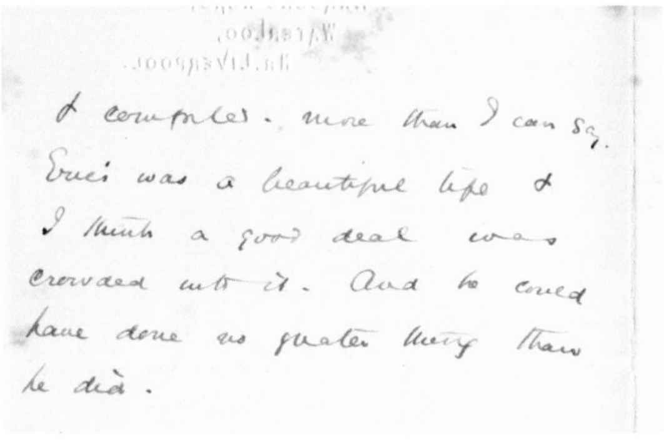

& comforted - more than I can say. Eric's was a beautiful life & I think a good deal was crowded into it. And he could have done no greater thing than he did.

Part of a letter from Reverend George Albert Brock, father of Eric, to Cradock-Watson.

A letter from Harold Wakeford to Cradock-Watson dated 28 March 1916. A week later, on 5 April 1916, he was killed in Mesopotamia.

Things ... but her ... pretty quiet just
now — but before long something will no
doubt. I expect. Returns at same
different ... and we are during now
... is ... of course. we
looking for ... of course. we
always ... afterward that we shall
never be able to get any — but we
must do something in our practice.
Though — ... however — Thaven, little
enough practice ... nowadays. Since
we landed in this place I have spent
only 6 complete nights in my bed out
of 20! Indeed, the other night I was
at midnight absolutely stuffed, I being
in stables where ... had eaten
through in a running torrent, &
could not sleep. we ... about
dawn very ...

Kindest regards to Mr Cadoc
... to yourself —
Yours very sincerely
[signature]

... to hand. It is — unmeasurable hard.
And moreover, I should not attempt
language than you in ... of the
boy, (but afterward who obtain a
common ... Itseems easier &
... to give command of men which
is so easy thing) as an inexperienced
youth, & to make it difficult for a
... (who has received sympathetic instruction
...) to obtain even junior
command. I can't help that my half.
Year in the ranks has meant of
infinitely more to me in the ... of
experience than any training I have
had as an officer. Cheerful that is
the appreciation of the point of view of
the rank & file — much ... & ...
youth will only acquire after hard experience.
True, active service is the ... of
all — but why wait till ... to

The medal group of Major J. C. Jack: Distinguished Service Order, Military Cross with second award bar, 1914/15 Star, British War Medal, Allied Victory Medal and the medal for the Delhi Durbar 1911.

The medals of brothers Arthur Ellis Johnson and Charles Edward Johnson. In spite of the note attached to his medals saying that he died of war disability in 1922, Charles' name does not appear on the memorial. No doubt, by then, the memorial was in the process of production.

St Michael's Terrace, Croston.

As a memorial to Godfrey Jackson, his parents and grandparents had a row of four almshouses built in Croston, Godfrey's mother's birthplace. They were built at St Michael's Terrace, Westhead, Croston in 1936.

Tank B30 (the number is visible, painted on the side of the tank) was commanded by Thomas Milbourn Mercer. The photograph shows the tank after it had been salvaged by the Germans.

HMS *Cordelia* was a light cruiser. An explosion aboard her caused the death of Alfred Vaughan.

HMS *Carmania* was a transatlantic liner belonging to the Cunard Line. During World War I she was requisitioned by the Admiralty, fitted with eight 4.7-inch guns and used as an armed merchant cruiser. William Somerville Limrick served aboard her and HMS *Arlanza* as assistant paymaster.

Limrick also served on HMS *Arlanza*, another liner converted into an armed merchant cruiser.

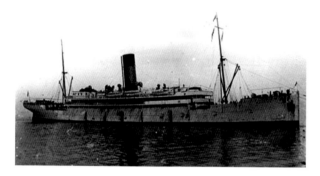

HMS *Patuca* on which Thomas Maitland Winslow served.

The memorial to those who lost their lives as a result of World War I contains 155 names. It was designed by L. B. Budden MA ARIBA, an Old Crosbeian and modelled by H. Tyson Smith. The names are engraved on brass which is mounted on a sill of Belgian marble and backed by green Westmoreland stone.

The memorial was unveiled on 2 October 1923 by Reverend Canon Samuel Crawford Armour DD who was headmaster from 1863 until 1903. It was mounted in what was then the main Hall, now the library.

Unveiling of the War Memorial,
BY THE
REV. CANON ARMOUR, D.D.,
AT
Merchant Taylors' School, Crosby,
Tuesday, October 2nd, 1923.

The Cadet Corps in July 1915. Formally recognised in March 1915, it was affiliated to the 6th (Rifle) Battalion of the King's Regime
at that time.

James Charles Jack
DSO, MC and bar, BA

Major
Royal Field Artillery
MTS 1886–95

James Charles Jack was the most highly decorated Old Crosbeian to die in the Great War. His father, Alexander Jack, was a shipbuilder and engineer who had served his apprenticeship in Glasgow and who, shortly after his return to Liverpool, became a partner in James, Jack, Rollo & Co.

Alexander Jack had married Sarah Hannah Hatton in 1874 and their first child, Muriel Agnes was born in 1875. James Charles entered this world on 22 August 1876 followed by Alexander Noel in 1877. The family was comfortably off and in 1881 they were living in a large house at 102 Princes Road in Toxteth Park and employed four servants. Their final child, Catherine Hester, arrived in 1883 when they were still living in Toxteth Park.

James's father died at the early age of 39 on 7 March 1886. Very soon after his father's death, on 3 May 1886, James set out from his home in Gores Lane, Formby to start his education at Merchant Taylors'; his brother started at the school the same year. Presumably because of his father's death and his easily recognised great potential, James was elected to a Harrison Scholarship at Christmas 1886. A year later, towards the end of 1887, James's sister Muriel died.

Little had changed by 1891, Sarah and her three surviving children were still living in Gores Lane and the two boys were still attending Merchant Taylors' where they were both developing into first class academics and sportsmen. James represented the school at rugby from 1893 to 1895 being captain in the last year. He also played for the school cricket XI in 1895. He left school in July 1895 and the school still benefits from his legacy: he started the house system which is practised today. He organised the boys into groups or 'sets', the purpose of which was to try to improve the sporting standards. The names of the sets, the present-day houses, have changed over the years but the principle behind them remains the same.

On leaving school, he went up to Oxford with a Classical Exhibition to Lincoln College, which he represented at rowing, cricket and rugby. In 1898 he captained the college cricket XI. Sir Gerald Berkeley Hurst KC in his autobiography, *Closed Chapters*, when talking of his Oxford days writes 'a far more obvious imperialist then at Lincoln was J C Jack whose passion for England had no half tones. He was a most engaging character, good at every game.' Graduating with honours he emerged from Oxford with a BA in history and entered the Indian Civil Service and in 1902 was appointed assistant settlement officer in Backergani, Bengal.

By 1912 he had risen to be director of Land Records in Bengal. While in India James had, between 1906 and 1910, been involved in carrying out a survey of Faridpur, a district of Bengal. His report on the survey was well received when it was published in 1916. In *The Cambridge History of India*, Mortimer Wheeler describes James as 'a brilliant and devoted settlement officer'.

In 1915 he was granted a commission in the Royal Field Artillery Special Reserve, being gazetted second lieutenant (on probation) on 24 May 1915. He went to France on 15 October 1915 and on 18 November was promoted to temporary lieutenant while acting as adjutant.

He was promoted to temporary captain on 26 April 1916 while commanding a battery of 4-inch guns. While in this rank he was awarded the Military Cross, gazetted on 28 September 1916. The citation reads:

> For conspicuous gallantry during operations. He directed the successful cutting of the wire from an exposed position under heavy shell fire. He was once partly buried. When his wires were cut he established communications by visual signalling and when the enemy counter-attacked in great force he was able to bring a heavy fire to bear on them which broke up their attack and inflicted heavy losses.

On 23 November 1916 he was further promoted to acting major whilst commanding a battery of 6-inch guns. As acting major he was awarded a bar to his Military Cross, which was gazetted on 13 May 1918. The citation this time reads:

> For conspicuous gallantry and devotion to duty. During a daylight raid on the enemy's trenches he went forward to observe and report on the artillery barrage and the progress of the raiding party. He remained at his post with great coolness and determination under an intense enemy barrage until he was severely wounded. He has always set a splendid example to all ranks.

His final award, the Distinguished Service Order, was gazetted posthumously on 27 July 1918:

> For conspicuous gallantry and devotion to duty. While his battery was being heavily gas shelled he superintended the removal of his guns to higher ground clear of the cloud of gas and continued to fire heavily throughout the bombardment. Another day when the enemy got close to the guns, he withdrew his guns without losing one. His fine courage and initiative throughout were a splendid example to his men.

While at the front he was wounded three times, on the last occasion fatally. On 31 May 1918, Major James Jack died of wounds at the casualty clearing station at Vignacourt while serving with D Battery, 150th Brigade, Royal Field Artillery.

He is buried in Vignacourt British Cemetery plot III row B grave 6. He was also Mentioned in Despatches on 23 December 1918 for distinguished and gallant service and devotion to duty.

On General Congreve's recommendation, James's promotion to the rank of lieutenant-colonel was agreed but was only received at Corps HQ on the day of his death and so he did not know of it. It was said that he was to be made brigadier general as soon as possible. Both those he commanded and his fellow officers praised his ability and leadership and he was highly respected by all those who knew him. This would undoubtedly account for his rapid rise from second lieutenant to lieutenant-colonel in a relatively short time.

GODFREY JACKSON

Lieutenant
1st/4th Battalion East Lancashire Regiment
MTS 1910–12

Godfrey Jackson was born and raised in Southport. His parents, George Jackson and Margaret (formerly Dalton) had four children but Godfrey was the only one to survive to adulthood. He was born on 12 January 1895. His father was a grocer but by 1901 he had retired, though still only 47, and Godfrey and his parents were living at 74 Roe Lane, Southport.

Godfrey entered Merchant Taylors' on 1 March 1910 as a boarding pupil having previously attended a private school called Southport College.

The 1911 census shows the family still living in Roe Lane but they had moved to number 17. Godfrey also sat, and passed, his Oxford Local Junior exam in 1911 and in the 1911/12 season represented the school as a member of the rugby XV. He left the school on 4 April 1912 and joined a solicitor's office.

He was gazetted as a second lieutenant in the 1st/4th Battalion East Lancashire Regiment with effect from 19 May 1915. The battalion spent the early part of the war in Egypt, Gallipoli and the Middle East but Godfrey seems not to have been with them. The battalion moved into France on 27 February 1917 and moved to the Western Front, initially at Épehy. According to Godfrey's record, he did not cross to France until 2 March 1917, at which time the battalion formed part of the 42nd (East Lancashire) Division. After serving at several places in the front line, they moved, in September, to the Ypres area. On 15 September 1917, the 4th Battalion East Lancashires attacked and captured Sans Souci, a German pillbox and strongpoint. It was probably during this attack that Godfrey was killed.

He is buried in Brandhoek New Military Cemetery No 3 plot I row G grave 31.

As a memorial to Godfrey, his parents and grandparents had a row of four almshouses built in Croston, Godfrey's mother's birthplace. They were built at St Michael's Terrace, Westhead, Croston in 1936.

ARTHUR ELLIS JOHNSON

Second Lieutenant
2nd Battalion York and Lancaster Regiment
MTS 1905–10

In the 1860s, Arthur's grandfather moved from Wisbech in Cambridgeshire to Liverpool and made an interesting change of career from 'bookseller and printer' to 'export bottler' i.e. a bottler of export beers. This move was clearly successful as in 1871 he was employing over twenty people. The firm lasted until well into the 20th century.

Arthur's father, William, who eventually took over the firm, married Alice Mary Tyrer in St Luke's church, Liverpool, 1882. They went on to have eight children. Arthur was the seventh of these. Only seven of the eight survived into adulthood. He was born on 2 May 1894, at 26 Richmond Terrace in Everton, into a family of three older sisters: Lydia Mary (born 1883), Alice Greta (born 1884), Katherine Delta (born 1888) and two older brothers: William Tyrer (born 1886), Harry Tyrer (born 1890). Another brother, George Tyrer had been born in 1892 but died in 1893. The last child, Charles Edward was born in 1896. All four boys attended Merchant Taylors'. By 1901, the family was living in 'Caradoc', a large house in Waterloo Park.

Arthur joined Merchant Taylors' on 17 September 1905 having previously attended 'Dunmore', a private preparatory school in Waterloo. He stayed at the school until 21 December 1910 having, that year, passed his Oxford Local Junior exam.

When Arthur left the school, he joined his father's firm and in 1911 was listed as a 'junior clerk'. The family still lived at Caradoc, with William working as a 'Manager' and Katherine as a 'typist'; one imagines in the family firm. Harry was a student at Liverpool University from which he graduated BSc in 1913 and MSc in 1914.

Details of Arthur's wartime career are rather vague. He initially joined the Liverpool Regiment as a private with the number 3638 though no battalion is given. He was still serving in this role when he was renumbered in 1917 and given the new number 201324, which indicates he was with the 5th Battalion.

He received a commission as second lieutenant on 28 March 1917 and was attached to the 2nd Battalion York and Lancaster Regiment. This battalion formed part of 16th Brigade, 6th Division. He crossed to France on an unrecorded date and was killed in action on 20 July 1917. The war diary of the 8th Battalion Bedfordshire Regiment which also formed part of the 16th Brigade records that 20 July was generally quiet but that the 2nd Battalion York and Lancasters carried out a night raid on enemy trenches and that Allied trenches were then shelled. Arthur could have lost his life as a result of either of these occurrences. If one of these, or some other, were the cause, it seems his body was not recovered as he has no known grave and he is commemorated on panels 105 and 106 of the Loos Memorial.

RODNEY RICHARD JOHNSON

Lance Corporal
20458
8th Battalion King's Own (Royal Lancaster)
Regiment
MTS 1910–12

Rodney and his parents were Londoners. Richard Johnson and Marguerita Brett married at St Saviour's church, Battersea on 14 September 1895. At the time of their marriage they were both living in Wandsworth and it was in the Lavender Hill area of the borough that Rodney was born on 18 February 1897.

He was baptised at St Barnabas church, Clapham Common on 11 April 1897 when the church would have been almost brand new. At the time of his marriage and of the baptism, Richard was working as a tinplate worker.

Although Rodney has been traced in the 1901 census as a visitor at 34 Chatham Road, Battersea, it has not proved possible to find either of his parents.

Rodney completed the earlier part of his education at Holden Street Council School in Battersea and having, presumably, moved to the north-west, he joined Merchant Taylors' on 14 September 1910, by which time his father had died.

On the day of the census in 1911, 2 April, Rodney, aged 14, was listed as the head of the household at 5 Hougoumont Avenue in Waterloo. A housekeeper appears to be looking after him. Meanwhile, his mother, Marguerite was listed as the housekeeper of the Exchange Hotel in Liverpool.

Rodney left Merchant Taylors' on 4 April 1912 and moved to Ellesmere College from where he went to the London and Liverpool Insurance Company as a clerk.

He enlisted in the army after about a year of war by which time he was 18, signing his attestation papers on 9 August 1915 and volunteering for the duration of the war. He gave his address as Ballarmona, St John's Road, Waterloo while his mother, given as next of kin, was still living at the Exchange Hotel.

He arrived at the depot of the King's Own (Royal Lancaster) Regiment on 16 August and was initially posted, after three days, to the 3rd Battalion in which he was advanced to lance corporal on 23 November 1915 and acting corporal on 15 May 1916. On 18 November he reverted to lance corporal when he was posted to the Expeditionary Force.

He was finally posted to France and joined the 8th Battalion in the field on 1 January 1917. The 8th was a New Army battalion which, by the date he joined it, was fighting with the 3rd Division. April and May found the division in the Arras area and it was here that Rodney was killed in action on 1 May 1917. A sergeant wrote to his mother, 'He had been helping to carry a wounded comrade down to the dressing station and on his return he was hit by a sniper and he died instantly'.

Presumably his grave was lost in the ensuing fighting as he has no known grave but is commemorated in bay 2 of the Arras Memorial.

HERBERT LEONARD JONES

Private
401072
12th Battalion Manchester Regiment
MTS 1911–17

Herbert Leonard Jones was born on 21 March 1899 at Mhow, a cantonment in Madhya Pradesh, India where his father, James David Jones, was serving with the 20th Hussars. James had married Alice Harriet Halpin at Christ Church Catholic church in Mhow on 15 February 1897 and when Herbert was born they already had one son, James John, born in 1898. Their next child, Alice Margaret, was also born in Mhow, in 1902 by which time the 20th Hussars and James had moved to South Africa to play their part in the Second Boer War. The 20th Hussars returned to England in 1904, which is probably when James decided to leave the army. The couple's fourth child, Arthur, was born in Waterloo in 1906 and their fifth, Nora Amelia, in 1908.

The 1911 census shows that up to that time, Herbert's parents had had six children, one of whom had died. The surviving five, along with their parents were living in 50 Norway Street, Waterloo and from where Herbert's father worked as a coachman.

Another sister, Kathleen, was born shortly before Herbert first entered Merchant Taylors' on 15 September 1911 having received his earlier education at Christ Church School, Waterloo and winning a scholarship to Merchant Taylors'. He was a member of the school's Cadet Corps and rose to the rank of sergeant. Outside of school he was a member of St John's church, Waterloo where he was leader of the choir. In 1913, the family grew again with the birth of Stanley.

Herbert worked well at school. In 1914 he gained a 2nd Class in his Oxford Local Junior exams, increased this to a 1st Class in 1915 and in 1916 passed his Senior exams.

He left the school on 2 April 1917 and, only just 18, joined the army. He enlisted at Seaforth and was eventually posted to the 12th Battalion Manchester Regiment. He went to France in February 1918 and was slightly wounded on 21 March – his 19th birthday. At 4 a.m. on 25 August 1918 the battalion advanced on the village of Martinpuich, halfway between Albert and Bapaume. They captured the village and cleared the enemy from it but were then stopped by heavy machine-gun fire. In the attack the battalion lost 28 other ranks killed, 112 wounded and 1 missing. Herbert was one of these casualties. It was not recorded whether he was the one missing or whether he was killed and his grave was lost. Whatever the reason, he has no known grave and is commemorated on panel 9 on the Vis-en-Artois Memorial.

His brother James was the first of the family to discover Herbert had been killed as he was serving with the Royal Army Medical Corps as a stretcher-bearer in the same division.

A final sister, Edna, who was never to know him, was born in 1920.

ALFRED JOSEPH KELSALL

Private
15410
17th Battalion King's (Liverpool Regiment)
MTS 1906–12

Alfred Joseph Kelsall was born in Cressington, Liverpool on 25 May 1896. He was the son of Alfred Richard Kelsall, a fish merchant, and his wife

Bessie Alice Ann Kelsall, formerly Wittaker. When Alfred was born they already had one daughter, Mary Beatrice, born in 1894.

His parents waited two years to have Alfred baptised, finally organising it for 28 June 1898 at St Peter's church, Liverpool, the long-demolished church after which Church Street is named. The baptism register shows they were still living in Cressington, a wealthy south Liverpool suburb then consisting of large, detached and semi-detached villas. In the same year, 1898, Alfred and Bessie had another son, Cyril Richard Adam, who died before his first birthday. Another brother, Gerald Richard, was born in 1900.

By 1901 the family had moved to 20 Broughton Drive, Garston. At the time of the 1901 census, Bessie must have been pregnant, as Muriel Alice was born towards the end of 1901. Muriel unfortunately died in the summer of 1902.

Alfred joined Merchant Taylors' on 17 September 1906 having previously attended a private school called Hoylake College. Another brother, Albert Ronald, was born in 1908 in Blundellsands.

Alfred and Bessie had eight children, four of whom survived childhood and by 1911 they were living in Elton Avenue, Blundellsands in a house called Glenhurst. Alfred left the school on 18 December 1912.

After the war broke out, Alfred enlisted in the army and was posted to 17th Battalion King's (Liverpool Regiment), the first of the Pals battalions. Following training the battalion left camp at Amesbury on 7 November 1915 and embarked on the SS *Princess Victoria* at 3 p.m., and arrived at Boulogne two hours later. After a brief stop at Ostreove rest camp they went by train and marched to Bellancourt and Vignacourt. Eventually they ended up on the Somme. Being part of 30th Division, they had 18th Division on their left and the French army on their right facing the village of Montauban. The attack on the village started at 7.30 a.m. on 1 July 1916 and by 10 a.m., the village was captured. Kelsall was probably killed during this attack.

His body was never recovered and he is commemorated on pier and face 1D 8B and 8C of the Thiepval Memorial.

Charles Kenneth Nuthall Kemp
MM

Lance Corporal
240452
1st/6th Battalion King's (Liverpool Regiment)
MTS 1907–12

Charles Kemp was born on 2 August 1896 in Darlington, County Durham. His father, Herbert Edwin Kemp married Jessie Nuthall at Holy Trinity church, Clapham on 10 August 1893 and described himself as a 'Traveller'. Later, in the census returns of 1901 and 1911 he described his occupation as 'Manufacturers' Agent dealing in drapers' goods'.

By 1898 Herbert had moved the family to Didsbury, Manchester, and his second son, John Herbert was born there in that year. They were living in Didsbury in 1901 at 5 Attwood Road, a large semi-detached house. At the end of 1901, still in Didsbury, Henry and Jessie's third child, Phyllis Mary, was born.

Around 1907 they seem to have undertaken another move, to the Liverpool area, for on 1 May 1907, Charles joined Merchant Taylors' having, according to the admissions register, previously been educated at a private preparatory school in Didsbury.

The 1911 census records show them living at Westfield, Jubilee Road, Formby. Charles Kenneth was actually entered on the form as Kenneth Charles so perhaps Kenneth was his preferred name. He left the school on 31 July 1912 and, according to the school's register, went 'into farming'.

Soon after the outbreak of war, Charles joined the army and was posted to 6th Battalion King's (Liverpool Regiment) as Private 1956. This battalion sailed for France on 24 February 1915 landing at Le Havre the following day to become part of 5th Brigade in 5th Division. As part of this division Charles would have taken part in the second battle of Ypres and the attack on Hill 60 in May 1915. After a brief spell with the Third Army at the end of 1915, the battalion was transferred to 55th (West Lancashire) Division on 26 January 1916 and relieved the French south of Arras. Later, in July 1916, they moved opposite the village of Guillemont on the Somme front. According to the 1/6th Battalion's war diary, an attack was made on 9 September on enemy positions in Wood Lane and on 10 September they were withdrawn from the trenches being relieved by New Zealand troops.

CWGC lists Charles as killed in action on 10 September 1916 though it is possible he was initially listed as missing as his medal index card shows he was renumbered as 240452 in 1917. The graves register initially listed him as an 'unknown British soldier'.

He is buried in Serre Road Cemetery in plot XXXIII row H grave 9.

Hugh Kennedy

Private
15793
17th Battalion King's (Liverpool Regiment)
MTS 1906–08

Hugh's father, Dodgson Kennedy, worked his way up from bank clerk to accountant and on his death in 1910 left, for that time, the not inconsiderable sum of nearly £16,000.

Dodgson had married Jane Halewood in 1879 and by 1891 when they were living in Holly House, Aughton, the couple had five children. Agnes was born in 1880 then Clement in 1882, William in 1884, Alan in 1886 and George Dodgson in 1890.

Hugh was born on 11 November 1893 and baptised at St Michael's church, Aughton on 10 December 1893.

Two more sisters arrived for Hugh in the following years: Frances in 1896 and Kathleen in 1900.

By 1901 Dodgson and his family were living in Winifred Lane, Aughton though Clement had moved out and was working as an 'Assistant Farmer' at Crookdake Hall in Cumberland and William and Alan were boarders at the Royal Grammar School in Lancaster.

When Hugh was only 12, his mother died, on 4 March 1906. At the time, he was attending the Grammar School in Ormskirk. Shortly afterwards he entered Merchant Taylors' on 17 September 1906 as a boarding pupil.

In 1907 his father remarried. His new wife, Ellen Ford, brought two more children from her first marriage to the family: 14-year-old Clement (see p.76) and 21-year-old Florence.

On 22 December 1908, Hugh left the school, ostensibly to become a farmer according to the school's register though the 1911 census shows him taking a different route having become a 'Stockbroker's Apprentice'.

Dodgson Kennedy, Hugh's father, died on 27 October 1910 and the following year finds Hugh living with his brother William in Aughton and, as stated, working as a 'Stockbroker's Apprentice'. Their two youngest sisters were both at boarding school in London.

Hugh signed his attestation papers on 2 September 1914, giving his occupation as 'Clerk'. He was then posted to 17th Battalion King's (Liverpool Regiment) and remained on home soil until 6 November 1915. While serving at home he married Elizabeth Harrison on 14 July 1915.

He sailed for France with the battalion on 7 November 1915. Shortly afterwards he would have received news of the birth of his daughter on 31 December 1915. Originally, the child was called Mary but a letter from Elizabeth to the regimental paymaster in January 1916 announced that she had changed the child's name to Jane! The child was baptised on 31 March 1916 while Hugh was no doubt at the front.

Having landed at Boulogne on 7 November and joined 30th Division, the battalion eventually arrived on the Somme. At 9 p.m. on 30 July 1916 they assembled for an attack on the German trenches between Guillemont and Falfemont Farm. This advance was held up by heavy machine-gun fire in the early hours of the following morning and at the end of a day of to-and-fro fighting, 60 of the battalion had been killed, 141 wounded and 95 were missing. Hugh was one of those wounded and was evacuated to the Field Ambulance. He was additionally diagnosed with shell shock and eventually moved to No 4 General Hospital. He rejoined the battalion on 15 September 1916.

About 2 p.m. on 12 October 1916, the battalion mounted an attack on the enemy front line but the preceding barrage had not cut through the barbed wire and the attack was unsuccessful. Heavy machine-gun fire caused many casualties with about 225 being wounded or missing. Hugh was classified among the missing and later, according to his record, 'death was assumed by the Army Council'.

He is commemorated on pier and face 1D 8B and 8C of the Thiepval Memorial.

ALLAN KNIGHT

Second Lieutenant
5th Battalion attached 11th Battalion South
Lancashire Regiment
MTS 1910–14

Allan's father was Frank Albert Knight who, throughout Allan's life, referred to himself as a 'Professor of Music'. Frank married Emily Margaret Barker in 1896 in Teesdale, probably Barnard Castle, her birthplace. They had four children of which Allan was the youngest. The eldest, Leonard was born in 1887, and his two older sisters were Margery (born 1889) and Doris (born 1893).

Allan was born in Southport on 20 July 1897 and in 1901, the family was still in Southport, living at 129 Manchester Road.

Allan's earlier education was provided by a private preparatory school in Sefton Park, called 'Parkfield'. An advertisement for the school in the *Liverpool Mercury* noted that 'Sons of professional men and merchants only are admitted'. He moved from Parkfield to Merchant Taylors' on 1 April 1910. This must have been a turbulent time for Allan. Not only did he have to deal with a new school but a week later, on 22 September, his brother Leonard emigrated to Australia, sailing from Liverpool to Sydney. Leonard emigrated for health reasons, and during the war he twice tried to enlist in the Australian forces but was twice rejected on the grounds of his health; he suffered from bronchitis and asthma.

Allan, his sisters and their parents were living at 66 Oxford Road, Waterloo in 1911. In 1913, Allan gained a 3rd Class in his Oxford Local Junior exams and the following year passed his Seniors. He left the school to work in an insurance office on 22 December 1914.

It is not clear whether Allan volunteered or was conscripted but he was granted a commission from an officer cadet unit, being gazetted second lieutenant with effect from 28 March 1917. Initially posted to the 5th Battalion South Lancashire Regiment, he was at some stage attached to the 11th Battalion, a pioneer battalion which formed part of 30th Division.

In March 1918, the German army launched its 'Spring Offensive', an attack against the Allied lines at various points on the Western Front. At the time of the attack, the 11th Battalion was concentrated in the village of Fluquières. It has not been possible to determine the exact place and nature of Allan's death but the 11th Battalion's war diary shows that he was killed on 23 March 1918. He was 20 years old.

His body was not recovered and he is commemorated on panels 48 and 49 of the Pozières Memorial.

ARTHUR KYRKE-SMITH

Captain
1st Battalion King's (Liverpool Regiment)
MTS 1889–94

Arthur Kyrke-Smith was a professional soldier before the Great War and though not the first Old Crosbeian to die in uniform during the war, he was the first to be killed in action.

Some records refer to him as Arthur Kyrke Kyrke-Smith and some as Arthur Kyrke-Smith. The 'single Kyrke form' appears in the school records and in the GRO birth records so this has been adopted here even though the 'double Kyrke version' appears in the *London Gazette* and on the war memorial in Farnham, Surrey.

Arthur Kyrke-Smith was born on 19 April 1878 and was the eldest child of Henry Kyrke-Smith, a rice and spice merchant with Wright, Crossley & Co, Liverpool, and his wife Anna Crossthwaite Kyrke-Smith (formerly Brown).

In 1881 Henry and his family were living at 17 Queen's Street, Waterloo and he had two children, Arthur and his sister Dorothy (born 1881). In 1882, Arnold Crossthwaite was born followed by Grace in 1883 and Annie Muriel in 1884.

Arthur came to Merchant Taylors' on 10 September 1889, his address was entered in the register as simply Kirkstone, Waterloo. This is expanded in the 1891 census to Kirkstone, Harbord Road, Waterloo where Henry, his wife and five children were living. At this time the household also included a governess and three servants, and so was, presumably, quite prosperous.

Arthur left Merchant Taylors' in July 1894, the nature of his employment after his departure is unknown. However, it is known that he joined the 4th Volunteer Battalion of the King's (Liverpool Regiment) and was granted a commission as second lieutenant on 31 January 1896. He was promoted to lieutenant on 11 November 1896 and to captain on 8 February 1899.

He went out to South Africa with the Volunteer Battalion to take part in the Boer War and while there, was granted the temporary rank of lieutenant in the army while serving with a volunteer company. He later transferred to the regular army being gazetted second lieutenant in the Liverpool Regiment on 5 May 1900. He served in South Africa until 6 November 1902 having seen action at Laing's Nek in June 1900, Belfast in August of the same year and other, minor operations. For his services he received the Queen's South Africa Medal with three clasps, Laing's Nek, Belfast and Cape Colony and the King's South Africa Medal with the usual two date clasps. While serving abroad he was promoted to lieutenant on 1 January 1901. Lieutenant Arthur Kyrke-Smith returned to the school in October 1902 to give a lecture to the Photographic Society on his experiences in South Africa, illustrating his talk with about a hundred lantern slides that he had taken in Natal and the Transvaal.

On 21 October 1904, Arthur's father Henry died a wealthy man, leaving an estate valued at over £26,000 in 1904. In the same year Arthur passed his examinations for promotion to captain.

On 30 April 1907, Arthur married Catherine Mabel Spittall at St Andrew's church, Southport and their first child, Violet Mabel was born in 1908.

In June 1910, he was appointed adjutant of 9th Battalion King's (Liverpool Regiment), a unit of the Territorial Force and later that year was promoted to captain. On 28 November 1910, his mother died at the family home, Kirkstone.

On 2 April 1911, Arthur was taking a break in Waterhead, Ambleside, staying in a boarding house with his wife and daughter and his parents-in-law.

His wife would have been expecting their second child at this time as their son Charles Arthur Murray was born before the end of the year.

Arthur gave up the adjutancy of the 9th Battalion at the end of October 1913 and returned to the 1st Battalion.

Being a first-line regular battalion, the 1st King's was one of those called on in the opening days of the war. On 12 August 1914, 27 officers and 1,016 men left Farnborough by train for Southampton where they embarked in the transport *Irrawaddy* and landed at Le Havre the following day, forming part of the original British Expeditionary Force. They then travelled by train and marched to a position between Hargnies and Givry where they experienced their first action of the war when they came under heavy shellfire and had to retire. Eventually, the Allies turned and forced the German army back until they reached the Aisne. It was near the village of Moussy on 20 September 1914 that Kyrke-Smith, in charge of C Company, was wounded. He died of his wounds on 23 September.

He is buried in grave A24 in Braine Communal Cemetery.

BERTRAM LE ROUGETEL

Corporal
477535
Royal Canadian Regiment
MTS 1894–1903

Le Rougetel is a Channel Island name; Bertram's father, Philip, was born in Grouville, Jersey in around 1848. Between 1871 and 1881 he found his way to Liverpool as in 1881 he was recorded as living in the house of his cousin in Toxteth Park, Liverpool. Later that same year he married Susan Harrison Jones.

Towards the end of 1882, their first child, Norman, arrived to be followed by Marie in 1885, Bertram on 14 April 1887, Elsie in 1888 and Arthur in 1890. All five children were baptised in St Paul's church, Princes Park, Bertram on 5 June 1887.

On the date of Bertram's baptism, the family was living at 27 Coltart Road, Toxteth Park. Between then and September 1888 when Elsie was baptised they moved to 13 West Albert Road where they were still living in April 1891, at which time Philip was working as a cashier, an occupation he followed in one form or another for his whole life.

Further additions to the family followed: twins Joan Cecilia and Mary Newman in 1894, Guy (see p.119) in 1896 and Kathleen in 1898.

Bertram joined Merchant Taylors' on 14 September 1898 and was awarded a Harrison Scholarship. The family was then living at 24 Courtenay Road, Waterloo. He started in the same year as his brother Arthur; his brother Norman had started in 1892 and left in 1898 while Guy would not start until 1905.

Bertram left the school in 1903 and at some point emigrated to Canada. He is certainly recorded as sailing from Liverpool to Halifax, Nova Scotia aboard the SS *Victorian* on 15 February 1907 and he does not appear in the 1911 census.

Bertram's mother died on 17 January 1913 and the following year he travelled back to England aboard the *Empress of Ireland*, arriving in Liverpool on 18 March. He returned to Canada on the *Teutonic* on 16 May.

Bertram served in the Great War with the Royal Canadian Regiment. He signed his attestation papers on 23 August 1915 at Halifax, Nova Scotia giving his occupation as 'Surveyor'. He was given the number 477535, which was based on the alphabetical order of enlistment. According to his form, he had previously served with the Corps of Guides – presumably the Canadian Corps of Guides, which was responsible for intelligence gathering. Probably on 26 August, the corps sailed for England aboard the SS *Caledonian*, disembarked at Plymouth and started training at Shorncliffe. The regiment entered France on 2 November 1915. After service near Ypres, Hooge etc, the regiment was ordered to the region of the Somme near Courcelette. After an attack on the Zollern Graben trench system on 16 September 1916, Bertram was posted as missing in action. His body was never recovered and he is commemorated on the Vimy Memorial as one of the 11,000 Canadians who died in France and Flanders and have no known grave.

GUY LE ROUGETEL

Private
33891
187th Company Machine Gun Corps
MTS 1905–12

Guy Le Rougetel was born on 7 January 1896 in Waterloo, Liverpool and was the youngest son and penultimate child of Philip and Susan Le Rougetel and brother of Bertram Le Rougetel (see p.118).

In 1901, the family was living at 24 Courtenay Road, Waterloo, Guy's father working as a cashier. Eight of Philip and Susan's nine children were still at home. The eldest, Norman, does not appear in the 1901 census but he does appear in the inbound passenger list of the SS *Orita* in November 1903 which shows that he boarded at St Vincent and disembarked at Liverpool so in 1901 he could have been working abroad.

Guy was the last of the brothers to join Merchant Taylors', arriving on 17 September 1905 from a private preparatory school in Waterloo.

By 1911, Guy's brother, Bertram, had emigrated to Canada while five of the children were still living at home (Marie, Arthur, Joan, Guy and Kathleen), which was now 2 Oxford Drive, Waterloo. In this year, Guy sat and passed his Oxford Local Junior exams and in 1912 passed the Seniors, leaving the school on 31 July that year to take up employment as a bank clerk.

During the war he initially enlisted as Private 4476 in the King's (Liverpool Regiment) but at some stage transferred to the Machine Gun Corps, specifically 187th Company which was attached to 37th Brigade, 14th Indian Division. The 14th Indian Division was formed in Mesopotamia in May 1916, and formed part of the army fighting the Turks in that country. Guy would probably have been in his battalion's machine gun section which would have been subsumed into the Machine Gun Corps on its formation in 1915.

The exact movements of 187th Company MGC are extremely difficult to trace as the records of the corps were largely destroyed by a fire shortly after World War I but it is known that Guy was killed in action on 4 February 1917 probably at the Hai Salient near Kut.

He is buried in Amara War Cemetery plot XVIII row H grave 15.

FRANCIS KIRKPATRICK LEVER

Midshipman
Royal Naval Reserve
MTS 1911–13

Francis Kirkpatrick Lever was the younger of the two sons born to Samuel Vernon Lever and his wife Amy (formerly Kirkpatrick). He was born on 7 July 1899 and was baptised at the church of St John the Divine in Fairfield on 10 September. On that date, the family was living at 54 Rufford Road, Liverpool, the same address at which they were living in 1901 when the census was taken. In that census, Samuel gave his occupation as 'Auctioneer's Clerk' and was sharing the house with his wife, Francis and his elder son Harold Vernon (born 1895).

By 1911, Francis's father's fortunes seemed to be improving, he now described himself as an 'Auctioneer and Valuer' and was living at 31 Cavendish Road, Blundellsands, a larger house than that in Rufford Road.

Both boys attended Merchant Taylors'. Harold started in 1907 and was joined by Francis on 15 September 1911 after attending Rossett School, a private preparatory school in Blundellsands.

Francis left school on 16 April 1913 to join HMS *Worcester*. Originally an 86-gun ship of the line called HMS *Frederick William*, she was a training ship for both Royal and Merchant Naval officers and was moored at Greenhithe on the Thames. As with all cadets of the *Worcester*, he automatically became a cadet in the Royal Naval Reserve. Having served eight terms on the *Worcester*, he was appointed midshipman in the RNR with seniority dating from 1 January 1916.

On 19 February 1916 he joined HMS *Centurion*, a relatively new battleship which formed part of the 2nd Battle Squadron at the battle of Jutland. He remained on the *Centurion* until November 1916 and was next posted to HMS *Onslaught*, a destroyer. Having completed a gunnery course at Devonport and obtaining a 2nd Class certificate he spent some time working on coastal motor boats before moving to his final posting, HMS *PC69*, in May 1918. This was one of a series of ships launched in 1918 to act as Q-ships and operated from Pembroke Dockyard. Q-ships were designed to look like merchant ships in order to lure enemy submarines into making a surface attack. When a submarine surfaced the ship would open fire with concealed weaponry.

He was recommended by the vice-admiral, Milford Haven, while serving aboard her, for recognition of his services. The record shows 'Their Lordships consider that the hunt and attacks on an enemy submarine on the 16–17 August 1918 were well executed and showed much tenacity and that an expression of their appreciation may be conveyed to him'.

On 8 October 1918, Francis was accidentally drowned at Milford Haven while serving aboard HMS *PC69*. He is buried in the churchyard of St Helen's church, Sefton in grave M 216.

WILLIAM SOMERVILLE LIMRICK

Assistant Paymaster
Royal Naval Reserve
MTS 1903–06

Having studied in Dublin and Edinburgh, William's father, also William Somerville Limrick, qualified as a doctor in 1870. He moved to Liverpool shortly afterwards to help in the practice of Dr Arthur May and on 17 April 1873 married his daughter Clara Elizabeth May at Sefton parish church. The couple had 12 children, three of whom died in infancy.

William Somerville Limrick was the couple's penultimate child, born on 17 February 1891 in Sefton. He was not, however the first in the family to be named William Somerville. His parents' fourth child, born in 1878 and who died the same year, had been given the same name. Their fifth child, Grace Marian also survived for a short time only, being born and dying in 1879. Their eighth child, Harold Bright, born in 1883, suffered a similar fate.

About two months after William's birth, the family was living at 5 Waterloo Road, Waterloo in what must have been a large house given the size of the family. Under the one roof lived William (practising as a physician and surgeon), his wife Clara and his remaining children: Frances Elizabeth (born 1874), Clara May (1875), Lucy Agnes (1876), Arthur Paul (1880), Nora Gladys (1882), Dorothy Skottowe (1885), Kathleen (1887) and William Somerville.

One final addition to the family, George Osborn Limrick, was born in 1893. Only the last two boys went to Merchant Taylors'.

In 1901 the family was living at 'Rose Bank', Crosby Road North; although Clara and Arthur had moved out. On 20 January 1903, William entered Merchant Taylors'. He stayed for three years, leaving in 1906. His brother, George, arrived at the school in 1905 and left in 1909.

After leaving school, William worked with a firm of Liverpool shipbrokers for four years and then became a purser with the Cunard Line.

By 1911, the remaining family had moved back to Waterloo Road, this time living at number 7. Nora and Dorothy had moved out, Dorothy having married in 1909. William (senior) died on 21 December 1911.

During the war William was granted a commission in the Royal Naval Reserve and joined HMS *Carmania* as an assistant paymaster at Gibraltar on 25 February 1915. *Carmania* was launched as a Cunard liner but was requisitioned by the Admiralty as an armed merchant cruiser in 1914. She was completing a refit when he joined her but was soon to return to her patrolling duties near the Canary Islands. She had a short spell in the Mediterranean and at the Dardanelles before returning for another refit and continuing to patrol the Canary Islands.

The nine surviving Limrick children.

In June 1916 she was returned to Cunard.

In December 1916 William joined HMS *Arlanza*. She was another liner converted for patrolling duties, forming part of the 10th Cruiser Squadron patrolling the area to the north of Scotland and from mid-1917 escorting Atlantic convoys.

William Limrick fell foul of the 1918 influenza epidemic. On 7 March, when the *Arlanza* was in Plymouth, he was moved to the Royal Naval Hospital where he died on 23 March.

He is buried in St Luke's churchyard in Great Crosby in grave A 25A.

HARRY KINDER LIVERSIDGE

Rifleman
1824
6th Battalion King's (Liverpool Regiment)
MTS 1909–13

Although not killed by enemy action, Harry Kinder Liversidge was the first Old Boy to be killed during the war.

Born on 19 May 1896, he was the eldest son of Herbert Campbell Liversidge and his wife Sarah (formerly Robinson). He was baptised at St Peter's church, Liverpool on 18 May 1896 at which time they were living in Soho Street, Liverpool from where Herbert went to work as a bookkeeper.

The following year, 1897, Harry's sister, Edith May, was born followed by Herbert Campbell, who was born in 1899 but died very soon afterwards.

The 1901 census shows Harry's father was working as a dock labourer and living with his wife and daughter Edith as boarders at 42 Washington Street, Bootle. Meanwhile, Harry was living with his widowed grandmother in Walton-on-the-Hill, a household in which his grandmother and her two daughters were all teachers.

Ethel Mary, a new sister for Harry, was born in 1904 at which time Harry was probably attending Arnot Street Council School in Walton, the school from which he entered Merchant Taylors' on 15 September 1909. A final sibling, Edmund George, arrived in the same year.

By 1911 Harry was still living with his grandmother and her daughters at 59 Rossett Road, Blundellsands while his father, now a foreman labourer in the docks, was living at 45 Luxmore Road, Bootle with his wife and three youngest children. His wife died of tuberculosis the following year.

Harry left Merchant Taylors' on 16 April 1913 to work as a bank clerk according to the school register but other sources say he became a surveyor's clerk.

He joined the 6th Battalion King's (Liverpool Regiment) very early in the war and was accidentally killed on the railway at Merstham, Surrey while on guard duty on 10 September 1914. According to family tradition, he was guarding the entrance to Merstham Tunnel when someone threw him a newspaper. When he stooped to retrieve it, he was hit by a passing train. He was 18 years old.

He is buried at Anfield Cemetery in grave XII C708.

HAROLD GEORGE LUNT

Private
624B
5th Battalion Australian Infantry
MTS 1907–11

Harold Lunt was born in Mildura, Victoria, Australia on 14 November 1895. He travelled to England with his parents, Harold Whitehead Lunt and Nellie Lunt, on the SS *Runic* in April 1904 and presumably settled in the Liverpool area where Harold attended Christ Church School, Waterloo before starting at Merchant Taylors' on 1 May 1907.

In 1911, Harold and his parents were living at 28 Kimberley Drive, Crosby and his father was working as a secretary and assistant manager of a bread, baking and flour dealing company.

Harold left school on 27 July 1911 and went abroad, initially sailing to Lyttleton in New Zealand on 24 August 1912 and then, in 1913, joining his father in Shepperton, Australia.

Harold enlisted at Seymour, Victoria on 23 February 1916, giving his occupation as 'Orchardist'. Initially posted to the 37th Battalion he embarked at Melbourne on the SS *Persic* bound for Europe on 3 June 1916. Having landed in England, he later went to France on 15 September and transferred to the 5th Battalion as part of a draft of reinforcements. At the end of March 1917, he was hospitalised suffering from influenza and was eventually admitted to No 8 General Hospital on 10 April.

On 16 April he was evacuated to England aboard the Hospital Ship *Aberdonian* suffering from 'skin fever', i.e. 'trench fever', and three days later was admitted to Reading War Hospital from which he was discharged after almost a month on 14 May. Having recovered, he was shipped out from Southampton and rejoined his unit on 31 July. Rejoining at this time meant he was just in time for the third battle of Ypres or Passchendaele.

On 20 September 1917, the 5th Battalion, as part of the Australian 1st Division, took part in the battle of the Menin Road. During this battle, Lunt was first posted wounded in action, then wounded and missing and finally killed in action. In statements made by his comrades in reports to their officers one stated:

> On 20 September at Ypres, Private Lunt was in my company on the way to the front when a shell exploded. I was wounded and Private Lunt was killed with the same shell. I recognised Private Lunt at the dressing station. He was dead.

Another report stated that:

> The battalion was moving into the line on 19 September 1917. My platoon was just outside the Menin tunnel dressing station near Hooge crater when a shell landed in the middle of the platoon putting the whole of the section in which was Private Lunt out of action. I immediately informed the AMC [Australian Medical Corps] men of the casualties and brought them to the spot. I saw Private Lunt lying on the ground; he was not dead but I could not stop to inquire the nature of his wounds. Had he lived he certainly would have been admitted to the above named dressing station. I reported the above named man as wounded.

A note on Lunt's service records says that he died and was buried at Verlick Farm, 100 yards east of Glencore Wood, east of Ypres. His grave was lost in the ensuing fighting. He now has no known grave and is commemorated on the Ypres (Menin Gate) Memorial.

HARRY READ MANSERGH

Lieutenant
1st/9th Battalion King's (Liverpool Regiment)
MTS 1908–10

Harry's parents, Thomas Read Mansergh and Emma Holgate, were married in Bury in 1889 and their first child, Gladys, was born the following year. From

1881 Thomas described himself as a 'Cowkeeper'; a description suggesting a somewhat rustic image for a man who owned a sizeable dairy business and who on his death in 1930 left an estate valued at about £29,000 (equivalent to £1.5–£2 million at present prices).

When Harry was born in Bootle on 1 September 1891, he was born into a reasonably well-off household living at 57 Queen's Road, Bootle. Harry may not even have remembered his two little brothers, who both died shortly after they were born: Frank in 1892 and Norman in 1893. Thomas and Emma then had three daughters: Doris in 1894, Irene in 1896, and Kathleen Mary in 1900. When Kathleen was born, the family was still living at the same address and running a dairy from there.

Harry came to Merchant Taylors' on 16 January 1908, having attended a day school in Bootle and a school in Bruges, probably Pembroke School. He left the school on 29 July 1910 having obtained a 3rd Class Honours in his Oxford Local Junior exam in 1909 and a 2nd Class in the Seniors in 1910. While at Merchant Taylors' he was a member of the Debating Society, giving his maiden speech to the society on 18 March 1910.

After Merchant Taylors' he went on to Liverpool University to study dentistry and it was while he was at Liverpool that his sister Kathleen died in 1911. Harry's father had by this time, retired and was living with his wife and remaining four children at 19 Breeze Hill, Bootle.

Harry joined up shortly after the outbreak of war, initially enlisting as Private 1262 in the King's (Liverpool Regiment). He was then commissioned as second lieutenant with the regiment early in 1915 probably into the 15th Battalion, a reserve battalion. He was transferred from the 15th to the 9th Battalion on 28 August 1915 and took part in the battle of Loos in September and October of that year.

The battalion's war diary records that Harry was accidentally wounded in early August 1916, was hospitalised and rejoined his unit on 4 September. He was again wounded, this time seriously, on 18 September and died of his wounds on 12 November.

He is buried in Étaples Military Cemetery plot I row A grave 66.

ADRIAN ROBSON MAY

Lieutenant
5th Battalion King's (Liverpool Regiment)
MTS 1909–09

Adrian Robson May was at the school only a very short time. His parents, Thomas James May and Fanny Blanche May (formerly Robson) were married in 1884 and he was their third son. Leslie Glynn had been born in Birkenhead in 1887 and Ernest Massey in 1888, also in Birkenhead. Between 1888 and 1891 the family moved from Birkenhead to Waterloo.

In 1891, Leslie and Ernest were living with their parents at 31 Neville Road, Crosby. Thomas was working as a 'Manager'. Marjorie Enid was born in 1891 but after the census. Adrian was born on 22 February 1897 in Waterloo and was followed by a sister, Phyllis, in 1898.

In 1901 Thomas and Fanny and their three youngest children were living at 9 Harbord Road, Waterloo. Leslie and Ernest have not been traced in the 1901 census, which is strange as both of them were attending Merchant Taylors' at the time, Leslie having joined in 1898 and Ernest in 1900.

Adrian entered Merchant Taylors' on 16 January 1909, coming to the school from Blundellsands School. However, he stayed for only six months leaving on 29 July 1909 to attend a private school in Llandudno. This was probably Woodlands in Deganwy, which he was attending in 1911.

After leaving school he became part-owner of a poultry farm, eventually rising to be joint manager.

Enlisting during the war Adrian initially served in 2/10th Battalion King's (Liverpool Regiment) as Private 4862 but seems not to have served overseas in this capacity. He was commissioned into 5th Battalion King's on 1 January 1916.

He was killed in action on 8 September 1916, dying from wounds received when the battalion's trenches came under intense shellfire.

He is buried in Dartmoor Cemetery Becordel-Becourt plot I row A grave 17.

John Stuart Mayer

Second Lieutenant
2nd/8th Battalion Manchester Regiment
MTS 1911–13

John Stuart Mayer's father, Walter Frederic Mayer, was a churchman, admitted to the Wesleyan ministry in 1888. He married Emily Gertrude Rhodes in Staffordshire in 1893 and they had four children, three of whom survived to adulthood: Donald Lawton, born in 1894, John Stuart born on 28 October 1895 in Bacup and Frederic Arthur, born in 1897, also in Bacup. Their father was minister of the Thorn Wesleyan Methodist Chapel in Alma Street, Bacup from 1895–97.

Walter was then moved to Rochdale and, in 1901, the family was living at 73 King's Road. In addition to the three boys and their mother, the boys' grandmother was living at the house. Their father was, on 31 March of that year visiting his father, John Mayer, a colliery secretary at Greenbank House, Burslem.

By 1911, Walter had been moved again, this time to a ministry in Blundellsands. He and his family now were living at 'Eversley', Eshe Road, Blundellsands. Donald and John were away from home boarding at Kingswood School in Bath, a school which catered for the education of the sons of Methodist clergymen and which John had entered in 1906.

John Stuart Mayer in the 1912/13 rugby XV. John is the left-hand boy in the middle row.

On 15 September 1911, six weeks short of his 16th birthday, John joined Merchant Taylors' and in the following year was awarded a Harrison Scholarship and gained a 1st Class in the Oxford Local Senior exams. In his last year at the school, 1913, he was awarded the Montefiore Prize for Classics and continued to represent the school as part of the rugby XV which he had done since arriving in 1911.

John left the school on 30 July 1913 to work for Scottish Widows Life Assurance and at about the same time, his father was relocated to Birkenhead where, sadly, he died at the early age of 49 on 11 October.

During the war John trained for a commission and entered the Inns of Court Officers' Training Corps as Private 3973 in June 1915. Having satisfactorily completed his training he was gazetted second lieutenant with effect from 6 December 1915 and posted to 2/8th Manchester Regiment. He crossed over to France on 17 March 1917 as part of the 66th Division and was attached to the 199th Trench Mortar Battery.

He was killed near Ypres on 29 January 1918 by splinters from an exploding shell. He is buried in Menin Road South Military Cemetery in plot III row F grave 4.

John's older brother Donald, who was not a former pupil, was killed two months later, on 6 April 1918.

DAVID MCDIARMID

Lieutenant
164th Company Machine Gun Corps
MTS 1908–10

Both David's parents, John and Isabella (formerly Fields), were born in Scotland and were probably married there given that his two older surviving siblings, Andrew (born around 1883) and Christina (around 1885) were born there too.

Sometime between 1885 and 1889, John moved his family down to the Lancashire area where Matthew was born in Audenshaw in 1888 and Jane in Droylesden in 1890. David was born on 7 April 1893. The final two children, Mary Malcolm and John arrived in 1895 and 1897 respectively. The last three were all born in Droylesden where John was working as a police constable. In 1901 the parents and five of their children occupied a small terrace house at 30 Droylsden Road, Audenshaw.

According to the school's admission register, David McDiarmid arrived at Merchant Taylors' having already attended the Central Council School, Morecombe and The Grammar School Lancaster. He arrived at Merchant Taylors' on 16 January 1908. In 1909 and 1910 he obtained Passes in his Oxford Local Senior exams and left the school on 29 July 1910 to go to Leeds University where he trained as a PE teacher.

Presumably his father's job brought him to Crosby about the same time that David came to Merchant Taylors' and he was still there in 1911, now promoted sergeant, seemingly living at the police station with his wife and four of his children. The census form records seven children having been born to the couple but three of them had died by 1911. Given that Christina, David, Mary and John are recorded on the census form, the implication is that Matthew, Jane and Andrew had died. The first two probably died in infancy and Andrew sometime between 1901 and 1911. David was, by 1911, 17 years old and a student teacher.

The outbreak of war interrupted his teaching career and in October 1914 he joined the Royal Army Medical Corps. On 27 March 1915 he was commissioned from an officers' training corps and granted a second lieutenancy in the 10th Battalion East Lancashire Regiment (a reserve battalion). In March 1916 he was attached to 164th Company Machine Gun Corps which had been formed in February of that year. The company formed part of the 55th (West Lancashire) Division.

He was involved in the advance on the Somme on 1 July 1916 and returned to the trenches with shell shock but after three weeks rejoined the corps and took part in another attack on 7 August. He was last seen 'leading a bomb attack with revolver in hand'. After the attack he was reported missing but later he was confirmed killed.

He is commemorated on pier and face 5C and 12 C of the Thiepval Memorial.

DUNCAN KEITH MCFARLANE

Trooper
50552
Imperial Camel Corps
MTS 1902–08

Duncan's father, Duncan Gray McFarlane, was born in Scotland, his mother Barbara Jane McFarlane (formerly Lewis) was born in Trieste, then part of Austria.

They married in Birmingham in 1884 and, in 1886, Barbara gave birth to their first child Agnes Marian, by which time they were living in Liverpool.

Their first son, Lewis Robert, was born in 1889 to be followed by Duncan Keith on 24 November 1890.

The following year finds Duncan (senior) working as a marine engineer and the family living at 3 Hornby Road, Bootle, a street of terraced houses. Their final child, Thomas Norman, was born in 1892.

Within ten years (in 1901) they had moved to 13 Claremont Road, Waterloo, also a terraced house, but distinctly larger than the house in Hornby Street.

Duncan started at the school on 16 September 1902 (at the same time as his brother Thomas) at which time they were living at 16 Fairholme Road, Crosby. He left the school in 1908. Although his parents and the rest of the family were still living at 16 Fairholme Road in 1911, there is no trace of Duncan (junior).

Duncan is next recorded by CWGC as having died on 25 January 1919 while serving with the 6th Company of the Camel Corps (part of the 2nd Camel Battalion). This company was a British company originally made up from members of the dismounted yeomanry brigade. The 6th was raised from the Cheshire, Shropshire, Montgomeryshire and Denbighshire Yeomanry. Each provided one officer and 35 men. According to *Lancashire Biographies* Roll of Honour he came from the Cheshire Yeomanry. The Camel Corps was disbanded in July 1918 but the 6th remained as a camel unit to support the campaign in the Hejaz.

Duncan died in Egypt on 25 January 1919 though exactly how is unknown. He is buried in the Alexandria (Hadra) War Memorial Cemetery grave G55.

WILLIAM EDWIN GORDON MEIN

Private
11420
1st Battalion Honourable Artillery Company
MTS 1910–15

William Edwin Gordon Mein was the eldest child of Thomas Gordon Mein and Mary Smith Mein (formerly Tucker). He was born on 25 September 1899 at Barry, Glamorgan.

In 1901, William and his parents were living in East Barry House, Broad Street, Barry, the home of William's grandparents. His father was working as a railway clerk. There seems to be a family connection to railways – William's grandfather, also William, was a railway secretary.

Two more children followed William, Joan Parrish Gordon was born in 1903 and Andrew Bentley Gordon in 1906.

As a young boy, William was privately tutored at home but later he joined Merchant Taylors' on 4 May 1910. By 1911, the family was living at Holly Bank, Coronation Drive, Great Crosby. William left Merchant Taylors' on 28 July 1915 and took up a post as a shipping clerk.

William had to wait until his 18th birthday in September 1917 before he could enlist. He then signed his attestation papers on 8 October. He was posted as a private to the 1st Battalion Honourable Artillery Company and served 'at home' from 8 October 1917 to 5 April 1918 and on the following day arrived in France.

He eventually formed part of the Army of Occupation in Cologne. While carrying out this duty he contracted pneumonia and he was evacuated to 44 Casualty Clearing Station, which had moved to Cologne in 1919. While hospitalised in 44 CCS he died, on 12 February 1919.

He is buried in Cologne Southern Cemetery plot II row C grave 6.

FRANCIS RIGBY MELLOR

Lieutenant
10th Battalion attached 6th Battalion East
Lancashire Regiment
MTS 1899–1905

The Mellor family had been brewers and rectifiers of spirits in Liverpool since 1823. Francis was part of the third generation to be involved with the business.

Francis's parents, John Mellor and Mary Elizabeth Kewley married in 1872 and over the course of the next 20 years had 15 children, 12 of whom survived to adulthood. Of these 15, ten were boys and all ten attended Merchant Taylors'. The eldest son, John, was born in 1873. He was followed by William in 1874 then Henry in 1875. Charles and Sydney seem to have been twins born just after Christmas in 1876 and though they attended Merchant Taylors' from 1886–7 they seem to disappear from the record and could be two of the three children who did not survive to 1911. Fanny Edith was born in 1877, Robert in 1879, Mary Lillian in 1881, James Douglas in 1884, Amy Margaret in 1885, Agnes Rose in 1887, Walter Samuel in 1888 and Frances Rigby on 10 July 1890. In 1891 the family was living in Grosvenor House, Crosby Road South, Waterloo. Another daughter, Alice Luna, was born in 1892.

Francis came to Merchant Taylors' on 2 May 1899, a few months after the death of his 13-year-old sister Amy Margaret. The family had moved to Rutland House, Nicholas Road, Blundellsands where they were still living in

1901. By then Francis's brother John was working as the brewery manager, Robert was a salesman for the wines and spirits produced and George was a warehouse clerk, also in wines and spirits.

Francis left the school in April 1905 and, inevitably, joined the family firm. He remained living at home – in 1911 eight of the children were still living or staying with their parents at Rutland House. In addition to Francis, John, Fanny, Mary, Agnes, Walter, now BA (Cantab) and a student for Holy Orders, Alice and Henry, now MA and a clerk in Holy Orders were at home. Francis was working as an assistant brewer. Francis's father died on 21 August 1911.

On the outbreak of war, Francis quickly gained a commission, being gazetted temporary second lieutenant with effect from 13 November 1914. He was posted to 10th Battalion East Lancashire Regiment, a reserve battalion of the regiment and was promoted to temporary lieutenant on 27 October 1915.

From the reserve battalion he was eventually attached to the 6th Battalion, which, as part of the 13th Division, had already fought at Gallipoli and had moved to Mesopotamia via Egypt in February 1916 to help relieve Kut al Amara. His record shows he landed at Basrah on 2 October 1916.

On 13 January 1917, possibly in the battle of Kut al Amara he was shot in the chest and died of his wounds on 16 January at 16 Casualty Clearing Station. He is buried in Amara War Cemetery, Iraq plot XXVI row D grave 1.

THOMAS MILBOURN MERCER

Second Lieutenant
Tank Corps
MTS 1904–10

Thomas Milbourn Mercer was born on 30 March 1893, the son of Hugh Thomas Mercer, a farmer of Croxteth, and his wife Isabella Margaret (formerly Milbourn). He was baptised at the church of St Michael and All Angels, Altcar on 28 May 1893.

He was the second child of four and his parents' first son. Their first child, Isabella Frances was born in 1891 a year after their marriage in 1890. Two years after Thomas, Charles Richard was born in 1895 and finally his sister, Phyllis May, was born in 1900.

Thomas's father, Hugh, worked Stand Farm on the Croxteth Park Estate, a farm whose origins can be traced back to the 17th century, though it now operates as a pub. He was farming there in 1901 employing six servants and labourers.

Thomas obtained his early education with private tuition at home and gained entry to Merchant Taylors' on 16 January 1904 where in 1908 he gained a Pass in his Oxford Local Junior exams. The following year he repeated this performance in his Senior exams. He left the school on 29 July 1910 to work on his father's farm.

By 1911, Hugh had been working Stand Farm for at least twenty years and the entire family was still living at home. Charles left school in this year and presumably went on to help his father.

On the outbreak of war, Thomas joined the newly formed 2nd Battalion King Edward's Horse enlisting as Private 382. He crossed to France with them on 22 April 1915 as part of the Canadian Cavalry Brigade. The battalion was replaced in that brigade by The Fort Garry Horse in December of that year. He became a lance corporal on 8 June 1916 and transferred to the Machine Gun Corps on 4 December. Thomas obtained his commission as second lieutenant on 30 January 1917 in the MGC (presumably Heavy Branch MGC whose B Battalion became B Battalion of the Tank Corps at the end of July 1917).

On 23 November 1917, Thomas took part in an attack on the village of Fontaine near Cambrai. B Battalion had 13 tanks in this action including B30 which was commanded by Thomas. His tank got into difficulties on the far side of the village and was later posted as missing. The tank had been put out of action by an enemy anti-aircraft gun and was later retrieved by the Germans. Thomas was posted as missing after the action. A photograph of his tank can be found in the plate section.

He is commemorated on panel 13 of the Cambrai Memorial.

ALLAN MACKENZIE MILLER

Private
540419
1st Battalion Canadian Machine Gun Corps
MTS 1906–07

Charles Carver Miller and Marian Barry married in Kinsale, County Cork in 1875. They went on to have ten children, four of whom had died by the time of the 1911 census. Two more would then die in the Great War.

They returned to England sometime between 1876 and 1879 and brought with them their first child, Norman Chambers, born in Ireland in 1876. Six more children arrived before Allan: Kathleen Nina Barry in 1879, Charles Carver in 1880 (thought to have died young). Leslie Bateman in 1883 (died in 1884), Marian Barry in 1885, Hettie Barry in 1887 and Eileen Nora in 1888.

Allan Mackenzie was born on 10 March 1891, thus just scraping into the census of that year which shows the family living in 1 Kimberley Street, Toxteth. Allan's father was working, as he always did and always would, as a wholesale fish salesman. In fact he went on to be part of the firm Harley and Miller and to own a number of trawlers sailing out of Liverpool.

The last two of Allan's siblings arrived in 1894 and 1895, Leonard Bateman Miller and Wilfrid Heard Miller (see below). Between their two births, Allan's sister Eileen died, aged six, at the end of 1894. The family had moved to 5 Courtenay Road, Waterloo by 1901 though Norman had left home and a year earlier had been made curate of a church in Birkdale. In 1903 Norman sailed for India possibly to take up a teaching post but the following year on 11 February he was struck down by typhoid in Andhra Pradesh.

Allan joined Merchant Taylors' on 2 May 1906 from the family home, 1 Sandheys Terrace, Waterloo, a large house overlooking the Mersey. He was not long at the school, leaving in July 1907. In 1911 Allan's parents were still living in Sandheys Terrace with Hettie, Leonard (now an apprentice engineer) and Wilfrid. Allan himself was working as a 'farm pupil' at Alstone Court in Somerset.

It is likely that Allan emigrated to Canada as he enlisted in the Canadian Expeditionary Force on 1 September 1915, giving his occupation as 'bank clerk' and claiming to have had experience in the Imperial Yeomanry and a cyclist company of the volunteer force.

He later fought as part of the 1st Battalion Canadian Machine Gun Corps, which supported the 1st Canadian Division towards the end of the war. Allan was killed in action near Arras (probably in the battle of the Scarpe) on 29 August 1918.

He is buried in Tigris Lane Cemetery, Wancourt, plot II row A grave 5.

WILFRID HEARD MILLER

Second Lieutenant
7th Battalion South Lancashire Regiment
MTS 1906–11

Charles Miller and his wife lost two sons during the war. Wilfrid, the youngest of their ten children, was the first to fall. Wilfrid was born on 8 May 1895 by which time his oldest brother, Norman, was almost 20.

By 1901, Wilfrid was one of the six of the surviving seven children (though the date of death for Charles (junior) is uncertain) living at 5 Courtenay Road, Waterloo.

Wilfrid came to Merchant Taylors' on 16 January 1906, a few months before his brother Allan. He had previously attended a private school referred to in the admission register as 'High School, Waterloo'.

Wilfrid acquitted himself well at school, particularly on the sports field. He represented the school at rugby 1908–11, being captain in the last year. *The School Review* for June 1909 records that he came into the team as full-back at the early age of 13½ and that even at this tender age, he kicked the ball 'splendidly' though his tackling was still rather weak and then, prophetically, 'will be great one day if he goes on as he is doing now.' In the June edition of 1911, his final year, he is described as a captain 'who has been a tower of strength to the team ... should be heard of again at full back'.

As a cricketer he was part of the school team from 1909 to 1911, again captaining the team in his final year, a post in which he 'set an excellent example to his team in all departments of the game'. He was a fine fielder and bowler, though his batting is often described as 'unorthodox'.

Not content with excelling at rugby and cricket, in 1911 he easily won the Open Tennis Singles competition and appeared in the final of the Handicap Doubles and Handicap Singles. The report of the tennis tournament in *The School Review* refers to Miller as the man 'who can only be described as an athletic demigod'.

To round off an excellent year, he won the Moss Cup on sports day. This trophy, which is still presented today, is awarded to the competitor who gains the highest number of points in Open events. This he did by taking first place in the 100 yards, 220 yards, the high jump and the 'throwing the cricket ball' and second place in the hurdle race.

Academically he gained a Pass in the Oxford Local Junior exams in 1909 and repeated this in 1910. In 1911 he gained a Pass in the Senior exams.

Gradually the family had been moving away from home. By 1911, in addition to 15-year-old Wilfrid, only his parents, a sister and a brother were living at home in Sandheys Terrace. His parents had also adopted an infant girl who had been born in London.

Following his successful school career, Wilfrid left Merchant Taylors' on 27 July 1911 and entered his father's fish merchant's company. Wilfrid continued his interest in rugby and played for Lancashire rugby XV in the 1913/14 season.

His medal index card shows that during the war, he initially enlisted as Private 1261 in the King's (Liverpool Regiment) though the battalion is not given. The listed date on which he went to France, however, 24 February 1915, would indicate that it was the 1st/6th Battalion. He was gazetted with a commission as second lieutenant with effect from 7 August 1915 and was posted to the 3rd Battalion South Lancashire Regiment, a reserve battalion. He was later transferred to the 7th Battalion, which had been in France since July 1915 so he clearly must have joined them after they had moved there.

Although the exact date of his joining the battalion is uncertain, it is known that he was involved in the attack on the village of La Boisselle in early July 1916 during the battle of the Somme. According to the battalion's war diary, he attacked with B Company and was killed early in the attack on 4 July 1916.

If he was recovered and buried, his grave has since been lost as he is commemorated on pier and face 7A and 7B of the Thiepval Memorial.

HERBERT HUGH MILLINGTON

Rifleman
1881
1st/18th Battalion London Regiment
MTS 1886–89

Herbert Hugh Millington's father, William, graduated BA from Brasenose College, Oxford in 1866 and the following year married Margaret Smith at St Luke's church, Chorlton. He was already a clergyman when he married and like many churchmen he moved around a considerable amount in the course of his career. His first posting was as curate at St Barnabas's church in Finsbury where his eldest child, Margaret Elizabeth Voysey Wilhelmina was baptised on 13 May 1869 at just a few weeks old. He then moved to St John's church in Penge where he remained from 1869 to 1871 during which time, in 1870, his second child, William Algernon was born. From 1871 to 1873 William was assistant chaplain at Wandsworth gaol and it was during his time here that his next two children were born, Florence Frances in 1872 and Herbert Hugh on 14 May 1873. In 1873 William moved out of London and became vicar of St Paul's in Southport. The final two additions to the family, Marion Grace and Charlotte Beatrice, arrived in 1875 and 1876 respectively.

In 1881 William and his family were occupying St Paul's vicarage in Southport. William was now MA, having obtained his higher degree in 1875. All six children, aged between four and 11, were living at home and there was a governess to look after them.

Hugh, as he seems to have been known, came to Merchant Taylors' on 8 September 1886 and stayed until July 1889 leaving, it seems, to become an apprentice corn broker. In 1891, all the children were still at home though only Hugh seems to have been working.

Between 1893 and 1899, Florence, Margaret and Marion all married and moved out of the family home and by 1901, William (junior) had become a teacher at 'Lindisfarne', a preparatory school in Blackheath and was living 'on site' and Hugh, still working as a corn broker, was living at 55 Little Dale Road, Seacombe. William (senior) who had by now become vicar of Cottingham in Northamptonshire was sharing the large rectory there with only his wife and youngest daughter, Charlotte. Hugh's father died suddenly on 3 May 1901, apparently of heart failure.

It seems that Hugh went abroad between 1901 and 1911 and studied at the mining college in Tucson, Arizona, later working as a mining engineer and surveyor in America. By chance he was on holiday in England when war broke out, and the following day enlisted at Chelsea into the 1st/18th Battalion The London Regiment, The London Irish Rifles as Rifleman 1881. This unit formed part of the 2nd London Division which landed at Le Havre on 10 March 1915.

The battalion took part in the action at Ginchy during the second battle of Ypres where Hugh was wounded on 16 May 1915. He died the following day. He is buried in Aire Communal Cemetery, plot I row B grave 6.

LAWRENCE FRANK MILNER

Lieutenant
9th Battalion King's (Liverpool Regiment)
MTS 1903–11

Lawrence Frank Milner was the youngest of three children born to Christopher Shepherd Milner and his wife Agnes (formerly Rigby). Married in Sefton parish church in 1880, their first child was a daughter, Agnes Eileen, born in Liverpool. Christopher was born in 1883 in Oswestry and finally, Lawrence was born on 17 October 1892 in Crosby.

Christopher worked as a bank clerk and by 1901 he and his family had moved to 179 Moor Lane, Crosby at which time Lawrence was attending Ballure House, a private preparatory school in Crosby. His father applied for him to enter Merchant Taylors' and, having satisfied all the requirements, he duly joined the school on 19 September 1903, being granted a Harrison Scholarship on entry.

His time at the school proved academically successful. In 1906 he sat his Oxford Local Junior exams and gained a 3rd Class, improving this in the following year to a 1st Class. He went on to sit the Senior exams in 1908 and obtained a 2nd Class. In 1909 he did better still and obtained a 1st Class with distinctions in English and French; a performance which permitted him to be excused responsions (the Oxford entrance exam). His reliability must also have impressed the staff as he was made a monitor in 1909, a post he held until he left in 1911.

He represented the school as part of the rugby XV in the season 1910/11, *The School Review* describing him as 'A thoroughly good forward, knows the game well and plays it, but is rather on the small side'.

In 1910 he was awarded the Windermere Prize for English and in 1911, the Tyler Prize for Ancient History. In his last year he was also Head of School.

In April 1911, approaching the end of his school career, he was living with his parents and sister at 8 Alexandra Road, Waterloo, his brother Christopher having preceded him to Oxford in 1901 after a time at school which saw him in the rugby, cricket and tennis teams.

Lawrence left school on 27 July 1911 and went up to Merton College, Oxford with a history scholarship of £80 per annum. He graduated with 2nd Class Honours in Classical Mods in 1913.

He enlisted as soon as war broke out and was granted a commission as second lieutenant on 22 August 1914 being posted to the 9th Battalion King's (Liverpool Regiment), which moved to Tunbridge Wells in October for training. When training was complete, they moved to France, landing at Le Havre on 13 March 1915, and becoming part of the 1st Division. In May the battalion took part in the failed battle of Aubers Ridge. They then spent time in reserve before training for their next attack in the battle of Loos. It was during this engagement that Lawrence was killed, on 25 September 1915. Another Old Boy reported seeing him binding the wounds of his orderly who had just been shot. Lawrence was kneeling in tall grass about 300 yards from the enemy trenches when he was shot in the head. He died about half an hour later.

He was buried near Lone Tree within a few yards of where he fell. His grave was subsequently lost and he is commemorated on panels 27 to 30 on the Loos Memorial.

VERNON MacDONALD MORRISON

Second Lieutenant
3rd Battalion attached 7th Battalion South Lancashire Regiment
MTS 1911–14

Born in Formby on 8 September 1897, Vernon MacDonald Morrison was the son of Matthew Morrison, a bookkeeper, and his wife Emily. He had two older sisters, Dorothy MacPherson, born in 1894 and Evelyn Parker, born in 1896. The children's dates and places of birth indicate a move from Formby to Waterloo between the end of 1897 and 1900 as Matthew and Emily's youngest child, Mabel Sansome, was born in Waterloo in 1900.

In 1901 the family was living at 17 Thorndale Road, Waterloo though on 31 March, when the census was taken, Matthew was a patient in Stanley Hospital.

By April 1911, Matthew and his family had moved house to 'Vennashar' in Mersey Road, Blundellsands and Vernon was attending Christ Church School in Waterloo. Having completed his studies at Christ Church he moved on to Merchant Taylors', which he entered on 15 September 1911. He obtained a 2nd Class in his Oxford Local Junior exams in 1914 and on 22 December of that year left school to join an insurance firm.

He was commissioned into the South Lancashire Regiment as a second lieutenant on 29 October 1915 but his medal index card shows he had previously risen to the rank of corporal in the King's (Liverpool Regiment) though it does not say which battalion and no number is stated. After commissioning he was probably posted to the 3rd Battalion of the South Lancashire Regiment, a reserve battalion which, on mobilisation in 1914, moved to Crosby and remained there throughout the conflict.

Eventually, he was transferred to the 7th Battalion, a service battalion that had been in France since September 1915 as part of the 19th (Western) Division. Vernon did not travel to France until some time in 1916. During the night of 13/14 November 1916, the battalion was involved in a raid on the enemy in the Ovillers region. Afterwards Vernon was posted as wounded and missing, believed killed.

His body was later recovered and is buried in Grandcourt Road Cemetery, Grandcourt in grave C76.

ROBERT NOEL MOUNTFIELD

Captain
8th Battalion attached 2nd/9th Battalion King's (Liverpool Regiment)
MTS 1899–1903

Known to his family as Robin, Robert Noel Mountfield was the eldest child of Robert Mountfield, who became manager of John Bacon, Ltd, a shipping company, and his wife Caroline (formerly Appleyard). Robert was born on 12 December 1887 and baptised at St Anne's church, Stanley on 8 March 1888, at which time he and his parents were living at 8 South Bank Road, Edge Lane, a small terraced house which was probably in keeping with his father's status at that time of 'shipping clerk'. A brother, John Maye, was born towards the end of 1889 but he died at the beginning of 1891 aged one.

By April 1891 the family had moved out from the city and was living at 23 Worthing Street, Blundellsands, still in a smallish house. Robert's sister, Caroline Blundell, was born in 1892.

Between 1891 and 1899, Robert (senior) must have been promoted. In his application for his son to join Merchant Taylors' he describes himself as 'Secretary' and they were living in a larger, semi-detached house at 32 Rossett Road, Crosby. Robert (junior) first arrived at Merchant Taylors' on 24 January 1899. Two years later, and still living in Rossett Road, Robert (senior) seems to have been further promoted to 'manager, steamship company'. Robert left the school in 1903, the year after his younger brother, Alexander Stuart, was born. Alexander would attend Merchant Taylors' from 1912 to 1918.

On leaving school, Robert became a clerk with the dock board and in 1911 was still living at home, which had been upgraded yet again to a double-fronted semi-detached house at 7 Eshe Road, Blundellsands.

Before the war, Robert spent four years serving with the Territorials as a rifleman. He enlisted again with the 6th Battalion King's (Liverpool Regiment) as a private on the outbreak of war. After a spell at Sevenoaks and Canterbury undergoing training, he was recommended for a commission and was gazetted second lieutenant in the 8th Battalion King's (Liverpool Regiment) with effect from 24 February 1915. He probably took part with the battalion in the battle of Festubert in May 1915. On 15 January 1916 he was invalided home suffering from 'trench fever' and while recovering was posted to North Wales to run training. When fit again, he was allowed a period of leave before rejoining the battalion in March.

Promotion to temporary captain followed on 26 June 1916. About a year later, on 7 June 1917, his substantive rank was increased to lieutenant and at the same time he relinquished the temporary rank of captain. On the same day he was given the acting rank of captain while commanding a company, holding this rank until 19 July when he handed over the company to someone else. He was later promoted to acting captain again and commanded another company from 17 September 1917. At an unknown date, he was seconded to the 2nd/9th Battalion King's (Liverpool Regiment) and he was serving in that battalion when he was killed. His death occurred during the handover between two battalions as the 9th was leaving the line. The German artillery had set up a heavy bombardment and he was hit by a shell splinter and died of his wounds the next day, 5 November 1917, in the dressing station at Brielen.

He was initially buried at Soult Camp Cemetery at 3 p.m. according to the war diary of the 2nd/9th and was later reburied in the Solferino Farm Cemetery in plot II row A grave 22.

RONALD HAMILTON WILLIAM MURDOCH

Second Lieutenant
21st Battalion attached 4th Battalion King's
(Liverpool Regiment)
MTS 1906–11

Ronald's father, David Hamilton Ball Murdoch (though he seems often not to have used the David), gained his Master Mariner's certificate in 1892 and consequently was at sea for much of his children's formative years. David had married Helen Christina McFarlane in Liverpool in 1889 and if they had any children before Ronald, they did not survive. Indeed the 1911 census shows that they definitely had two children who died while young.

Born on 3 July 1895 and baptised at Holy Trinity church in Toxteth Park on 1 September of that year, Ronald and his parents lived at 43 Kingsley Road until they moved to Waterloo between 1895 and 1901.

Ronald's sister Helen Hamilton was born in March 1901, on the day of the census (31 March) she was one month old. They were living at 5 Thorndale Road, Waterloo and although Ronald's father appears to have been at sea, his mother, Helen had a 'visitor', Margaret McFarlane, staying with them. She was probably Ronald's grandmother, visiting to help with newborn Helen.

Before coming to Merchant Taylors', Ronald spent some time at the Merchant Taylors' Girls' School Preparatory department and Christ Church School in Waterloo. He arrived at Merchant Taylors' on 16 January 1906 and stayed until 27 July 1911. In his time at the school, he sat and passed the Oxford Local Junior exam in both 1910 and 1911. In the latter year he also acquired a new brother, Hamilton B., while the family were living at 53 Kimberley Drive, Crosby. Hamilton did not attend Merchant Taylors'.

Ronald joined the Inns of Court Officers' Training Corps as Private 5948 early in the war and trained for a commission. This he obtained on 2 June 1916 being gazetted second lieutenant and was initially posted to 21st Battalion King's (Liverpool Regiment), a reserve battalion. He was then reposted to the 4th Battalion, which had been in France since March 1915. At the time he joined them the battalion would have been part of 33rd Division. On 28 October 1916 the battalion took part in an attack on Dewdrop Trench. After the attack, Second Lieutenant Murdoch was posted 'Missing in action'.

Presumably his body was never recovered as he is commemorated on pier and face 1D 8B and 8C of the Thiepval Memorial.

FRANCIS ERNEST NEALE

Company Sergeant Major
2706122
13th Battalion Canadian Garrison Regiment
MTS 1892–93

Francis's father, Thomas Binley Neale came to Liverpool from Bilston in Leicestershire in about 1870 as an apprentice in the timber trade. He took up residence in the Bootle area and on 11 September 1877 married Frances Elizabeth Peat at St John's church in Bootle.

Francis Ernest was their first child. Born on 13 November 1879, he was baptised in St John's church, Bootle on 11 January 1880 at which time he and his parents were living at 12 Oriel Road, Bootle. On 3 December 1880 Francis's brother Harold Douglas was born. In April 1881, they were still living in Oriel Road and the following year a sister, Norah, was born followed by Florence Peat in 1884.

By 1891 they had moved to 11 Marine Terrace, Waterloo, though the two boys were boarding with a schoolteacher at 17 Cambridge Road.

Francis joined Merchant Taylors' on 1 March 1892 but stayed for only a year, leaving at Easter 1893. His brother, Harold, who joined the same year stayed until 1896, after which he became a timber merchant's clerk, probably in his father's company. It is not recorded what Francis did in the years after he left school, though it is known that he went to South Africa and took part in the Boer War where he was a trooper (number 33055) in the 93rd Company of the 23rd Battalion Imperial Yeomanry which was based at Bloemfontein, tasked with guarding the lines of communication between Cape Town and Pretoria. They arrived in South Africa in March 1901. Following the war he also spent three years as a trooper (number 906) in A Division of the South Africa Constabulary.

Early in 1906, Francis's mother died and before the end of the year, his father had married again. His new bride was Beatrice Mary Hill who bore him another son, Arthur Hill, in 1909.

After South Africa, Francis moved to Canada although exactly when is unknown. The indications are that he settled in British Columbia, where he signed his attestation papers on 1 August 1918 giving his occupation as clerk and his address as Morrissey, British Columbia. He claims on his form that, in addition to his military experience in South Africa, he had spent time with the 107th Regiment and the 30th British Columbia Horse, both reserve units. His attestation papers are stamped 11th Canadian Garrison Regiment whereas the CWGC record has him serving with the 13th Regiment. The Canadian

Garrison regiments were formed for guard duty at home and each military district produced a battalion. The 11th was based in British Columbia (where he lived) and the 13th in Alberta (where he died) so it may be that he was initially serving with the 11th but transferred to the 13th. When he died of influenza on 26 November 1918 he was buried in Calgary Union Cemetery.

His father predeceased him, dying on 1 November 1918.

GEORGE GASTON NICKEL

Second Lieutenant
20th Battalion King's (Liverpool Regiment)
MTS 1895–1900

Some sources list George's initials as G. A. G. Nickel and his full name as George Anne Gaston Nickel. This, indeed, is the way he appears in all references by the school.

Albert Victor Prosper Nickel married Adelaide Peachey Cartmel in 1881 and they seem to have lived in France for some time after the wedding as their sons Oswald and George were born there, the former on 11 July 1882 and the latter on 31 July 1883. The family may have stayed there for a number of years as they do not appear in the 1891 census and although Albert is listed as 'deceased' in the school's admission register, there is no record of his death at the General Record office.

George and Oswald both came to Merchant Taylors' on 11 September 1895 while they were living in Manley Road, Waterloo. Their time spent living in France meant they both became fluent in French and they were well known for performing scenes from French plays on Speech Day. George is said to have possessed marked talent as an actor, a talent of which he seems to have made good use while delivering speeches to the school's Debating Society. In his Oxford Local exams he achieved first place in French and was awarded a Harrison Scholarship in September 1899. He left school in July 1900, a year after his brother and became a clerk in a shipping office.

George underwent a change of occupation between 1901, when he was still working as a clerk and living at 10 Amberley Street in Toxteth Park, Liverpool, and 1911, by which time he was working as a journalist and living with his mother and brother at 159 Bedford Street, still in Toxteth Park.

On the outbreak of war he joined the King's (Liverpool Regiment) as Private 22192 but later underwent officer training in the Inns of Court Officers' Training Corps in which he became Corporal 5348 and was eventually commissioned, being gazetted second lieutenant on 27 December 1915. His medal index card records no overseas service while serving in the ranks.

The 20th Battalion had moved to Boulogne six weeks before George was commissioned so he must have joined them after they had gone to the front, though exactly when is uncertain.

George was killed in action on 31 July 1917, probably during the battle of Pilckem Ridge, the opening move of the third battle of Ypres, Passchendaele. The battalion's war diary records that he was liaison officer with 3rd Battalion Rifle Brigade.

He is commemorated on panels 4 and 6 of the Ypres (Menin Gate) Memorial.

IORWERTH AP ROWLAND OWEN

Second Lieutenant
Royal Flying Corps
MTS 1907–14

Iorwerth's father, Rowland Owen was a physician and surgeon. He married his second wife, Margaret Owen, in 1895. Iorwerth was born on 22 July 1896, making him over ten years younger than his half-brother Trevor. A younger sister, Mona Eiluned, was added to the family in 1899. Combining the names of his children with his origins on Anglesey points to a certain nationalist tendency in Dr Owen.

In 1901 Rowland, Margaret and their two children were living at 37 Sandy Road, Seaforth, being looked after by a cook, housemaid, and with a nurse to take care of the children. As a small child, Iorwerth attended Blundellsands School, a private preparatory school and then entered Merchant Taylors' on 1 May 1907. His brother Trevor had previously attended Merchant Taylors' from 1896 to 1900.

By 1911, the entire family, parents and three children, was back under one roof at Sandy Nook in Seaforth. As the children were older, they now had a governess and two servants. Iorwerth made his first attempt at his Oxford Local Junior exams in 1911 and gained a Pass. He tried again in 1912 and obtained a 3rd Class. He left Merchant Taylors' on 30 July 1914 and moved to Mill Hill School having boarded with Mr J. H. Milton and his wife for six years. His intention was to go to London University and study medicine.

While at Mill Hill he joined the school's Officers' Training Corps and, foregoing his medical training, eventually moved to the Inns of Court Officers' Training Corps as Private 5631. He obtained his commission in September 1916 and then attended flying school at Oxford until 8 November 1916. He was then posted to a reserve squadron on Salisbury Plain followed by a further posting where he gained his wings on 31 March 1917. Iorwerth was allowed a short period of leave before being ordered to France where he joined 13 Squadron, a reconnaissance squadron flying BE2c aircraft. On 7 May 1917, Iorwerth took off from Savy airfield at 10.40 a.m. flying aircraft number 4595 on a photographic mission. While flying this mission he was engaged by five enemy aircraft. His observer AM2 Reginald Hickling died from gunshot wounds. Iorwerth, though wounded in the head and chest, managed to land the plane near Fresnoy. He died later that day in a field ambulance. He was buried the next day with full military honours in grave D17 of St Catherine British Cemetery near Arras.

His many friends described him as a lover of all sports, a good musician and chess player and an excellent shot.

DOUGLAS KENNETH PARKES
MB, CHB

Captain
Royal Army Medical Corps
MTS 1899–1903

Douglas Parkes was at least the third generation of his family who showed 'medical leanings'. His grandfather described himself as a 'Medical Galvanist' while his father, Robert John Parkes called himself a 'Medical Electrician' throughout his life. Both these occupations were connected with the therapeutic use of electricity.

Robert John Parkes married Sarah Ellen Stanger in Derbyshire in 1884 and Douglas, their first-born, arrived on 18 July 1885 in Buxton. In 1887, also in Buxton, Reginald followed. Between the beginning of 1887 and the end of 1888, Robert moved his family to Southport where they took up residence in a large house at 2 Church Street, a house in which they lived for at least the next twenty years.

In 1888, Douglas's brother, Stanley, was born and in 1890 his sister, Dorothy Hilda. In 1891, Robert was clearly prospering in his profession as not only did he live in a large house; but he employed an assistant electrician, two nurses and a maid. Douglas's youngest brother, Harold Robert, arrived in 1892 and his youngest sister, Muriel Florence in 1897.

Douglas entered the school on 24 January 1899 shortly before his mother died in the summer of the same year and in July 1900 he was elected to a Harrison Scholarship. In 1901, Reginald appears to have been living in the school boarding house run by J. H. Milton in College Road whereas the other five children, including Douglas, were still living at the family home in Church Street. Reginald started at the school in 1901 and Stanley in 1902.

In July 1903, Douglas left Merchant Taylors' and is next heard of completing his MB, ChB at Liverpool University in 1914. Unless he took 11 years to complete his degree, what he did between leaving school and the start of his course is not known. He does not appear in the 1911 census. The 1915 medical register notes him as contactable via Messrs Stevens & Parkes, solicitors of 22 Bedford Row, London.

He gained a commission in the Royal Army Medical Corps and was gazetted as temporary lieutenant from 7 June 1915. This commission he seems to have relinquished on 10 June 1916 before being reappointed on 23 October. He was promoted to temporary captain from 23 November 1916, went to work at Crowthorne War Hospital, a prisoner of war camp used for mentally ill German soldiers (now part of Broadmoor Hospital) and relinquished this commission on 24 October 1917.

He went to work at Knockaloe internment camp on the Isle of Man at an unknown date and died there on 3 January 1919, being buried on 6 January.

FREDERICK PHILLIPS PEARSON

Corporal
2881
1st/6th Battalion South Staffordshire Regiment
MTS 1892–97

Frederick's father, Edward, was born in Whitchurch in Shropshire, moved to Liverpool about 1870 and spent his whole life as a draper. He married Maria Phillips at St Nicholas's church in Liverpool in 1872 and they had seven children, five of whom survived to adulthood. Frederick was the fifth of the seven.

Their first two children both died young, Henry was born in 1873 and died in 1876, and Arthur Edward was born in 1875 and died the same year. The first surviving son was Edward Percy, who was born in 1876. He was baptised in St Luke's church, Liverpool on 7 May 1876 by which time Edward and Maria had moved from their earlier home at 43 Beaumont Street to Myrtle Street where they lived until at least 1891, initially at 5A and later at 17. A daughter, Gertrude Harriet, was born in 1877 and then Frederick Phillips Pearson on 11 May 1880. Both, like Edward, were baptised in St Luke's church, Frederick on 4 June 1880. In 1881 the family was still living at 17 Myrtle Street.

Frederick's sister Ada Mary was born in 1882 and the final child, Constance, was born in 1885 and, as with the other children, was baptised at St Luke's.

Although the family's address for Constance's baptism was given as 14 Caledonia Street, the 1891 census shows they were still living at 17 Myrtle Street.

Frederick entered Merchant Taylors' in 1892 and while he was at the school, represented it as a member of the rugby XV in 1895, 1896 and 1897 before leaving in 1897. On leaving the school he joined the National Provincial Bank and worked in a branch in Chester. While working in Chester, he joined the ranks of the 2nd Volunteer Battalion of the Cheshire Regiment. On the outbreak of the Boer War in South Africa he volunteered for service and served with the 1st Volunteer Company of the Cheshires as Private 7519. He sailed for South Africa aboard the *Britannic* on 7 January 1900 and arrived in the Cape on the 27th. For his services in the war he was awarded the Queen's South Africa Medal with the clasps for Orange Free State, Cape Colony and Transvaal.

By 1901, the draper's business had clearly become a family concern employing Edward, Edward (junior) and Gertrude with the family living at 16 Oxford Road, Waterloo.

Returning from South Africa Frederick went back to his banking career and 1911 finds him boarding at 38 Frederick Street, Stetchford, near Birmingham and working as a bank clerk. By this stage his father had retired and had moved back to Whitchurch with Maria and daughter Ada; Edward (junior) had taken over the running of the business.

When war broke out in 1914, Frederick was still working for the National Provincial Bank and was based in Wolverhampton. It was here that he enlisted in September 1914 into the 6th Battalion of the South Staffordshire Regiment. He went to France with the battalion in March 1915 and soon found himself in the Ypres Salient and in early July was in the trenches at Zillebeke where he was killed in action on Wednesday 7 July, a period referred to in the battalion's war diary as 'quiet except for artillery duels'. He fell foul of one of these shells. His lieutenant wrote:

A shell came over which did not explode but crashed in a dugout burying two men one of whom was lying in the debris wounded. Pearson and another man at once got to work to dig them out and had just succeeded when another shell came over and a bit struck Pearson on the head. I took him up myself but all to no purpose, he was hit badly.

He is buried in Sanctuary Wood Cemetery in plot V row C grave 10.

WALTER LESLIE PRINGLE

Private
61440
12th Battalion Manchester Regiment
MTS 1912–13

Walter was the second son of Walter Richard Pringle, a bookkeeper and a native of Birmingham and his wife Emma (formerly Christian). His parents had married in St Thomas's church, Seaforth on 6 July 1895 and their first son, William Arnold was born soon afterwards in 1897. Walter Leslie, their second son, was born on 17 October 1898.

By 1901, a daughter, Mabel Roberts, had been added to the family, which was living at 23 Ferndale Road, Waterloo, a street of terraced houses a few minutes' walk from the school. Walter (senior) was working as a clerk in a soap manufacturers. In 1908 another sister, Isobel Dora, was added to the family.

Three years later, in 1911, Walter and his family had moved to 30 Winstanley Road, Waterloo, from which Walter (senior) set out each morning to do the same job as a clerk.

Walter Leslie Pringle entered Merchant Taylors' on 18 September 1912 having previously attended Christ Church Church of England School in Waterloo. He did not stay at the school very long, leaving aged 14 on 30 July 1913 to work in a 'cotton office'.

Details of Walter's service in the war are scarce. His service record was one of those which did not survive the bombing raids of World War II and his medal index card simply shows that he initially joined the South Lancashire Regiment and was given the number 43611 and later transferred to the Manchester Regiment with number 61440. The Commonwealth War Graves records show he served with the 12th Battalion of the Manchester Regiment. Comparison with other soldiers of the 12th Battalion with similar numbers indicate that he might have transferred between regiments early in 1918 and so might have been with them when they had to withstand and then defeat the German Spring Offensive, following which they took part in the Allied attacks in August.

Walter was killed in action on 1 September 1918 aged 19, probably at the battle of Bapaume.

He is buried in Bancourt British Cemetery, section V row K grave 18.

CLARENCE PUGH

Private
109154
1st Battalion Nottinghamshire and Derbyshire
Regiment
MTS 1910–15

Clarence was one of two sons born to Reginald Clifford Pugh and his wife Elizabeth (formerly Dewhurst) whom he had married in 1898 in Bolton. He was born in Bolton on 25 May 1899.

In 1901, Reginald, who was working as a 'Grocer's Assistant' was living at 237 Bridgman Street, Bolton with his wife and son. No doubt to make his income stretch a little further, Reginald had taken in a boarder. Reginald's second son, Reginald Clifford, was born in Bolton in 1902.

The family probably moved to Merseyside in 1910 as Clarence came to Merchant Taylors' on 14 September 1910 having previously attended The Grammar School, Bolton. His father gave his occupation as 'Clerk' which he expanded upon in the census of the following year to describe himself as an 'Oil Merchant's Clerk'. The family was living at 30 Beech Grove, Seaforth. Clarence left the school on 28 July 1915 to become a 'Cotton Clerk'.

Clarence would have been 18 on 25 May 1917 and, having attested on 26 January 1917 giving his occupation as 'clerk', he was mobilised on 13 August. After basic training he was initially posted to the Manchester Regiment in December and embarked at Folkstone on 31 March 1918, arriving in Boulogne on the same day. He was posted to 1st Battalion Nottinghamshire and Derbyshire Regiment on 4 April 1918. This battalion at that time formed part of 8th Division and in May took part in the fighting on the Somme where, on 27 May, Clarence was reported missing in action. It was soon realised that he had been made a prisoner of war and he was presumably sent to Niederzwehren prisoner-of-war camp near Kassel, Germany.

While in the camp, Clarence died of wounds on 22 August 1918 and was buried in Niederzwehren Cemetery plot VIII row A grave 16.

Edward Rhodes Pugh

Captain
30th Battalion Northumberland Fusiliers attached
King's African Rifles
MTS 1899–1903

When Thomas Edward Pugh married Sarah Jessie Rhodes on 1 June 1880, he styled himself as 'Book Keeper'. By April 1881, they were living at 3 Austin Terrace, Liscard, and he stated his occupation as 'Commercial Clerk, Shipping Office'. Their daughter Mary Elizabeth was born in the month before the census, and their second daughter, Wemyss Gertrude, was born in 1884.

In about 1885 Thomas was appointed representative and manager of the Orient Steamship Company, originally in Adelaide but later in Melbourne. So it was that Edward Rhodes Pugh was born on 16 September 1888 at 2 Park Place, Toorak Road, South Yarra, Melbourne. He was baptised at Christ Church, South Yarra on 20 February 1889.

Edward's father suffered from health problems and to help alleviate these he switched his base of operations to Sydney and then took a voyage to Colombo. Recovering somewhat he set out to return to Australia aboard the SS *Carthage* of the P&O Line but died in November 1889 during the voyage, being buried at sea outside King George's Sound in Western Australia.

His wife and family returned to England shortly after his death, as by 1891, they were living at 6 Derwent Square, West Derby. It seems Sarah was left reasonably well off as she is described as 'Living on her own means' at this time. Edward was only two years old. It would be another eight years before he came to Merchant Taylors', in 1899.

By 1901, Sarah and the three children had moved to 10 Rossett Road, Crosby and two years later, in 1903, Edward left Merchant Taylors'.

What Edward did between leaving Merchant Taylors' and the start of the war is not clear. Though his mother was staying at a boarding house in Southampton in 1911 according to the census, Edward does not appear.

It appears that at the start of the war he enlisted as a private (No 2026) in the 6th Battalion of the King's (Liverpool Regiment) but saw no overseas service in this role. He was later granted a commission. Originally gazetted as a second lieutenant in the *London Gazette* of 10 December 1914, this was later cancelled with effect from 10 December and he was gazetted temporary lieutenant in the supplement to the *London Gazette* of the 12th of that month. The commission was to date from 5 November 1914, the date of formation of the 24th Battalion

Northumberland Fusiliers, the battalion to which he was posted. He was gazetted as temporary captain in March 1915, the captaincy to date from 25 November 1914.

In the supplement to *London Gazette* of 8 December 1915 he was moved from the Service Battalion (the 24th) to a reserve battalion (presumably the 30th Battalion as listed by CWGC). The move was dated 20 November 1915. While with this battalion, he was appointed adjutant from 1 September 1916.

In April 1917, he was attached to the King's African Rifles with whom he saw out the war. He died of influenza in Zomba Hospital on 2 December 1918 while still attached to the King's African Rifles and is buried in grave number 64 in Zomba Town Cemetery in what was then Nyasaland, present-day Malawi.

AMYAS LEIGH RADFORD

Captain
9th Battalion King's (Liverpool Regiment)
attached 8th Battalion Lancashire Fusiliers
MTS 1886–91

Amyas's parents, Samuel Leigh Radford and Mary MacLeod, were married in Edinburgh on 8 January 1873. Before the year ended, their first child, Samuel Collins, was born in Waterloo, Liverpool. Amyas was their second child, born on 26 December 1874, at Burlington House, Waterloo. This was probably a large house standing on the site of the present Burlington House office block. Their final child William MacLeod was born at Ben Rhydding in Yorkshire in 1878.

By 1881, Samuel had moved his family to Mill House in Willaston on the Wirral. On the night of 3 April, Amyas and his two brothers were being cared for by the family's servants, a nurse, a cook and a maid while their parents were away visiting the Hydrotherapy Establishment at Ben Rhydding near Ilkley. The connection with Ben Rhydding was a long one. It had been founded in 1844 and later taken over by Mary's father, William MacLeod, Amyas's grandfather who became manager there in 1847 and later became its owner. In fact, Mary herself had been born at Ben Rhydding.

Amyas first came to Merchant Taylors' in 1886, two years after his brother Samuel started and two before his brother William who arrived in 1888. He left the school in 1891 and entered the family business. By this time the family had moved to 6 College Avenue, Crosby, a house later to be taken over (with others) and used as a boarding house for the school. His older brother Samuel had left school the previous year and was now working as a shipbroker's apprentice while his father was still working as a merchant dealing in corn and flour.

Amyas's first connection with the military came in 1900 when, on 7 March, he was commissioned as second lieutenant in the 6th Volunteer Battalion of the King's (Liverpool Regiment).

By 1901, Samuel had moved the family yet again and was living in The Serpentine South, Blundellsands. This was a larger house and housed quite an extended family. Not only Samuel and Mary were living there along with Amyas (now a cashier in the flour trade), William (a salesman in the flour trade) and Samuel (junior) (also a salesman in the flour trade) but Samuel's wife, Mabel, their children Walter (see p.154) and Collins (both of whom attended Merchant Taylors') and Mary's widowed sister and two servants were also in residence.

Amyas was promoted to captain in the volunteer reserve on 17 December 1907.

Amyas's father died on 14 May 1910 by which time he had moved house yet again; this time to Raasay, Hall Road East, Blundellsands. The following year only his widow, Amyas (now styling himself 'Corn Merchant') and Mary's sister, Constance were living at 'home'.

At some point, Amyas was transferred to the 1st/9th Battalion King's (Liverpool Regiment) and was then attached to the 8th Battalion Lancashire Fusiliers, a Territorial battalion which in August 1914 was stationed at Salford. In September 1914 the battalion sailed as part of the 42nd Division and landed in Egypt on 25 September; their aim being to guard the Suez Canal. On 1 May 1915 they embarked once again, this time at Alexandria and on 5 May landed at Helles on the Gallipoli peninsula being ferried ashore by trawlers under the cover of the SS *Clyde*. On 11 May the battalion relieved the Australians in trenches at Krithia Road and stayed there until 16 May apparently suffering slight loss, chiefly from fatal head wounds. Whatever the cause, Amyas was one of those killed. He died on 12 May. By the end of August, of the 32 officers who landed on 5 May, only three remained and they were all wounded.

He is commemorated on the Helles Memorial.

Amyas was a cricketer and golfer and was a member of Northern Cricket Club, Freshfield Golf Club and Liverpool Conservative Club.

WALTER CYRIL LEIGH RADFORD

Private
G/16826
2nd Battalion Royal Sussex Regiment
MTS 1908–13

Walter Cyril Leigh Radford was one of five members of a family who attended Merchant Taylors' over two generations. He had been preceded by his father Samuel Collins Radford and two uncles, Amyas Leigh Radford (see p.152) and William MacLeod Radford. His brother Collins Hector MacLeod Radford was a contemporary. Walter appears to have been referred to within the family as Cyril (just as Collins seems to have been known as Hector).

Walter's father, Samuel Collins Radford married Mabel Ann (formerly Minns) in 1897, and Walter was born on 3 March 1898 at Union Mills on the Isle of Man. Walter's grandfather, Samuel Leigh Radford, was a corn and flour merchant and lived in a large house in The Serpentine South in Blundellsands. In 1901 Walter was living in this house with his grandfather and grandmother, his two uncles, parents and brother. His father and uncles had joined the family flour firm on leaving school. While the family were living here, three more siblings for Walter arrived. They were known, at least familiarly, as Molly (born around 1902), Kitty (born around 1904) and Norma (born around 1910).

As a young boy, Walter attended a private preparatory school in Blundellsands, the name of which is not given in the school records. He entered Merchant Taylors' on 16 September 1908.

In 1910, Walter's grandfather died and whether or not this was the cause, by 1911 the family home had been split up with Walter's immediate family living at 1 Cambridge Drive, Crosby.

Leaving school on 20 December 1913, Walter joined Parr's Bank in Castle Street, Liverpool as an apprentice, in the following year. He presumably continued to work here until his 18th birthday after which he enlisted in the army. According to de Ruvigny's *Roll of Honour* he joined 31st Battalion Royal Fusiliers as Private 16826. The school's biographical register states he served with them from April 1916. However, other records say that he enlisted on 3 June 1916. This could be the date on which he transferred to the 2nd Battalion Royal Sussex Regiment. He served with the Expeditionary Force in France and Flanders from 9 May 1917, working as a signaller. On 22 November he was part of D Company, 2nd Battalion Royal Sussex Regiment, operating near Passchendaele as a runner. While carrying a message, he was wounded. Taken to No 4 Casualty Clearing Station at Lozinghem, he died of his wounds the same day. He was 19 years old.

He is buried in plot V row C grave 2 of the Oxford Road Cemetery, Ypres.

LEOFRIC REES

Lieutenant
4th Battalion attached 1st Battalion Royal
Warwickshire Regiment
MTS 1899–1901

Leofric Rees was the youngest child of James Price Rees and his wife Ida Gwendoline Rees (formerly Phillips) who had married in 1874. Leofric had six older siblings: Elsie (born 1875), Oswald (1876), Harry Arthur (1878), Roderick (1879), Muriel (1881) and Gwendoline (1884). Leofric was born on 10 July 1885. All the children were born in Southport. Leofric's father was working as a 'Central America Merchant'.

In 1891, five-year-old Leofric was living with his parents and siblings in Park Avenue, North Meols, Southport in what was probably a large house and with three servants to cater for their needs. In 1895, aged 20, Leofric's sister Elsie died.

Merchant Taylors' opened its doors to Leofric in 1899 and he left two years later in 1901 aged 16. He was still living at home with his parents, Harry, Muriel and Gwendoline. Oswald had married in 1899 and had moved to Little Sutton on the Wirral. There are indications that Roderick might have gone to India as a tea planter.

By 1911, Leofric was working as a 'Mercantile Clerk in the Cotton Trade' and was still living with his parents and sister Gwendoline in Melling Road in Southport.

On 4 October 1915 he was commissioned as second lieutenant (on probation) in the Royal Warwickshire Regiment and was confirmed in the rank on 25 November 1916. He was initially posted to the 4th Battalion the Royal Warwickshire Regiment. This was a training unit which remained in England throughout the war. He was later posted to the 1st Battalion and entered France on 24 July 1917. He appears on the roll call of officers in the 1st Battalion at the end of July.

On 4 October 1917, the battalion took part in the battle of Broodseinde, which was part of the Passchendaele offensive. Leofric Rees was wounded in the engagement and the battalion's war diary records that he died of his wounds on the same day.

His grave was lost in the ensuing fighting and he is commemorated on panels 23 to 28 and 163A of the Tyne Cot Memorial.

155

ARTHUR ROBERTS

BA

Captain
15th Battalion London Regiment
MTS 1901–08

Arthur Roberts was born on 14 December 1890 at Sefton, Lancashire. He was the son of John Brining Roberts (a cotton broker) and his wife Catherine (formerly Hunt). By the time that Arthur was born, they already had three children: Charles (born in 1883), Catherine Grace (1885) and Margaret Hunt (1888). In 1891 Arthur was living at 1 Wesley Street, Waterloo and his father was, at that stage, working as a manager in a cotton broker's office.

The fourth and fifth children, John Brining and Harold David, were born in 1897 and 1900 respectively. All four boys attended Merchant Taylors'.

In 1901, all six children were still living with their parents at 19 Queen's Street, Waterloo. The eldest boy, Charles, having left school in 1899, was working as an apprentice in the timber trade.

Arthur came to Merchant Taylors' in 1901 and proved a most worthwhile acquisition. He was given a Harrison Scholarship in 1904; played rugby for the school XV 1906–08; cricket for the XI 1906–08, being captain in the last year; was a monitor from 1906–08; and was awarded the Derby Prize for Modern Languages in 1907. He left school in 1908.

Taking the Civil Service exam, he entered the Treasury and Audit department in 1910 and was working there as an 'examiner' in 1911 having once described his reason for taking this post as the need 'to earn a modest bread and cheese'. His work required him to live in London and in 1911 he was boarding at 6 Trefoil Street, Wandsworth.

Before the war he had joined the 15th (County of London) Battalion (Prince of Wales's Own Civil Service Rifles) and on 16 August 1911 was promoted from private to second lieutenant within the battalion. He certainly made good use of his time when in London. Not only did he play rugby for Richmond, Blackheath and the Civil Service; in 1912 he also managed to graduate BA with honours in French from London University. On 15 July 1913 he was promoted to the rank of lieutenant.

When war broke out, the 15th Battalion formed part of 2nd London Division and on mobilisation it moved, in November, to billets in Watford. On 17 March 1915, the battalion entrained at Watford and was given a great send off by the local people as they travelled to Southampton, then sailed to Le Havre, arriving on 18 March. The battalion marched to camp at

Harfleur and the following day entrained for Berguette. Arthur Roberts and 59 other ranks were left behind to act as first reinforcements.

In November 1915, he suffered a fall from his horse and returned to England for four months to convalesce. When he returned to D Company of the battalion in May 1916, he recognised only one officer who had survived with the battalion from 1914. His return was greeted by a German attack on Vimy Ridge on 21 May.

On 15 September 1916 the battalion took part in the capture of High Wood on the Somme. Before the attack the men lay in no man's land in front of their trenches. Captain Roberts had crawled close to the enemy's trench and as he stood to give the order to charge, he was shot through the head. During the attack, 80 per cent of the Civil Service Rifles became casualties.

Arthur's remains were not discovered until 1925 and he was buried in Cerisy-Gailly French National Cemetery, plot I row H grave 15.

HAROLD ROSS

Second Lieutenant
5th Battalion Lancashire Fusiliers
MTS 1892–97

Sometime between 1871 and 1879, Harold's father William Henry Ross sailed to South Africa where he settled in King William's Town. It was here in 1879 that he and Mary Catherine Barton were granted a licence to marry. Their son Harold was born in King William's Town on 22 August 1880. His sister Gladys was born in 1883, also in South Africa. William and his family returned to England between Gladys's birth in 1883 and the birth of their son Cyril in Seaforth in 1885.

In 1887, another son, William was born. Unfortunately, William did not survive infancy, dying on 9 May 1887 aged 10 days. He survived the birth two days longer than his mother, Mary, who died on 7 May aged 42.

Harold's father remarried in 1889. He and his new wife, Sarah, were married in St Luke's church, Crosby and the 1891 census shows them living at 18 Myers Road West, Crosby. Harold's father was working as a cashier.

Harold joined Merchant Taylors' in 1892. He gained his rugby colours and, in 1896, won the Open Hurdles on Sports Day before leaving in 1897. After he left school, he became a mercantile clerk, as shown in the 1901 census return. At that time, his brother Cyril – also a 'Merchants' Boy', who would later go on to be

President of the Old Boys' Association and a governor of the school – was staying with his grandmother at 133 Liverpool Road, Crosby while the rest of the family was living at 31 Sandringham Road, Seaforth. William was still working as a bookkeeper, at this time for the Liverpool Gas Company. Shortly after the census was taken in 1901, Harold's stepmother died.

By 1911, Harold's father had retired and Harold himself was working as a 'marine freight clerk'. They, and the other two children, were still living in the same house in Sandringham Road.

Harold received his commission as second lieutenant on 29 August 1917, being commissioned from an officer cadet unit and posted to the 5th Battalion Lancashire Fusiliers. The battalion had returned to France from Egypt in March of that year; he would have joined them probably in the Ypres area at the beginning of September or on the Belgian coast at Nieuport. They remained in Nieuport in relative peace and quiet until, in November, they moved to Givenchy as part of the 3rd Army and in March had to face the German Spring Offensive.

There is some confusion over the date and manner of Harold's death. He seems to have been posted 'Missing' on 21 March 1918 but was later reported 'Wounded and a Prisoner of War'. Later still he was reported to have 'Died in German Hands' with his medal index card and CWGC giving his date of death as 8 April 1918.

He is buried at Le Cateau Military Cemetery, plot III row D grave 4.

DAVID ROWATT

Second Lieutenant
Royal Field Artillery
MTS 1901–07

David's father, David Crawford Rowatt married Eleanor Sergenson in 1889 and over the next 20 years they had 11 children. All of their six sons attended Merchant Taylors' and of these boys, two were killed in the Great War, one was very seriously wounded and one died in the flu pandemic of 1918.

David was David and Eleanor's eldest child. He was born on 12 April 1890 into a family of wealthy tobacco merchants; his grandfather, David Allison Rowatt being a partner in the firm of Lyon and Rowatt who are believed to have had the only tobacco import licence for Liverpool and who later developed links with British American Tobacco.

In 1891, aged 11 months, David was living with his parents in a house called Kenilworth in Waterloo Park; a house they still occupied in 1901. By then it was more fully occupied. David's brother Robert had arrived in 1892, his first sister,

The Rowatt children just before the war. From the left Jean, Allison, Stewart, Agnes, Crawford, Eleanor, Edmund, James, Marion, Robert and David. David and Edmund were to die in the war, Robert was badly wounded and Stewart died in the flu pandemic of 1918.

Marion, in 1893 then James in 1895, Edmund in 1897, Eleanor in 1898 and Crawford in 1900. His father also employed a cook, waitress and two nurses.

David joined Merchant Taylors' in 1901 and was undoubtedly a successful student. He was granted a Harrison Scholarship in 1905 and represented the school as a member of the rugby XV and cricket XI in 1906 and 1907, captaining the cricket XI in 1907, when he got the best out of a poor side. He left school in 1907 and in his last year was awarded the Davis Prize for Mathematics and an English essay prize.

Almost inevitably, after leaving school he joined his father's firm, Messrs Rowatt and Lyon, Tobacco Importers. David also maintained his interest in sport becoming a well-known member of both Northern Cricket Club and Waterloo Rugby Club.

While he was at Merchant Taylors' his mother had given birth to twins, Agnes and Stewart in 1901 and later to Allison in 1903. (The spelling reflecting her grandfather, David Allison Rowatt's middle name). His final sibling, Jean, was born in 1909.

By 1911, the Rowatts had moved to 23 Esplanade, Waterloo. David was still working in the family firm as a clerk and had been joined by Robert who was doing a similar job. The family employed five servants.

On 21 August 1913 David married Sadie Harvey-Gibson, the daughter of Robert John Harvey-Gibson, Professor of Botany at Liverpool University.

David was commissioned as temporary second lieutenant on 30 September 1915 and posted to A Battery, CL Brigade, Royal Field Artillery which was a County Palatine brigade serving with the 30th Division. He crossed to France on 30 November 1915 according to his medal index card. Before the war, David, Robert and their father had been members of Anfield Bicycle Club. At Christmas 1915 the club sent various presents to its members at the front; David and Robert were sent 'Peterson pipes and some tobacco' (particularly apt in their case!). David wrote back from 'Somewhere in France' expressing his appreciation and saying:

The town I am in at present boasts a canteen which, however, never seems to have any stock, and as the last shelling cleared out most of the civilians we are dependent on home supplies for extras. We only use the back rooms of the house I am billeted in as the front ones are too draughty. It ought to be a safe billet if the theory is correct that the best place to hide in is the latest shell hole.

David Rowatt was killed in action on the first day of the battle of the Somme, 1 July 1916. It is recorded in the August circular of the Anfield Bicycle Club that 'his battery had just taken up its new advance position when a shell landed on top of it killing him and two other officers instantaneously as well as mortally wounding a fourth'.

He is buried in Peronne Road Cemetery, Maricourt plot II row E grave 36.

EDMUND ROWATT

Private
15578
17th Battalion King's (Liverpool Regiment)
MTS 1908–14

Edmund was the younger brother of David Rowatt (see p.158). Born on 20 April 1897 he was the fifth child and fourth son of David Crawford Rowatt and his wife Eleanor.

Edmund entered Merchant Taylors' on 1 May 1908, coming to the school from a private preparatory school in Waterloo called 'Dunsmore'.

Like his brother he demonstrated a degree of sporting prowess while he was at school. He played for the school rugby XV in 1912, 1913 and 1914, the cricket XI in 1914 and won the Moss Challenge Cup for the competitor with the highest number of points in Open events on Sports Day in 1912–14. For a number of years he held the school record for the ¼-mile being timed at 54.6 seconds.

He left the school on 30 July 1914 and as soon as the 17th Battalion was formed, he enlisted. The 17th was the first of all the Pals battalions to be formed and was established by Lord Derby on 29 August 1914. Edmund's papers show he enlisted at Liverpool and attested on 31 August 1914. In March 1915 he spent three days in Rainhill Hospital suffering from influenza. In April 1915 the 17th Battalion became part of 89th Brigade, 30th Division which initially contained all four of the Liverpool Pals battalions, the 17th, 18th, 19th and 20th. In the same month, they were moved to Grantham to continue their training where, on 23 June, Edmund was appointed lance corporal but reverted to private at his own request on 23 August.

The battalion remained at Grantham from 29 April 1915 to 4 September before moving to Larkhill on Salisbury Plain where, on 7 September, he was confined to barracks for three days for missing a stable parade.

On 6 November, Edmund sailed across the Channel with the battalion and landed in France on the 7th.

Edmund reported sick to 55 Field Ambulance on 12 April 1916, was sent to Highland (No 51) Casualty Clearing Station where he was diagnosed with German measles and on 14 April was admitted to the Isolation Hospital at Le Havre. He rejoined the battalion on 21 May 1916.

He was proposed for membership to the Anfield Cycle Club – to which his father and brothers already belonged – in the July 1916 issue of the circular.

On 30 July 1916 at 4.45 a.m. the 17th Battalion went into an attack against the village of Guillemont in support of the 19th and 20th Battalions but the attack was held up by machine-gun fire. In the course of the attack, 56 other ranks were listed as killed, 130 wounded and 95 missing. Edmund, 19 years old, was presumably among the missing as his body was never recovered. Not a month had passed since the death of his brother David.

He is commemorated on pier and face 1D 8B and 8C of the Thiepval Memorial.

The confirmation of his membership of the Anfield Cycle Club was posted in the August 1916 issue of the circular.

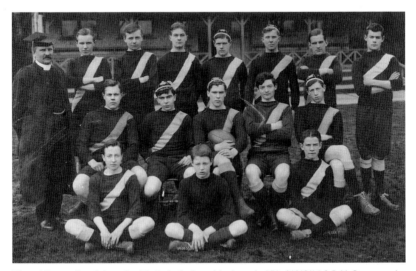

Edmund Rowatt (fourth from the right in the back row) in the rugby XV of 1913/14. S. B. McQueen, on the right of the front row, later played for Scotland.

CHARLES CONWAY SHAW

MC

Lieutenant
Machine Gun Corps
MTS 1912–13

Charles Conway Shaw was born in Rainhill, Lancashire on 19 February 1897. His father, Henry Clayton Shaw, was an engineer and chemical works manager.

Henry had married Martha Ann Hallworth in 1889 and before Charles was born she had given birth to three daughters: Hilda in 1890, Beatrice in 1892 and Vera Margaret in 1896.

In 1901, Henry, his wife and children and his 75-year-old mother-in-law were living in Holly Cottage in Rainhill.

The family, other than Charles, does not appear in the 1911 census. He was a boarder at South Lawn, Liverpool Road, Crosby, in the home of Edward Hartley and his wife. Edward Hartley was a member of staff at Merchant Taylors' and was at that time providing boarding for a number of boys (seven in the 1911 census). Among the other boys boarding with Hartley was Harry Rostron, son of Arthur Rostron, who as Master of the *Carpathia* was to become famous in 1912 for his rescue of the survivors of the *Titanic*.

Given the address noted for Charles's parents in the CWGC records – Les Ombrage, Chemin de Capeyon, Caudéran, Gironde, France – it may be that they had, by 1911, already emigrated.

Charles came to Merchant Taylors' in 1912 aged 15 and stayed only a short time, leaving in 1913.

He was another of the Old Boys who joined the colours shortly after the outbreak of war, enlisting with the 6th Battalion King's (Liverpool Regiment) in November 1914. On 25 October 1916 he was granted a commission as temporary second lieutenant (on probation) in the Machine Gun Corps.

As a second lieutenant he was awarded the Military Cross. The citation in the *London Gazette* reads:

T/2 Lt Charles Conway Shaw MGC
For conspicuous gallantry and devotion to duty. He directed the fire of his machine guns with great judgement and precision under heavy shell fire engaging enemy troops and transport and a field gun battery with great effect. Later he successfully covered the retirement of other troops. His high example of cheerfulness and courage inspired his men with a splendid fighting spirit.

The citation appears in the supplement to the *London Gazette* dated 16 September 1918 and post-dates his death. The date of the act for which he was awarded the MC is not given but the reference to 'the retirement of other troops' might indicate it took place during the German Spring Offensive.

Charles was promoted to temporary lieutenant on 24 April 1918.

At the time of his death on 31 August 1918 he was, according to CWGC, with 39th Battalion Machine Gun Corps. At the end of August, the army was moving forward to control the crossings of the Cojeul and Sensée rivers. The move began at 3.30 p.m. on 30 August 1918 and no reports were received until the following morning from two sections which had passed through heavy shelling. One of these was under the command of Lieutenant Shaw who, along with his sergeant, had been killed during the night.

He is buried in Vis-en-Artois British Cemetery in Haucourt, plot VI row G grave 2.

FRASER MORTON SHEARD
MC

Captain
18th Battalion King's (Liverpool Regiment)
MTS 1905–12

Fraser's parents, Theodore Senior Sheard and Mabel Pemberton, were married at St Saviour's church, Liverpool on 28 December 1893.

Almost exactly nine months later, on 29 September 1894, the first of their three sons, Fraser Morton, was born. He was followed in 1896 by Geoffrey Senior (see p.165) and in 1897 by Rowland Theodore. All three boys attended Merchant Taylors'.

Fraser was baptised on 10 March 1895 at St Saviour's church. At this time his father was working as a chartered accountant and the family was living at 125 Canning Street, Liverpool. By 1901, the family had moved out of Liverpool city and was living at 175 Moor Lane, Crosby.

As the eldest, Fraser was the first of the Sheard boys to come to Merchant Taylors', arriving on 17 September 1905 having previously attended Ballure House, a private preparatory school in Crosby.

A note in the admissions register shows that he was absent from school for the spring term of 1906 and for the spring and summer terms of 1909; absences as yet unexplained.

In 1911 Fraser, his parents and brothers were still living in Moor Lane,

Crosby and in that year, Fraser passed his Oxford Local Senior examination. He also represented the school as part of the cricket XI and rugby XV, being vice captain of cricket in 1912.

Fraser left the school on 31 July 1912 to work, according to the records in a 'General Merchant's Office'.

The following year, on 27 August 1913 he sailed from Liverpool to Montreal aboard the Allan Line's SS *Virginian*. The passenger list gives his occupation as 'Clerk' and he set up, according to the biographical register 'in business in Montreal'. How long he intended to stay in Canada is not known nor if his return was occasioned by the outbreak of war but return he did, arriving in Liverpool aboard the SS *Megantic* on 16 November 1914.

He must have volunteered to serve almost straightaway as he was gazetted as a second lieutenant with the 18th Battalion King's (Liverpool Regiment) with effect from 11 February 1915. This battalion, as part of 89th Brigade, 30th Division, landed at Boulogne in November 1915. On Christmas Day 1915 it transferred to 21st Brigade.

On 30 May 1916 Fraser was transferred to the General List for service with a trench mortar battalion and was promoted to acting captain on 10 July 1916 while commanding such a battalion. This acting rank lasted until 20 November 1916 when he relinquished it on ceasing to command a trench mortar battalion and reverted to second lieutenant.

Fraser was awarded the Military Cross, the award being gazetted in the supplement to the *Edinburgh Gazette* of 1 January 1917, though no citation is given and no date of the act resulting in the award is noted.

Substantive promotion followed on 1 July 1917 when he was raised to temporary lieutenant. He was granted a return to acting captain rank on 24 August 1917 when he took over command of a company. His final promotion came on 2 November 1917 when he was promoted to temporary captain.

On 22 March 1918, at about 10.30 a.m., the battalion's war diary records him as leading No 3 Company along the Germaine River to Stevens Redoubt after which it records him as wounded and missing. He was actually taken prisoner and died of his wounds while a prisoner of war on 2 April.

He is buried at the British Premont Cemetery, plot IV row B grave 38.

GEOFFREY SENIOR SHEARD

Second Lieutenant
3rd Battalion Cheshire Regiment
MTS 1910–13

Theodore Senior Sheard and his wife Mabel had three sons: Fraser Morton (see p.163), Geoffrey Senior and Rowland Theodore. Rowland was the only one to survive the war.

Geoffrey was the second son, born in Liverpool on 1 March 1896. In 1901, Geoffrey was living with his parents and brothers at 175 Moor Lane, Crosby.

Geoffrey received the early part of his education at Ackworth, an independent Quaker school near Pontefract, leaving there to enter Merchant Taylors' on 21 January 1910. Later that year he obtained a Pass in his Oxford Local Junior exam. The family had moved by 1911 to 'Waverley', Moor Lane, Crosby.

Geoffrey again sat the Oxford Local Junior exam in 1912 and, again, obtained a Pass. He represented the school as part of the cricket XI in 1913 and left Merchant Taylors' on 30 July 1913 to go into farming.

According to *The School Review*, Geoffrey joined the 6th Battalion King's (Liverpool Regiment) on 7 August 1914 but his medal index card gives his first unit as 1/1 Western Division Cyclist Company as Private 1771. Whatever he actually did at the beginning of the war his record shows that he did not see any overseas service while serving in the ranks.

In 1915 he gained a commission in the Cheshire Regiment being gazetted second lieutenant (on probation) on 23 March and being confirmed in the rank on 20 November. The *London Gazette* shows him being posted to the 3rd Battalion, the same battalion he was serving with at the time of his death according to CWGC. However, this battalion was a reserve battalion, a training unit and was in the UK throughout the war. His medal index card shows the first theatre of war he served in was Gallipoli, which makes it more likely he was attached to 1/4th or 1/7th Battalion, both of which landed at Suvla Bay on 9 August 1915. According to *The School Review*, while at Suvla Bay he contracted enteric fever and dysentery. Having recovered from these he went to France where he could have served with a number of battalions, though his burial place makes the 1/5th look the most likely. The 1/5th was a pioneer battalion which, late in June, was constructing trenches at Telegraph Hill near Arras. Several men were killed or wounded there, all of them buried in the cemetery at Etrun.

At the end of June Geoffrey was severely wounded and died of his wounds on 26 June 1917. He is buried in Duisans British Cemetery, Etrun, plot IV row N grave 2.

Reginald Singlehurst

Captain
24th Battalion attached 9th Battalion King's Royal Rifle Corps
MTS 1892–95

Born in Liverpool on 11 September 1882, Reginald was the son of Paul Robert Singlehurst and his wife Harriette Anne (formerly Brodie). He was the only one of his parents' six children to be born in England. Four of the others were born in Parnaiba, Brazil where his father seems to have settled and was working as a merchant. Reginald was baptised in St Luke's church, Liverpool on 13 December 1882; the family's address being given as Parnaiba, Brazil.

In 1891, Reginald was living in Edinburgh at 3 Greenbank Terrace with his mother, Harriette, who is described as 'Living on Private Means' and his brothers and sisters: Percy Brodie (born around 1880), Linda Hardell (around 1881), Robert Bruce (around 1884), Muriel Rhoda Dick (around 1886) and Frieda Catherine Jessie who was two months old. In this census return and that for 1911, Frieda is listed as born in Edinburgh though in the 1901 return it says Brazil.

In late 1891 or early 1892, the family must have moved to Liverpool, as Reginald joined Merchant Taylors' in 1892 and left in 1895. Three years later, on 13 June 1898, his father died in Parnaiba.

By 1901, the family was living at 2 Sefton Drive, Toxteth Park. Reginald was working as an insurance clerk.

No further trace has been found of Reginald until he was commissioned in 1915. He was originally commissioned into the Prince of Wales's Own (West Yorkshire Regiment) as a temporary second lieutenant on 28 December 1915 and was transferred to the King's Royal Rifle Corps on 26 May 1916. His first posting was to the 24th Battalion King's Royal Rifle Corps, a reserve battalion based in the north-east of England and he transferred to a service battalion (the 9th) on 3 November 1916. The 9th Battalion formed part of the 14th (Light) Division and during 1917, Reginald would have taken part in the various battles of the Arras Offensive and Passchendaele.

Reginald was promoted to temporary lieutenant on 15 April 1917 and then on 15 November 1917 to acting captain while commanding a company. The post of company commander and its associated acting rank he relinquished in 1 January 1918 but was quickly promoted to temporary captain a week later on 7 January.

On 21 March 1918, the Germans began their Spring Offensive. The battalion's war diary records the following:

> At 10 a.m. a runner came from C Company to say that the enemy had come over in the fog and were already on the Pechine Line (our main line of resistance in the outpost line). Immediately afterwards a runner from A Company came in to say that the Company Commander, Captain Singlehurst, had been killed, and that the Germans had reached the St. Quentin Road.

In the chaos and disorganisation that followed the attack, Reginald's body was lost and his record has him 'missing in action'. He is commemorated on panels 61 to 64 of the Pozières Memorial.

ROBERT BRUCE SINGLEHURST
MC

Captain
12th Battalion Northumberland Fusiliers
MTS 1892–95

Born in Parnaiba, Brazil on 9 January 1884 to Paul Robert Singlehurst and his wife Harriette, Robert was the younger brother of Reginald (see p.166).

In 1891, Robert was living in Edinburgh at 3 Greenbank Terrace with his mother and siblings. After the birth of Frieda in 1891, Harriette must have moved the family to Liverpool for, in 1892, Robert and Reginald started their studies at Merchant Taylors'. Robert left the school in 1895 and continued his education at Liverpool College. It seems their father, Paul, remained in Brazil as he died in Parnaiba on 13 June 1898.

By 1901, the family was living at 2 Sefton Drive, Toxteth Park. Robert was working as a chartered accountant's clerk. In 1909, Robert married Margaret Ashburner and their first child, Robert Maurice Ashburner Singlehurst was born early in 1911, just before the census was taken. This shows Robert living with his family at 18 Lytton Grove, Putney and working as a chartered accountant.

On 28 January 1914, Margaret gave birth to a daughter, Beryl Margaret. When the war started, Robert was quickly granted a commission being gazetted temporary second lieutenant with effect from 20 December 1914. He was posted to the 12th Battalion Northumberland Fusiliers which formed part of 21st Division. In May 1915 the division was stationed at Halton Park and 26 July 1915 saw the birth of Robert's second son George Basil (who, in World War II, would be awarded the DSO and DFC).

After basic musketry training the battalion moved to Witley Camp on 9 August. The majority of the division crossed to France on 7 September. Their baptism of fire came at the battle of Loos at the end of September where the division lost over 3,000 casualties. Robert was promoted to temporary captain on 26 October while commanding a company.

In March 1916, the award of the Military Cross was gazetted. The citation reads:

> For conspicuous gallantry when leading a raid on the enemy trenches. Several of the enemy were killed or taken prisoners. Captain Singlehurst, with great coolness and bravery, remained on the enemy's parapet till all his men had been withdrawn and later went out again under fire to search for and bring in the wounded.

On 13 April 1916 he handed over the command of the company and consequently relinquished the rank of captain. On 30 April 1916, six men of the 12th Battalion Northumberland Fusiliers were killed by shellfire. One of these was Robert Bruce Singlehurst.

He is buried in Serre Road Cemetery No 2, plot XX row A grave 11.

ALLAN WENMAN SMITH

Lieutenant
Royal Flying Corps
MTS 1906–12

Allan Wenman Smith was born in Crosby on 28 July 1896. His father, Frank Thomas Smith was a 'Merchant's Manager' and had married his wife, Jean Bell Thomson in 1893. Allan had an older brother and sister, Charles Frederic (born 1894) and Ethel Wenman (1895).

In 1901, the family was living near the school at 12 College Road. While they were living there, Allan gained two younger sisters, Jean Bell in 1904, and Margaret Wenman in 1908.

Allan received his early education at a private preparatory school in Mersey Road, Blundellsands called 'Sandholme' before moving on to Merchant Taylors' on 1 May 1906.

In 1911, the family was still living in the same house in College Road. He left school on 31 July 1912 and started work in a timber merchant's office, probably with his brother.

At the start of the war he enlisted in the 6th Battalion King's (Liverpool Regiment) as Private 1359 and on 25 February 1915 landed, with the battalion, at Le Havre to form part of 15th Brigade, 5th Division. According to a report of his death in the *Crosby Herald* of 31 March 1917 he soon 'distinguished himself for his self-sacrifice and great bravery taking part in the charge of the Canadians when the French line was broken by the first German gas attack [in March 1915], and came out of it with only three others of his platoon'. He later took part in the division's attack on Hill 60 in May 1915 surviving the action in which a number of Old Crosbeians were killed. According to the same newspaper, 'Later he organised a search party for wounded at Hill 60, and brought in wounded himself. For this he was recommended by his officers for distinction, and received the Russian Order of St George.'

He was commissioned into his own battalion, being gazetted second lieutenant with effect from 29 August 1915. He transferred to the Royal Flying Corps in January 1916 and was appointed second lieutenant flying officer (observer) on 29 April 1916. While acting as observer in No 1 Squadron, he was photographing the German lines on 17 June 1916 when his pilot Captain Malcolm Bell-Irving and he were wounded by anti-aircraft fire while flying a Morane BB number 5164; a plane produced in France for use by the RFC. They landed safely.

Having returned to England to train as a pilot he gained his aviator's certificate on a Maurice Farman biplane at Brooklands on 8 October 1916. He was promoted temporary lieutenant on 1 November 1916 with seniority from March 1916 and was granted his wings in February 1917.

On 18 March 1917, Allan was part of 34 Reserve Squadron and flying from Market Drayton when he was killed in a flying accident.

He was buried in Sefton churchyard in grave O33 on 22 March 1917.

JOHN GREGG SPEERS

Lance Corporal
3737
1st/10th Battalion King's (Liverpool Regiment)
MTS 1896–1900

John Gregg Speers' father, John Reid Speers, was born in Bombay, India in about 1845 and was shipped back to Liverpool when he was very young (by 1851) where he lived with his uncle, also John, a corn merchant, for many years. He married Amy Halsall in 1880 and they had four children. John Gregg was born on 14 July 1884, and he had two older siblings, Halsall (born in 1881) and Kathleen Lavens (1883). John and Amy's final child, Archibald, was born in 1894.

In 1891 the family were living in Gladstone House, Liverpool Road, Formby, but by 1901 they had moved house to 2 Wicks Lane, Formby.

Both of the older boys went to Merchant Taylors'. Halsall seems to have attended only in 1896, while John started in 1896 but stayed on until 1900. When they left school, Halsall and John both became apprentices, Halsall in the grain trade and John in the timber trade. Kathleen became a schoolteacher.

It seems that Halsall emigrated to Canada between 1901 and 1906 as he appears in the 1906 census for Edmonton, Alberta. This is perhaps not surprising for someone in the grain trade. However, by 1911, the family seems to have split up. John Gregg was boarding at 51 Coltart Road, Liverpool and was working as an accountant. John's father, John Reid Speers, was also a boarder, at 47 Falkner Street. Amy and the rest of the children seem not to appear in the 1911 census, however, there are good indications that they might all have followed Halsall to Canada. On the army records produced after the war concerning John Gregg's death, his brothers Halsall and Archibald have the same address as their mother: c/o Post Office, Namao, near Edmonton, Alberta.

Coltart Road in about 1900.

170

Moreover, Archibald attested at Edmonton in Canada in December 1914 giving his occupation as 'Farmer' and his next of kin as his mother Mrs J. R. Speers of Namao, Alberta. Kathleen Speers married a Canadian, Thomas Stuart Hay, and served in France as a nurse after her husband was killed in action. Archibald lost a leg during the war.

Meanwhile, John Gregg enlisted at Liverpool and signed his papers on 15 September 1914 giving his address as 51 Coltart Street and his occupation as 'Salesman'. On his papers he claimed to have already spent six years and eight days with the Scottish Volunteer Battalion King's (Liverpool Regiment). He was posted to the 1/10th Battalion (the Liverpool Scottish), which had already moved to France in November 1914 as part of the 3rd Division. John himself embarked at Southampton and landed in France on 12 February 1915. On 16 March, he seems to have had a fall which resulted in damage to his knee serious enough to have him taken for treatment to 85th Field Ambulance and then to 12 General Hospital, Rouen. He stayed there until 31 March before being discharged to duty. He was promoted to acting lance corporal on 1 April 1915.

It was not long before the battalion had its first major experience of warfare. This took place on 16 June 1915 in the encounter known to the Liverpool Scottish as the battle of Hooge. The battalion strength before the attack was 542. During the action the battalion gained about 1,000 yards of territory but the cost was 79 men killed, 212 wounded and 109 missing – 400 casualties in total.

John Gregg Speers was one of the missing. He is commemorated on panels 4 and 6 of the Ypres (Menin Gate) Memorial.

John's mother seems to have remained in Canada; she died there in 1922 and is buried in Namao Cemetery. His father died in Liverpool in 1925.

WILLIAM SHUTTLEWORTH STANDRING

Second Lieutenant
12th Battalion East Lancashire Regiment
MTS 1909–13

William was the youngest of five children born to Robert Standring and his wife Alice, only four of whom survived to adulthood. Robert and Alice had married in Rochdale in 1887. Their eldest surviving child, Mary was born in Rochdale in 1889. She was followed by two more girls, Helen in 1890 and Alice in 1892. William was born on 15 June 1895.

In 1901, when William was five years old, the family was living at 36 Edenfield Road, Rochdale from where his father worked as a registration agent for the Conservative party. Between 1901 and 1909 they moved to Southport where Robert continued to act as agent for the Conservative party and in 1909 William joined Merchant Taylors'. He had previously been educated at Rochdale Secondary School. By 1911 William was living at 159 Portland Street, Southport with his mother and three sisters, each of whom had entered the teaching profession. Robert was presumably working away. William proved to be a good sportsman while at Merchant Taylors', representing the school as a member of the cricket XI in 1913 and the rugby XV in 1912/13. He left school in 1913 and continued with his rugby, playing for Southport Rugby Club.

He seems to have been a pre-war member of the Territorial Army Service Corps with the rank of private and the number 1000. Later, he was renumbered S4/252880 indicating that he was a member of Kitchener's Fourth New Army. It appears that he rose to the rank of corporal before being commissioned as second lieutenant in the 14th Battalion King's (Liverpool) Regiment on 3 June 1915. It seems he had no overseas service while serving in the ranks. A year later, in June 1916 William was transferred to the East Lancashire Regiment. He crossed to France on 14 July 1916 being posted to 30 Base Depot and was then attached to the 17th Battalion King's (Liverpool Regiment), reporting for duty with four other second lieutenants on 27 July. The battalion was at that time on the Somme.

After only a few days at the front, the 89th Brigade, of which 17th Battalion formed a part, was involved in the attack on Guillemont village on 30 July. The 17th was in support of two other Pals battalions – the 19th and 20th. When his company advanced, those on either side of them were delayed by barbed wire and as a result, his men were exposed to enemy fire. The commanding officer sent Standring and two runners back to clarify what he was expected to do. The area they had to cross was exposed to machine-gun fire and one of the runners was killed by shrapnel. William was seen to be wounded about 8.00 a.m. and was treated at a field ambulance but was not seen after the action. In 1917, his grave was discovered about 2,000 yards south of Guillemont.

He was later reburied in Guillemont Road Cemetery, Guillemont, plot XIII row D grave 4.

ARNOLD BRACEY STEPHENSON

Lieutenant
4th Battalion King's (Liverpool Regiment)
MTS 1892–97

The name 'Stephenson, A B' appears on the school's war memorial. However, the biographical register contains no reference to a pupil with this name. The only boy to have entered the school with this surname and initials and who appears in the admissions register is Arnold Bracey Stephenson, brother of Arthur Theodore Stephenson (see p.174).

No casualty with this name appears in the CWGC list and his medals were claimed in 1919. His medal index card shows him entitled to a Silver War Badge, which was issued to those who had been honourably discharged due to wounds or sickness. It may be that he passed away as a result of the injuries or illness for which he was awarded this badge.

Arnold's father, Reverend Robert Stephenson, a graduate of Gonville and Caius College, Cambridge, took over as vicar of St James, Birkdale in 1874. He had previously been curate of St George's, Birmingham 1856–7 and vicar of St James, Ashted, Birmingham 1859–74.

While he was in Birmingham he married his first wife, Charlotte Lucy Taunton in 1857. The couple had five children. Charlotte died in 1877 and Robert married Philippa Sarah Bracey in 1878.

Arnold Bracey Stephenson was born on 12 September 1880, the eldest son of Robert and Philippa. In 1881 they were all living at 26 Lulworth Road, Birkdale, the vicarage of St James's church where they continued to live until 1905 when Robert retired. Robert and Philippa had two other sons: Charles Harold in 1882 and finally Arthur Theodore in 1884.

Arnold began his career at Merchant Taylors' in 1892, stayed five years and left in 1897. He went to the Victoria University of Manchester to study medicine but did not complete the course, leaving in 1900 for reasons unknown, though he is said to have fought in the Boer War.

In February 1901, Arnold was gazetted as second lieutenant in the 6th Battalion King's (Liverpool Regiment). He was advanced to lieutenant in the 4th Battalion on 1 June 1902 and resigned his commission on 26 November 1904.

In 1907 he married Esther James and in 1912, Esther gave birth to a son, Robert David Bracey Stephenson.

Arnold was readmitted to the regiment as a lieutenant on 13 January 1916 and seems to have served with the 4th Battalion. He was wounded on the Somme in 1916 and returned to Merchant Taylors' as a member of staff and an officer of the cadet corps from September to December 1917.

Another son, Theodore, seems to have been born in 1917. Two years later, in November 1919 Arnold died, as noted in the staff register of the school.

Arnold's son Robert died in Italy in World War II as a Pilot Officer in the Royal Air Force Volunteer Reserve.

ARTHUR THEODORE STEPHENSON

Lieutenant
7th Battalion King's (Liverpool Regiment)
MTS 1896–97

Arthur was brother to Arnold Bracey Stephenson. He was born on 3 July 1884 and baptised on 29 July by his father. He was the third son of Robert and Philippa and his early life would largely have mirrored that of his two older brothers. They spent their formative years living in the vicarage of St James's, Birkdale in Lulworth Road, no doubt attending church regularly while finding time to play on the beach.

All three boys of Robert's second marriage attended Merchant Taylors', Arnold from 1892 to 1897, Charles from 1893 to 1899 and Arthur for one year only, 1896–97. When they left the school, Arnold eventually joined the army, Charles became a law student and Arthur a student of music. He was, apparently, a gifted pianist who often gave recitals in Southport.

Robert continued as vicar of St James's until 1905 when he retired and moved out of the vicarage settling by 1911 in Leyland Road, Southport. Arthur's occupation in this year is not recorded. He is simply described as existing 'on private means'.

When the war began, Arthur was quick to answer the call. He was gazetted as second lieutenant in the 7th Battalion King's (Liverpool Regiment) from 4 October 1914. The 7th was a Territorial battalion which went to France in March 1915 but his records show he did not cross the Channel until 17 June 1915. He was wounded on 21 June, just four days after his arrival. Promotion to temporary lieutenant followed on 12 November 1915 though this was 'backdated' to 7 April 1915. He probably took part in the battle of Loos in September and October 1915. In January 1916, the battalion transferred to 55th Division and settled down to a period of 'standard trench warfare' – trench raids etc. During 'quiet times' when they were behind the lines on rest periods or training etc, Arthur was well known for his piano concerts.

He wrote home on 21 January 1916 and announced: 'We had a Brigade Inspection yesterday, which went off very well. The Brig.Gen is quite a good sort. He asked if we had anyone who could tune a piano at Brigade HQ... I am going, probably on Tuesday.'

The war diary records that on 28 June 1916 there was a raid on the German trenches by a 'Special Party', which involved Arthur Stephenson. After the raid he was reported 'Missing presumed killed'.

His body must have been discovered later as he is buried in Gommecourt Wood New Cemetery at Foncquevillers in plot IV row D grave 9.

JOHN NELSON STEWART

Second Lieutenant
5th Battalion King's (Liverpool Regiment)
MTS 1906–12

John Nelson Stewart was the eldest child of John Inglis Stewart and Lily Nelson, who married on 8 November 1893 at St Mary's church in Bootle. John was born on 18 June 1895 in Liverpool, followed two years later by Roy Morris (1897).

In 1901, John (senior), Lily, their two sons and John Nelson's 71-year-old grandfather were living at 74 Warbreck Road, Walton on the Hill. Lily must have been expecting her next child when the census was taken as Cecil Ince was born in August 1901.

John and his brother Roy started their time at Merchant Taylors' in 1906.

By 1911 John (senior) had moved his family to 9 Alexandra Road, Waterloo, and he now described his occupation as 'accountant' rather than 'bookkeeper'. The following year John left school, the same year in which his brother Cecil started.

John's war service started with the 2/6th Battalion King's (Liverpool Regiment) as Private 3317. This was a second-line battalion which served at home until early 1917. However, before the battalion was sent overseas, John was discharged to a commission, being gazetted second lieutenant (on probation) from 25 October 1916. He was posted to 1/5th Battalion which, at the time, was serving with 55th Division and which, in October 1916 was ordered to the Ypres salient.

John was confirmed in his rank of second lieutenant on 30 January 1917. The battalion spent the first half of 1917 in the salient where it underwent a 'quiet time' which didn't involve any major engagements but would have seen the men subjected to constant artillery bombardment, sniping and raids. It was during this time, on 9 April 1917, that John Stewart died of wounds, presumably received during one of the artillery bombardments.

He is buried in Neuville-Vitasse Road Cemetery, row B grave 18.

CLIFFORD STOCKDALE

Private
266447
2nd Battalion South Lancashire Regiment
MTS 1906–14

Clifford was the fourth child of Richard Stockdale and his wife Sara (formerly Laycock). Both Richard and Sara had Yorkshire roots and had married in Skipton in 1892. Between then and 1893 they had moved to Liverpool where their first child, William was born in October to be followed by Doris Mary in 1895, Eric in 1896 and Clifford on 2 August 1898.

By 1901 Richard, who described himself as a chemist, had opened a pharmacy at 17 Blundellsands Road West, a house which still has the word 'Pharmacy' carved in the lintel above its door. On census day, 31 March, he and his family were being visited by a Matthew Laycock and his wife Lucetta who, to judge by their ages, would appear to be Sara's uncle and aunt.

Clifford arrived at Merchant Taylors' on 17 September 1906 having previously attended a private preparatory school in Blundellsands Road called 'Hendre' which was run by two sisters, the Misses Kyrke. The following year, on 5 March 1907, his father Richard died aged only 39.

In 1909, his mother remarried, her new husband being another pharmacist, George Harold Cole. They continued to live in the same house in Blundellsands Road, though by 1911 it had a name – Aireville.

Clifford passed his Oxford Local Junior exam in 1913 and in the 1913/14 season represented the school as a member of the rugby XV. He left the school on 22 December 1914 and, according to the school's records, found employment in the offices of the Dock Board.

Clifford enlisted as a private (No 5888) in the 1/10th Battalion King's (Liverpool Regiment), the Liverpool Scottish and attested on 2 December 1915 aged only 17 though this did not prove a problem as his battalion was a Territorial battalion which allowed enlistment at 17. He embarked at Southampton on 9 June 1916 and disembarked at Le Havre the following day. He eventually joined his unit, which had been in France since November 1914, on 20 June. At this time, the 1/10th formed part of the 55th Division and was opposite the village of Guillemont on the Somme. He survived unharmed for two months until he was admitted to hospital on 18 August 1916 with a gunshot wound to the back. Discharged from hospital on 3 October, he returned to England to convalesce and spent six months in Norfolk on light duties. In 1917, following the renumbering of the Territorial Force he was given a new number, 357110.

Having recovered from his wound, he was transferred back to the BEF and re-entered France on 5 April 1918 being posted this time to the 2nd Battalion South Lancashire Regiment which he joined on 8 April 1918 with a new number 266447. On 10 April, the enemy attacked the front line between Armentières and Ploegsteert and it was in this action, the battle of Messine, that Clifford was killed in action, aged 19. His body was never recovered and he is commemorated on panels 6 and 7 of the Ploegsteert Memorial.

His eldest brother, Lieutenant William Stockdale (see below), was also killed in the war.

WILLIAM STOCKDALE

Lieutenant
2nd/6th Battalion Duke of Wellington's (West Riding Regiment)
MTS 1903–11

William's parents, Richard and Sara Stockdale, moved to the Liverpool area shortly before the birth of their first son, William, on 31 October 1893. By 1901 they had three more children, Doris Mary, (1895), Eric (1896) and Clifford (1898, see previous page). William's father was a chemist and was, in 1901, running a pharmacy in Blundellsands Road West.

William joined Merchant Taylors' on 1 May 1903 having come from 'Hendre' private preparatory school in Blundellsands Road, the same school attended by Clifford.

On 5 March 1907, when William was 13, his father died. Nonetheless, in the same year he gained a Pass in his Oxford Local Junior exams and followed this with a 3rd Class in 1908. Two years later, in 1910, he sat his Senior exams and gained a 1st Class. He was rewarded with a Harrison Scholarship. He did well, not only academically, but also on the sports field, playing for the 1st XV in the 1910/11 season being described in *The School Review* as a 'Dashing forward'. He also took part in the annual swimming competition.

In 1909 his mother remarried, her new husband being another pharmacist, George Harold Cole. In 1911, Sara, her new husband and her four children were still living in Blundellsands Road West.

William left Merchant Taylors' on 27 July 1911 and began training as a chartered accountant. He was still working towards his final exams when war broke out and he immediately enlisted in the 6th Battalion King's (Liverpool Regiment) with the rank of private and the number 2072. He accompanied the battalion to France on 4 February 1915 taking part in the second battle of Ypres in April and May 1915 including the attack on Hill 60. After 12 months' service he was recommended for a commission and following the necessary period of training he was promoted second lieutenant on 20 December 1915.

He was posted to the 2nd/6th Battalion Duke of Wellington's (West Riding Regiment), which was a second-line battalion and did not cross to France until February 1917. After taking part in several actions in the Ancre and Arras area, the 62nd Division made an attack on Bullecourt on 3 May 1917 during which they suffered heavy losses. Among those posted missing on this date was William Stockdale, his death was later presumed.

He is commemorated on bay 6 of the Arras Memorial.

GILBERT STOTT

Fourth Engineer Officer/Assistant Engineer
Mercantile Marine/Royal Naval Reserve
MTS 1901–03

Gilbert Stott was the only son of James Stott and his wife, the exotically named Dorcas Wavell Stott (formerly Burnett). He was born on 26 April 1888 in Great Crosby about a year after his parents were married. His sister Dorothy arrived in 1890.

In 1891, Gilbert's father was working as a 'manager' and living with his family at 2 Amherst Villas, Fairholme Road, Crosby. Two more baby girls arrived in the following years, Wavell in 1892 and Jean in 1895. In 1897 Gilbert joined Merchant Taylors' and in 1901 he was living with his parents and sisters, still in Fairholme Road, at number 5.

He left the school in 1903 and although there had been no signs of him being an outstanding athlete, he left on a high note by winning the obstacle race on Sports Day and winning it, according to Lawrence Grensted who wrote the account of the day in *The School Review* 'in very good style. He showed especial pace in diving under the tarpaulins and altogether deserved his win'. In addition, although he did not win a prize, he was honourably mentioned on Speech Day for his drawing work.

Although it is not mentioned in the school records it is likely that he joined the merchant navy. On 19 December 1914 he received a commission as assistant engineer RNR.

On 5 May 1917 he was fourth engineer officer aboard the SS *Feltria* of the Cunard Line sailing from New York to Avonmouth with a general cargo. At 7.30 p.m., she was sighted and torpedoed by the German UC48 8 miles south-east of Mine Head, Waterford. Four of the six lifeboats were successfully launched. The U-boat's captain stopped to record details of the vessel he had just sunk and began to sail away but stopped again, this time to pick up Gilbert who was transferred to one of the lifeboats in an exhausted condition. By midnight three of the boat's crew, including Gilbert, had succumbed to exposure. Out of *Feltria*'s crew of 69, 45 had lost their lives by the time the survivors reached shore.

Gilbert Stott was buried at sea and is commemorated on the Tower Hill Memorial.

THOMAS BROWN STOWELL
MC BA

Second Lieutenant
3rd Battalion attached 8th Battalion South Lancashire Regiment
MTS 1900–09

Born on 11 July 1890, Thomas was the penultimate child of Joseph Talbot Stowell, a cotton broker's salesman, and his wife Margaret, whose maiden name was also Stowell.

Joseph and Margaret had married in 1877 and within the year their first child Elsie Margaret was born (in 1878). She was followed by Ernest Redmond in 1879, Joseph Douglas in 1881, Hugh Talbot in 1883, Harold Gordon in 1885, Muriel Louise in 1887 and then by Thomas in 1890. In 1891 they were all living in Hoscote Park, West Kirby, Wirral, a road consisting, at the time, of large Victorian semi-detached villas. Thomas's younger sister, Dorothy Talbot was born in 1894 by which time the family appear to have moved into the Waterloo area. Tragically Dorothy died in 1895 at the age of one and Harold died in Ramsay on the Isle of Man aged 13 in 1898.

Thomas joined Merchant Taylors' in January 1900, coming to the school from a private preparatory school in Blundellsands called 'Marina'. In the following year he was elected to a Harrison Scholarship. On his admission to the school the family was living in Harbord Road, Waterloo, the road in which they still lived (at number 11) in 1901 by which time Ernest and Hugh had both left school and were working as 'Cotton Merchant's Salesmen'.

There is no doubt that Thomas entered wholeheartedly into the life of the school and benefitted greatly from the experience. In 1902 he gained a 1st Class in the Oxford Local Preliminary exams which he followed with a 1st Class in the Junior exams in 1903, a 2nd Class in the Senior exams in 1904 and a 1st

Class in 1905. He resat the Senior exams in 1909, not only gaining a 1st Class but taking second place in the whole of England with distinctions in Religious Knowledge (first place in England), English (first place in England), Latin (first place in England), Greek and French. As a result of this performance he was excused responsions (the Oxford entrance exam).

His academic abilities gained him a number of prizes while he was at school. He won the Montefiore Prize for Classics in 1906, the Graves Prize for History in 1908, the Tyler Prize for Divinity, the Windermere Prize for English Literature and the Great Crosby Scholarship in 1909.

He held a number of positions of responsibility both on and off the sports field. He was a member of the 1st XV 1905–09, being captain in 1907, 1908 and 1909. *The School Review* described him as 'a hard working forward who has captained the team with success'. However, earlier comments imply that he was a rather small player. In one set of comments on 'Characters of the XV' it was said that he had 'all the makings of a first class forward except size' and in another that he 'had made an inspiring captain. Only fault is that he won't grow taller'.

He represented the school as part of the cricket XI 1906–09 acting as captain in 1909. In 1908 he was awarded both the Killey Cup and the Whately Simmonds Bat for having the highest batting average for the season. In 1907 he was also captain of swimming and winner of the Swimming Challenge Cup. Tom was a monitor 1905–09 and, unsurprisingly, Head Boy 1908–09. External awards were also visited upon him. In 1905 he was awarded a County Senior Exhibition. In 1907 he was awarded a County Senior Scholarship of £60 per annum for three years and in 1909 he was granted a Classics Scholarship to Oriel College, Oxford. He was also given a Bible Clerkship for Classics at Oriel College valued at £100 per annum.

He left the school on 29 July 1909 and went up to Oxford later in the year to study Classics. In the first part of his studies he gained, in 1911, 1st Class Honours in Classical Mods and two years later, in 1913, he completed the course gaining a BA after achieving a 1st Class in Greats. Following his graduation he took the Home and India Civil Service exam and gained 35th place, being appointed on 23 January 1914 to the post of second class clerk in the Office of Works.

Following the outbreak of the war, Thomas made a number of attempts to apply for a commission but each time he was rejected on the grounds of extremely short sight. Eventually he did manage to enlist as Private 2875 in the 19th Battalion London Regiment (St Pancras Rifles) and landed with the battalion at Le Havre on 10 March 1915 after which they eventually became part of the 47th Division and took part in several engagements in 1915, most notably the battle of Loos at the end of September.

While with the St Pancras Rifles, Thomas was promoted to lance corporal and then sergeant but seems to have reverted to private on transfer to the 3rd Battalion East Lancashire Regiment. Eventually he was accepted for a commission and was gazetted as second lieutenant (on probation) with the 3rd Battalion South Lancashire Regiment with effect from 22 November 1916. This was a reserve battalion that remained in the UK during the war. For his overseas service he was attached to the 8th Battalion. This unit took part in the battle of Messines in June 1917. On 7 June C Company had a hard fight for Lumm Farm which was heavily defended by machine guns. It was eventually rushed by a platoon led by Second Lieutenant Stowell. It was probably for this act that he was awarded the Military Cross. This was announced in the supplement to the *London Gazette* of 8 August 1917. The citation reads:

> For conspicuous gallantry and devotion to duty, during an advance he kept his platoon well together under heavy shell and machine gun fire, showing great initiative and grasp of the situation, whereby he was enabled to capture two machine guns and a strongly fortified post.

On Monday 19 November 1917, the war diary records that Second Lieutenant T. B. Stowell MC died of wounds received while on duty in the Canal sector near the town of Bethune. Details of his wounding are not given though it is noted that the previous night they had been subject to bombardment by *minenwerfer* (short-range mortars).

He is buried in Bethune Town Cemetery, plot III row J grave 20.

BASIL EVERY TEAGUE

Private
3009
10th Battalion King's (Liverpool Regiment)
MTS 1904–08

Basil's father, Thomas Teague, was a Cornish-born manager of a tin smelter. He had married Marian Gray Every in 1887 in St Michael and All Saints' church in Chiswick, describing himself as a 'Merchant' from Truro. Shortly after the wedding they returned to Cornwall and took up residence in Perranarworthal, a small village about 5 miles from Truro. It was there that Basil was born on 3 July

1891. Basil's brother Thomas (see p.183) had been born about two years earlier, and a sister, Katherine Every Teague, followed in 1893.

By 1901, the family was living in Penpol House in Feock, Cornwall and Thomas was managing the tin smelting works, presumably those at Penpol. They were clearly doing well as the family employed a governess and two servants. By this time, however, the Cornish tin smelting industry was in decline and the firm of Harvey & Co moved their works to Merseyside, initially to Birkenhead in 1901 and then to Bootle in 1905 and this may be why the Teagues moved into the area.

Basil entered Merchant Taylors' in 1904 and left in 1908. In his last year he played for the cricket XI but just failed to get his colours. He went on to become a prominent member of Waterloo Rugby Cub and Northern Cricket Club. After school he became a clerk, at least this is the way he is described in the 1911 census when he and his parents were living at 12 Victoria Road, Waterloo, a large, double-fronted three-storey detached house.

When he attested in 1914, he was working as a clerk for J. Lionel Barber & Co Ltd, South American Merchants and Bankers, Liverpool. He signed his attestation forms on 5 August 1914, the day after Britain declared war. He served 'at home' with the 10th Battalion King's (Liverpool Regiment) until 31 October 1914 and embarked for France on 1 November 1914 on the SS *Maidan*, landing at Le Havre the following day. The battalion went into the trenches near Kemmel, south of Ypres and over the next few months was badly depleted as a result of weather conditions, illness and casualties. The November return of 26 officers and 829 men was by January 1915 reduced to 370 officers and men. Basil Teague was not immune to illness and on 9 February 1915 he was admitted to No 7 Field Ambulance at Locre suffering from jaundice. Following his recovery he was discharged to duty with his unit on 14 February. On 25 February, Basil received a wound to the head and died in No 7 Field Ambulance on 28 February. In the war diary he is simply listed as killed in action at a time when the battalion was handing over the trenches to another unit so his death may have been the result of shelling or a sniper.

He is buried in Locre (now Loker) churchyard, plot II row F grave 8.

Thomas Every Teague

Corporal
1638
1st/6th Battalion King's (Liverpool Regiment)
MTS 1904–07

Thomas was the oldest child of Thomas Teague and his wife Marian. He was born on 1 July 1889 in Perranarworthal, Cornwall two years after his parents' marriage in 1887. The family was still living in Perranarworthal in 1891 at Pinewood House from where Thomas (senior) was working as a tin smelter. Thomas's brother Basil (see p.181) was born here in July 1891. A move to Feock near Truro followed sometime between 1891 and 1893 in which year, Thomas's sister Katherine Every was born.

The Teagues moved to the Bootle area and Thomas and his brother Basil entered Merchant Taylors' in 1904. He left three years later in 1907 by which time he had represented the school at rugby in the 1906/7 season, and cricket in 1907. In 1906 he also won the Killey Cup and the Whately Simmonds Bat, topping the tables for batting average, bowling average and number of catches taken. After leaving school he spent some time in South America.

On his return to London from Antofagasta, Chile on 23 March 1914 aboard the SS *Esmeraldas*, the ship's papers listed his occupation as 'assayer'. At the start of the war, his records show that he had already been with the 6th Battalion King's (Liverpool Regiment) for four years and confirm his occupation as 'assayer' working for himself. He attested on 4 August 1914, the day war was declared, and was promoted to lance corporal on 9 September 1914. The battalion remained at home until 24 February 1915 when it embarked at Southampton aboard the SS *City of Edinburgh* disembarking at Le Havre the following day – the day that his brother was fatally wounded. Two days after disembarkation he was promoted to acting corporal.

The battalion moved to the Ypres area and on 5 May 1915 fought off an attack by the Germans on Hill 60. It was during this attack that Thomas Teague was killed in action. According to the regimental history, 'He was in the first line and was shot in passing a message having raised himself on his elbow'.

His body or his grave became lost in the subsequent fighting as he is commemorated on panels 4 and 6 of the Ypres (Menin Gate) Memorial.

WILLIAM TRAMPLEASURE

Private
883730
187th Battalion Canadian Infantry
MTS 1900–02

William's father, Joseph Clare Trampleasure, was a clergyman of the Church of England and married Hannah Lucinda Devenish in Bumlin parish, Roscommon in 1884. Joseph and his new wife then returned to Birkenhead where he had been appointed curate of St Anne's church. It was while living in Birkenhead that William was born on 13 February 1885 and was baptised on 20 February at St Anne's.

In 1885, Joseph was transferred to the parish of St Mary's, Dodleston where he remained until 1901. William's sister Lilian Clare was born in the nearby village of Higher Kinnerton on 27 January 1886 and towards the end of the year, their mother Hannah died.

Joseph remarried on 13 February 1890 to Annie Harriet Anwyl Richards and the following year they and Joseph's two children were living at The Quarry House, Higher Kinnerton, Flintshire. Joseph and Annie had two children of their own: Muriel Clare born in 1895 and Beatrice Anwyl Clare in 1899.

William came to Merchant Taylors' in 1900 and as his parents were living in the parsonage at Kinnerton, he stayed with his uncle, also William, and his wife Sarah, at 67 Handfield Road, Waterloo. In 1902, William left the school and his father was moved to be vicar of St Luke's Lower Whitely, Cheshire, where he was living with his wife and three daughters in 1911.

William does not seem to appear in the 1911 census. He may already have emigrated to Canada where he became a farmer. He was certainly working as a farmer and living in Morningside, Alberta when he enlisted on 16 October 1916. He was posted to the 187th Battalion of the Canadian Infantry, an Alberta-based unit, which, in December 1916 sailed for England with 24 officers and 774 other ranks. He must have been taken ill before he could move to France for he was admitted to Aldershot Hospital and died there on 25 January 1917.

He is buried in Aldershot Military Cemetery in grave AF 2044.

JAMES WILLIAM TURNBULL

Private
184057
3rd Battalion Canadian Infantry
MTS 1889–93

James's father, also James William Turnbull, married Anne Young at Newcastle on Tyne in 1873. By the time their daughter Anne Mary was born in 1874 they had moved to the north-west where James William (junior) was born in Liverpool on 12 November 1877. He was baptised in St Saviour's church, Everton on 30 December 1877, at which time the family was living at 89 Stanfield Road.

By 1881 they had moved to 79 Salisbury Road, also in Everton, from where James (senior) worked, as he did throughout his life, as a customs officer. James's youngest brother, Alfred Walter, was born in 1884.

James entered Merchant Taylors' in 1889 and by 1891 he and his family were living at 4 Neville Road, Waterloo. He left school in 1893.

In 1901, James bought a farm in Calgary, Canada and started farming, a career he continued until after the outbreak of the war. While living in Canada he married his wife, Mary. He enlisted at Calgary on 1 December 1915 and in January 1916 joined the Machine Gun Section of the 3rd Battalion Canadian Infantry. Although the battalion had originally arrived in England in 1914, James joined them in France in October 1916. He would then have taken part in the battle of the Ancre Heights at the end of 1916 and the battle of Vimy at the beginning of 1917.

In May 1917, the 3rd Battalion took part in the capture of Fresnoy starting on 3 May 1917. On this day James was wounded in the trenches and died of his wounds at the 3rd Canadian Ambulance.

He is buried in Sainte Catherine British Cemetery, grave M21.

EDWIN SYERS TURNER

Lieutenant
Royal Naval Volunteer Reserve
MTS 1891–94

When George Edwin Turner married Catalina Syers in Sefton church in February 1877, he gave his place of residence as Port Said and it was in

Port Said that his first child, Edwin Syers, was born on 11 June 1878. George was a merchant, possibly born in Bombay, and his movement around the world would probably account for the birth of his children in many locations: Dorothy was born in 1880, also in Port Said, Norah was born in Penang in 1884 and George Perim was born in 1886 on Perim Island in the Red Sea.

By 1891, Catalina and her family had settled back in England and were living at 5 Sidney Street, Bedford. They must have moved to the Crosby area about this time as Edwin started at Merchant Taylors' in 1891 and stayed until 1894. After leaving school, Edwin was employed as a timber broker's clerk and was working as such in 1901 when he and his brother appear to be living on their own at 6 Sandringham Road, Seaforth.

On 17 March 1906, Edwin's father died while living in Essex. Five years later, in 1911, Edwin was working as a salesman in the timber trade and was living with his mother and sister Norah in Southminster, Essex.

Edwin was a small boat sailor of some note and did a great deal of cruising in his boats *Bab* and *Rani IV*. Making regular contributions to *The Yachting Monthly*, he became known as a 'good man incapable of a mean thought or action, and to know him was to like and admire him'. Given his love of the sea, it is not surprising that he volunteered for the RNVR and was appointed sub-lieutenant in June 1915, being promoted to lieutenant on 30 May of the following year; a promotion not seen by his mother as she died on 19 March 1916.

Following a course at HMS *Fisgard* he was initially posted to a motor launch of the Auxiliary Patrol (ML 4), being transferred on 23 March 1916 to ML 70. He took command of this on 17 June 1916 and on 27 September 1916 was given command of ML 360. This post he seems to have held for the rest of the war. On 17 December 1917 he married Myra Hilda Tom Johnston at St Patrick's church, Port of Spain, Trinidad while he was stationed in the West Indies.

When the war ended he came back to Liverpool in March 1919 and was clearly unwell. Some sources say he died in Fazakerley Hospital on 6 March from complications following pneumonia and some say he died aboard his ship.

He was buried in the churchyard of St Bartholomew's, Huyton-with-Roby, grave 507A. Two months later, on 4 May, his daughter, Edwina Rosemary Turner, was born in Trinidad.

RICHARD TURNER

Private
21637
19th Battalion King's (Liverpool Regiment)
MTS 1909–12

Richard's parents, Robert Frank Turner and Frances (formerly Jarvis) were married at St Mary's church, Walton in 1887. Over the next 20 years they had seven children, five of whom survived into adulthood. Eleanor was born in 1890, Frank in 1891, Richard on 28 June 1896 in Walton, Alison in 1899, Ernest in 1901 and Malcolm in 1906. The seventh child has not been identified.

In 1901, when Richard was four years old, the family were living at 11 Sandon Road, a small terraced house in Waterloo. Robert was working as a clerk for a shipping line.

On 15 September 1909 Richard first joined Merchant Taylors'. He was made a Harrison Scholar. By 1911 the family had moved house to 42 Oxford Road, Waterloo and in the same year, Richard gained a Pass in the Oxford Local Junior exams, a performance he repeated in the Senior exams the following year before leaving school on 31 July 1912 to start work in an insurance office.

Richard, a clerk, enlisted in the 19th Battalion King's (Liverpool Regiment), one of the Pals battalions, in September 1914 and following training, landed with them at Boulogne on 7 November 1915. Here they formed part of 30th Division and would have taken part in the battle of Albert at the beginning of July 1916. On 30 July the battalion took part in the attack on the village of Guillemont; an attack which resulted in the battalion losing 76 other ranks killed, 172 wounded and 177 missing. Richard was one of the wounded. He eventually arrived at the Royal Herbert Hospital, Woolwich where he died of septic poisoning on 7 December.

He was buried with full military honours on 12 December 1916 in West Derby Cemetery, Liverpool in plot VII grave CE 1310.

Alfred Francis Campbell Vaughan

Sub-Lieutenant
Royal Naval Volunteer Reserve
MTS 1904–10

Alfred's father Frederick Splatt Vaughan was a master mariner who gained his Master's certificate in 1872. He and his wife Elizabeth were living in Valparaiso, Chile when Alfred Francis Campbell and his brother Frederick Vivian, who also attended Merchant Taylors', were born. Frederick (junior) was born in 1887 and Alfred on 26 October 1893.

When his mother applied to have Alfred admitted to Merchant Taylors', his father had already died. Coming to the school on 17 September 1904 from 'Hendre', a private preparatory school in Blundellsands, he gained a 3rd Class in his Oxford Local Junior exams in 1909 and a Pass in the Senior exams in 1910. He demonstrated some skill in sport, winning the Swimming Cup in 1910 having taken first place in the 2-lengths, 6-lengths, 25-lengths races and the 'long plunge' along with second place in the 1-length race. In the same year he was chosen for the rugby XV. Though described as a 'Steady half' it seems he tended to pass too high. He was also a member of the Debating Society and proposed or seconded motions on a number of occasions. He left the school on 14 April 1910 to start work in a merchant's office.

His connection with the Royal Naval Volunteer Reserve started on 27 January 1913 when he became a midshipman in the Mersey Division based at HMS *Eagle* where his brother had been an officer for a number of years. He was promoted to acting sub-lieutenant on 30 October 1913 and was absorbed, along with others from the RNVR into the Royal Naval Division late in 1914. Posted to Howe Battalion in the 2nd Brigade he fought in the defence of Antwerp from 6 October 1914 until ordered to retire on 8 October when he subsequently escaped to England.

Following his return he was appointed to HMS *Cordelia,* a relatively new light cruiser. On 1 March 1915 an explosion occurred aboard the cruiser, which destroyed a number of cabins and split the quarter deck. There was only one fatality, Alfred Vaughan. According to a marine who was a member of the crew and who wrote an article in the *Western Mail* in June 1941 describing the explosion, Alfred was writing a letter at the time of his death.

He is buried in the churchyard of St Helen's church, Sefton in grave O36.

JOHN VAUGHAN

Second Lieutenant
20th Battalion King's (Liverpool Regiment)
MTS 1909–15

John's father, also John, graduated MA from the University of Glasgow in 1891, was ordained into the Presbyterian Church in 1895 and was appointed to St James's church, Sunderland, the same year that he married Mary Ann Webster. Their first child, Mary, was born in Sunderland in 1896 and their only son, John, was born on 6 May 1898. A second daughter, Constance, was born in 1901. In that year the family were living at 45 Otto Terrace, Sunderland and they remained in the town until John (senior) was transferred to Blundellsands on 25 February 1904.

John started at Merchant Taylors' on 15 September 1909 and was awarded a Harrison Scholarship. He had previously attended a private preparatory school in Blundellsands. In 1910, his younger sister Constance died.

By 1911 they had moved to a house called Skethtock in Blundellsands and in the following year, John gained a 3rd Class in the Oxford Local Junior exams following this in 1912 with a 1st Class then a 2nd Class in the Senior exams.

John left the school on 28 July 1915 but not before he had played for the rugby XV (1914/15), been appointed a monitor (1915) and a sergeant in the Cadet Corps (1915). He also spoke at Debating Society meetings.

After school he went to Liverpool University to study medicine, joined the Officers' Training Corps and was granted a commission on 7 August 1915, initially commissioned to the 15th Battalion, a reserve battalion. He was offered a position training NCOs but turned it down saying he preferred to go to the front. Presumably as a result of this he transferred to the 20th Battalion and probably landed, with them, at Boulogne in November 1915. His proficiency in French resulted in him being appointed as liaison officer. The battalion took part in the battle of Albert in July 1916 but their most devastating engagement was the attack on the village of Guillemont on 30 July in which seven officers were killed, four wounded and five missing along with 59 other ranks killed, 179 wounded and 119 missing. John Vaughan was one of these casualties. It was reported that he was killed by machine-gun fire while at the head of a charge over a German parapet. Either his body was not recovered or his grave was lost in subsequent fighting as he has no known grave and is commemorated on the Thiepval Memorial on pier and face 1D 8B and 8C.

EDGAR SAMUEL VEEVERS

Second Lieutenant
1st/4th Battalion King's Own (Royal Lancaster)
Regiment
MTS 1905–11

Edgar Samuel Veevers was the second youngest of five children born to Samuel Veevers, a cotton broker, and his wife Florence Mary (née Barrell). Their eldest, Norman Barrell, was born in 1890, about a year after their marriage in 1889. He was followed by John Noel in 1892, Edna Florence in 1893, Edgar Samuel on 25 April 1896 and Doris Elizabeth in 1897.

By 1901, their family completed, Samuel and Florence were living in a large house called 'Normanton' in Francis Road in Blundellsands.

Only two of the three boys attended Merchant Taylors', Edgar and John. John arrived in 1903 and Edgar followed on 1 May 1905, having been taught until then at the preparatory department of Merchants' Girls' School. He left on 11 May 1911 by which time the family had moved to 14 Eshe Road North and Norman and John had followed their father into the cotton trade.

Originally a private, number 24982, in the King's (Liverpool Regiment) Edgar crossed to France on 22 December 1915. Later, having undergone training as part of an officer cadet unit, he was gazetted as second lieutenant with effect from 30 May 1917 and was eventually posted to 1st/4th Battalion King's Own (Royal Lancaster) Regiment. He would probably have taken part, with this unit, in the battles for Pilckem Ridge, Menin Road Ridge, Estaires and Hazbrouk.

On 30 July 1918 he was killed by a sniper and was buried in Houchin British Cemetery, plot II row B grave 8.

HAROLD WAKEFORD

Second Lieutenant
10th Battalion attached 6th Battalion South Lancashire Regiment
MTS 1904–12

Harold's father, Alfred Joseph Wakeford, seems to have tried a number of occupations in his lifetime and to have moved around quite a lot which accounts for his family being born in such diverse places. Born in Cardiff, he married Eliza Jowett in Bradford in 1886 (where he seems to have been a salesman for a paper manufacturer).

His daughter Grace Edith was born in Sowerby Bridge in 1887; his first son, Charles, in Ripponden in 1889; then Frank in 1893 in Wells, Somerset; and Harold in Bristol on 12 February 1895.

Between 1895 and 1901 they moved to the north-west where they were living in the latter year at 45 Ashdale Road, Waterloo where Alfred was working as a 'Commercial Traveller'.

On 16 January 1904, Harold started his first day at Merchant Taylors' where he had been admitted as a Harrison Scholar having received the earlier part of his education at Christ Church School in Waterloo. He seems to have taken his academic education in his stride progressing gradually through his exams as the years passed. In 1908 he obtained a Pass in the Oxford Local Junior exams, in 1909, a 3rd Class and in 1910 a 1st Class. In his Senior exams in 1911 he gained a 2nd Class.

By 1911, Harold's father had undergone another change of occupation as he is listed in the census as a 'Sweet and Chocolate Manufacturer'. The whole family was still living at home, which was now 5 Galloway Road, Waterloo with Grace and Charles helping in the sweet business while Frank had become a student teacher.

In his final year at school, Harold gained not only a 1st Class in his Senior exams but also won the Swimming Cup and the Windermere Prize for English.

Harold left school on 31 July 1912. He took and passed the Civil Service exams and on 15 February 1913 was appointed a clerk of the Second Division, being assigned to the Department of Agriculture and Technical Instruction of Ireland.

About two years later, his family almost suffered the loss of his father and brother. Alfred Joseph Wakeford was travelling as a first-class passenger and Harold's brother Charles was working as assistant purser aboard the *Empress of Ireland* when she sailed from Quebec on 28 May 1914. The next day, she was in collision with another ship in the St Lawrence River and sank in 15 minutes. Of the 1,477 on board, only 465 were saved, including Harold's father and brother. (Interestingly, the captain of the *Empress of Ireland*, Henry Kendall, had a son at Merchant Taylors' at the time.)

Shortly after war was declared, Harold enlisted, joining the Black Watch (TF) on 18 August 1914 but was quickly given a commission being made second lieutenant on 29 December and initially posted to 10th Battalion South Lancashire Regiment, a reserve battalion. He was then transferred to the 6th Battalion, which he joined in Gallipoli on 17 November 1915. Evacuated from Gallipoli in December 1915 he moved to Egypt and then to Mesopotamia in February 1916. He wrote an article in 1916 describing the evacuation of Suvla which appeared in *The School Review*.

Harold was killed in action near Kut on 5 April 1916 and was buried at Falahizeh but the grave was later lost and he is now commemorated on panel 23 of the Basra Memorial. General Maude wrote 'he died most gallantly leading his men in a night assault and we found him after the capture of the enemy position almost on the parapet of the Turkish trench to which he had advanced under a very heavy fire.'

Harold's brother Charles also lost his life in World War I when HMS *Champagne* was torpedoed and sunk in October 1917.

ROBERT STAPLETON WATT

Second Lieutenant
13th Battalion East Yorkshire Regiment
MTS 1907–09

Robert's father, also Robert, was a Glasgow-born Board of Trade inspector who married his wife Kate Smith in 1890. They had three children, all born in the Liverpool area: Doris May in 1892, Kathleen Cunningham in 1894 and Robert Stapleton on 8 February 1896. In 1901, the family was living at 8 Brooke Road, Waterloo.

Robert came to Merchant Taylors' on 17 September 1907 having attended a private preparatory school in Waterloo. He left on 7 April 1909 to go to Mostyn House School in Parkgate, Cheshire. He was still at the school in 1911. While at Merchant Taylors' he gained the prize for singing, being the possessor, it was said, of a 'remarkable soprano voice'.

On leaving school he started work in the offices of Messrs J. T. Duncan & Co, shipowners of Cardiff.

Robert was gazetted a second lieutenant with the East Yorkshire Regiment on 11 January 1915. Training followed at several places including Beverley, Ripon and Salisbury Plain until the battalion sailed for Egypt in December 1915 as part of 31st Division. However, Robert did not sail with them. Being deemed too young, he was ordered to Clipstone Camp to join a reserve battalion, probably the 14th. He later became attached to the 15th Battalion at Seaton Delaval where he was engaged on the HQ staff of General Westmacott. The 13th Battalion moved from Egypt to France in March 1916 and Robert rejoined them in September of that year.

On 13 November 1916 at 5.45 a.m., began the battle of the Ancre. During this battle, Robert Watt was wounded and passing through the system of field ambulances and casualty clearing stations he eventually arrived at 24 General Hospital at Étaples, where he died of his wounds on 20 November. He was 20 years old.

He is buried in Étaples Military Cemetery, plot I row B grave 7.

NORMAN LUTHER WATTS

Major
9th Battalion King's (Liverpool Regiment)
MTS 1900–04

Norman's father, Luther Watts, was a successful draper and silk mercer. He married Bertha Priest in 1886 and they went on to have three sons: Norman Luther on 7 November 1887, Thomas William (see p.194) in 1890 and Douglas in 1898 and a daughter, Ada Priest, in 1892. The two older sons both went to Merchant Taylors' and both were killed in the war.

Norman may well have started his life in Toxteth Park but by 1891 he, his parents and brother Thomas, had moved to Rye Ground Lane, Formby where his father employed a nurse to help look after the two boys.

Norman came to Merchant Taylors' in 1900 and stayed until 1904 by which time Ada and Douglas had been added to the family and they had moved house (between 1892 and 1898) to Woodstock, College Avenue, Formby. On leaving school he not only followed in his father's footsteps and became a silk mercer but he also maintained the family connection with the Liverpool Volunteers with which his father had been associated, being commissioned as second lieutenant in the 6th Volunteer Battalion King's (Liverpool Regiment) on 10 May 1907. With the Haldane reforms of 1908 and the formation of the Territorial Force, the 6th VBKLR became the 9th Battalion King's (Liverpool Regiment) and on 6 November 1909, Norman was promoted to lieutenant in this battalion. In 1911 his parents had moved again, this time to Huyton where they again named their house Woodstock. It is not clear whether Norman was still living with them as on the Sunday evening of the census return he was staying at the Ivanhoe Hotel in Bloomsbury Street, London.

On the outbreak of war, he and his battalion were mobilised and, after training, landed at Le Havre on 13 March 1915 becoming part of 1st Division. During the training period, it was decided that Norman's father, Lieutenant-Colonel Luther Watts, who commanded the battalion was too old for foreign service and he stayed in the UK commanding a reserve battalion. The 9th transferred to the reformed 55th Division in January 1916 and on 13 August, Norman was promoted to major. This division saw much fighting after they moved to the Somme in August 1916: the battle of Guillemont, battle of Ginchy and the battle of Flers-Courcelette and then the battle of Morval which began on 25 September 1916 and involved an attack from Flers towards Gueudecourt. It was in this attack that Norman was killed at the head of his company, the second of the family's sons to be killed. It was a year to the day after the death of his brother.

He is buried in Danzig Alley British Cemetery, Mametz, in plot I row E grave 12.

THOMAS WILLIAM WATTS

Second Lieutenant
9th Battalion King's (Liverpool Regiment)
MTS 1900–06

Thomas William Watts was born on 4 February 1890, the son of Luther Watts and his wife Bertha. Luther was a draper and silk merchant and an officer in the 6th Volunteer Battalion King's (Liverpool Regiment) later to become commanding officer of its successor, the 9th Battalion.

Thomas's father was successful in his career and by 1891 was living in Rye Ground Lane in Formby with his wife and two sons, Norman (born 1887, see p.193) and Thomas. In addition to the 'standard' servant of the day, he also employed a nurse to help look after the two boys. Two further children followed: Ada Priest in 1892 and Douglas in 1898.

Thomas came to Merchant Taylors' in 1900 and in 1901 the family is recorded as living in Woodstock, College Avenue, Formby, a secluded road of large Victorian villas. Leaving school in 1906, Thomas seems to have gone to work in his father's shop. He is described in the 1911 census as a 'Shop Assistant'. At the time he was living with his parents and siblings at Woodstock, Huyton.

Unlike his brother, Thomas was not a pre-war member of the Territorials. Instead he enlisted as a private in the 9th Battalion on 8 August 1914 with number 2380. He did not remain long in the ranks, however, being gazetted second lieutenant in the 9th Battalion King's (Liverpool Regiment) on 11 November 1914 and embarking for France, with his brother, on 12 March 1915. On 25 September 1915, the opening day of the battle of Loos the battalion took part in the attack on the German line. The war diary for 25–27 September makes the simple statement that the casualties for those day amounted to 11 officers and 223 other ranks with no names given. Thomas Watts was one of these casualties, killed in action while attacking the enemy trenches. The front line had moved so little by the following year that on the first anniversary of his death, his older brother would be killed within 10 miles of where Thomas fell.

He is buried in St Mary's ADS Cemetery, Haisnes, plot I row E grave 14.

HAROLD BENNETT WHINYATES

Second Lieutenant
2nd Battalion South Lancashire Regiment
MTS 1907–09

Harold's father, Thomas, was an accountant with a chemical firm and married Clarissa Annie Worrall in Runcorn in 1889. Harold was the third child of six. He had two older sisters, Ada (born 1890) and Clarissa (born 1892), and three younger brothers, Stanley (born 1897), Thomas Edwin (born 1902) and Edgar Worrall (born 1914).

By 1901, Thomas had risen to be head bookkeeper with his employer and had moved into 39 Birchdale Road, Waterloo with his wife and children.

Harold started at Merchant Taylors' on 17 September 1907, having, as with so many old boys, previously attended Christ Church School in Waterloo. He stayed for less than two years, leaving on 4 June 1909 to go into 'Commerce'. Before leaving Merchant Taylors' he was confirmed by the Bishop of Liverpool on 25 March at St Mary's church in Waterloo.

Harold's brothers Stanley, Thomas and Edgar also attended Merchant Taylors' though Stanley left in 1910 to become a chorister at St James's Chapel Royal. In 1911 the family was still living in Birchdale Road, Waterloo but had moved four houses along the road to number 31. Harold was at this time working as an apprentice in a shipping office.

On the outbreak of war, Harold enlisted with the King's (Liverpool Regiment) as a private, number 1776. His later renumbering to 240354 shows that he belonged to the 6th Battalion and it was with this battalion that he landed at Le Havre on 25 February 1915 as part of the 5th Division. He would, most likely, have taken part in the second battle of Ypres, the capture of Hill 60 and the battle of the Somme, though, fortunately they missed the opening day of this battle, on which British casualties were 20,000 killed and about 40,000 wounded or missing. Harold was chosen for a commission and on 1 March 1917, having undergone training with an officer cadet unit, he was gazetted as second lieutenant.

On 10 August 1917, while serving with the 2nd Battalion South Lancashire Regiment, he was employed with a divisional pack company taking stores to positions east of Ypres when he received gunshot wounds to his head, knee and shoulder. He was evacuated to No 17 Casualty Clearing Station at Remy Siding but died of his wounds on 14 August.

He is buried in plot XV row A grave 17 of Lijssenthoek Cemetery.

Bernard White

Lance Corporal
27252
11th Battalion King's (Liverpool Regiment)
MTS 1906–08

Little is known about Bernard White. He was born on 15 July 1895 the son of Walter White, a draper of Southport and his wife Martha. By the time Bernard was born they already had three children: David Reginald (born 1888), Walter (1891) and Marjorie Alice (1894). Bernard had one younger sibling, Dorothy (1897).

In 1901 they were living at 12 Cumberland Road, Southport, a large Victorian detached house.

Bernard was accepted into Merchant Taylors' and first attended in 1906. His stay was not a long one, as he left in 1908 to go to Ashville College in Harrogate. He was boarding there in 1911 and left in the same year.

After leaving Ashville College, he probably returned to Southport where he enlisted in and served with the 11th Battalion King's (Liverpool Regiment). He crossed to France on 15 July 1915 following the battalion which had landed on 30 May having been converted to a pioneer battalion in January of that year. In 1915, he would have been present for the attack on Hooge and Bellewaarde. He was killed in action on 18 August 1916, probably at Delville Wood.

His body was never recovered and he has no known grave, being commemorated on pier and face 1D 8B and 8C of the Thiepval Memorial.

Herbert John Whitehead

Private
88896
1st/7th Battalion King's (Liverpool Regiment)
MTS 1911–15

Herbert's father, Joseph Simeon Whitehead and his grandfather, Thomas were both born in Nottingham but his grandfather 'emigrated' to Liverpool with his family and set up a business as auctioneer and valuer. Thomas later followed him into the business.

Joseph married Lizzie Knight, a music teacher, in 1896 and the following year she gave birth to their first child, Thomas Hope. Herbert John was born on

13 November 1898. In March 1901, Lizzie gave birth to twins, Edith Agnes and Frank Mason. No doubt as a result of the recent birth and possibly also due to the frailty of the new babies, the two older boys were 'farmed out'; Thomas to his Knight grandparents in White Rock Street, Liverpool and Herbert to his grandfather, Thomas Whitehead, in Sandringham Drive, Liscard. Meanwhile, Joseph, Lizzie, the new twins and Lizzie's mother were at the family home at 25 Alton Street, Liverpool. A few months later, Frank died.

Three more brothers and sisters followed: Kathleen Florence in 1903, Bertha Frances in 1904 and Ralph Gordon in March 1911. (Ralph also attended Merchant Taylors', 1919–24.) At the time of Ralph's birth the family had moved out to Crosby and was living at 20 Rossett Road.

Herbert received his early education at Christ Church School in Waterloo and moved on to Merchant Taylors' on 15 September 1911 where he was given a Harrison Scholarship. He obtained a 1st Class in his Oxford Local Junior exams in 1914 and a Pass in the Senior exams in 1915, his last year at school. In the 1914/15 season he was a member of the rugby XV. His speeches to the Debating Society clearly impressed his fellow members as he was described as a 'promising speaker with a nice manner and voice'. He left the school on 28 July 1915 to work for an insurance company.

Herbert enlisted at Seaforth and was posted to 1st/7th Battalion King's (Liverpool Regiment). His service record was among those destroyed by enemy action in World War II so it is not clear if he volunteered in 1915 (he could volunteer for the Territorials at 17) or was conscripted in 1916.

The CWGC lists him as being killed in action on 9 August 1918 which, according to the battalion's war diary, was a day in which they were moving out of the trenches to Vaudricourt but with no mention of casualties.

He is buried in Houchin British Cemetery, plot II row A grave 29.

WILLIAM FREDERICK WHITEHEAD

Private
17496
19th Battalion King's (Liverpool Regiment)
MTS 1908–10

Samuel Whitehead married Alice Maud Harrison in the district of Romford, Essex at the beginning of 1895 and on 4 October of that year, William was born in Forest Gate, Essex. He was to be the eldest of five children.

His sister Lucy Isabel was born in Harlesden, Middlesex in 1899 and between then and 1901 Samuel moved his family to Waterloo where they lived at 38 Lyra Road from which he went to work as a 'Commercial Traveller'. Before William started at Merchant Taylors', two more sisters arrived, Alice in 1904 and Frances May in 1907.

William's first day at the school was 16 January 1908, when he joined, like many others, from Christ Church, Waterloo. He stayed just over two years, leaving on 29 July 1910 to go to Bootle Technical School where, if the occupation given on his attestation forms is accurate, he probably studied some form of engineering. He was probably still attending this school in 1911 when the family was living at 3 Hougoumont Avenue, Waterloo. Another brother, Charles Samuel, was born in 1912.

On leaving Bootle Technical School, William became an apprentice engineer at H. T. Boothroyd's in Bootle, a firm specialising in the manufacture of electrical machinery. He was due to complete his apprenticeship on 4 October 1916 but instead signed his attestation papers on 2 September 1914, still only 19 years old. He was posted to the 19th Battalion King's (Liverpool Regiment), the third of the Pals battalions and landed at Boulogne on 7 November 1915 as part of the 30th Division.

There are slight discrepancies over the details of his death. According to his army record, which has survived, he suffered gunshot wounds on 23 January 1916 resulting in fractures to the bones in both of his lower legs. He was evacuated to No 21 Casualty Clearing Station at Corbie and died there on 4 February 1916. However, according to the battalion's war diary, on 22 January a bombardment by *minenwerfer* wrecked a dugout killing a lance corporal, seriously wounding Private Whitehead and slightly wounding five others. It is likely that the culprit was a *minenwerfer* round which hit the dugout and broke both his legs.

He is buried in Corbie Communal Cemetery in plot I row D grave 40 and commemorated in St Luke's, Crosby churchyard.

His youngest brother Sub-Lieutenant Charles Samuel Whitehead RNR was killed on 3 May 1941 when HMT *Alberic* was in collision with HMS *St Albans* off Scapa Flow.

(WILLIAM) HERBERT WILLIAMS

Lieutenant
Unit unknown
MTS 1897–1902

Considering he spent five years at the school, there seems to be little on record concerning Williams. The school records list him simply as Herbert Williams but other sources indicate that his full name was William Herbert Williams.

His parents, Rowland Jones Williams and Anne Margaret Jones, were married in 1883. Born on 6 February 1886 in Bootle, he was the second of their three children. The eldest, Ella Constance, was born in 1884 and the youngest, David Eric, in 1899.

In 1891, Rowland, his wife and two eldest children were living at 17 St Catherine's Road, Bootle, a sizeable semi-detached dwelling from where he worked as a timber merchant.

Herbert came to Merchant Taylors' in 1897 and by 1901 the family had moved to 31 Merton Road, Bootle. He left the school in 1902 and joined his father in the timber merchant business. At some time between 1902 and 1911, Rowland moved his family out of Liverpool and settled near Chester.

During the war, the school's biographical register records he was killed in action as a lieutenant in 1917. No other information, including his battalion, regiment or date of death has been traced.

JOHN HEBER WILLIAMS

Private
2661
9th Battalion Royal Warwickshire Regiment
MTS 1908–10

John Heber Williams was born in Southport on 26 March 1896. His sister, Dorothy Grace, was about six years old when he was born. Their father, John Williams was a clergyman who, with his wife, Sarah, was running, by 1901, a 'Ladies' School' in Argyle Road, Southport where the family lived.

John initially attended Clive House, a private preparatory school in Southport from which he came to Merchant Taylors' on 16 September 1908. He left on 16 April 1910 to attend Wellingborough School, no doubt as a result of his father being moved to another parish. The family was living in the vicarage in Moulton, Northamptonshire in 1911.

When war broke out, he enlisted at Warwick and was posted to the 9th Battalion Royal Warwickshire Regiment as Private 2661. They became part of 13th Division which gathered at Blackdown, Hampshire and shipped out to Gallipoli where he disembarked at Cape Helles on 13 July 1915. The battalion returned to Mudros at the end of July and landed at ANZAC Cove at the beginning of August.

John was killed in action on 10 August 1915, probably at the battle of Sari Bair, and is commemorated on panels 35 to 37 of the Helles Memorial. The army appears to have known him simply as John Williams.

JOHN RAYNER WILLIAMS

Private
230254
10th Battalion King's Shropshire Light Infantry
MTS 1905–11

John Rayner Williams was born on 23 September 1894 in Trinidad, West Indies. He was the son of Reverend John Williams and Lucy Helen Williams (formerly Rayner) who had married in the registration district of Conway in 1891.

John's father died between 1894 and 1901 by which time Lucy and her son had returned to the UK and were living in Brynrhedyn, Conway with his cousins, including Lucy's sister's son Thomas H. R. Daniels (see p.58) who was also lost in the war.

John Rayner Williams joined Merchant Taylors' School in 1905 and stayed until 1911 though he was absent through illness for the whole of the spring and summer terms 1908. In view of the fact that his mother was a widow, the governors agreed to remit the fees for this period.

On the night of the census, 2 April 1911, John and his mother were living at 21 Alexandra Road, Crosby with Lucy's sister, Florence Daniels, who had also been widowed.

During the war John enlisted initially into the 1/1st Shropshire Yeomanry and was given the regimental number 1894. This unit was dismounted in November 1915 and on 4 March 1916 he sailed for Egypt on the SS *Arcadian*.

At Cairo on 2 March 1917, the 1/1st Shropshire Yeomanry merged with the 1/1st Cheshire Yeomanry to become the 10th Battalion King's Shropshire Light Infantry in 231st Brigade, 74th Division. John was issued with the new number 230254.

The 10th Battalion was involved in General Allenby's move into Palestine and took part in the battle of Gaza, the capture of Jerusalem and the occupation of Jericho.

The division received a warning order to leave Palestine on 3 March and began embarkation at Alexandria on 29 April. They landed at Marseilles on 7 May 1918. On 21 August 1918 the battalion, following a rest period, was ordered back into the trenches at St Floris, north of Bethune.

John was killed in action on 19 September 1918 and, having no known grave, is commemorated on panel 8 of the Vis-en-Artois Memorial. He probably died in the battle of Épehy when the 74th Division attacked the Hindenburg Line in pouring rain under a creeping artillery barrage.

He is also commemorated on the Port of Spain Cenotaph.

THOMAS MAITLAND WINSLOW
RD

Lieutenant Commander
Royal Naval Reserve
MTS 1882–86

Thomas Maitland Winslow was the oldest Old Crosbeian to be killed during the war. He was born in Liverpool on 21 December 1872 and was baptised on 16 January 1873 at St Barnabas' church, Liverpool when his parents were living at 22 Falkner Street. His father, Charles de Blois Winslow, was a clergyman and graduate of Cambridge who had been at St Barnabas since 1867, initially as curate and later, from 1871 to 1879 as vicar. In 1879 Charles was moved to be vicar of St Nicholas's church, Blundellsands.

In 1881, Thomas and his family were living in the Serpentine, Blundellsands. The family was by then composed of Charles and his wife Eleanor Lucy, (formerly Hayes) and their seven children, Charles Frederick de Blois (born 1870), Aubrey Isaac de Blois (born 1871), Thomas Maitland, Emily Mary (1875), Grace (1877), Isabel (1879) and Arthur (1881).

Thomas arrived for his first day at Merchant Taylors' in 1882 and left in 1886, the year in which his brother Lawrence was born. His time at the school predates the publication of *The School Review* so any school successes have not been recorded. All five of his brothers attended Merchant Taylors': Charles 1880–89, Aubrey 1880–87, Arthur in 1893 and Lawrence 1896–1902. Presumably the arrival of the older boys coincided with their father's move to Blundellsands.

Charles (known as Fred) seems to have emigrated to South Africa and is recorded as a miner sailing for Cape Town in 1895. He later became a stockbroker and died and is buried in Bulawayo (now in Zimbabwe). Aubrey also emigrated shortly after leaving school, in his case to Australia, dying and being buried in Albany, Western Australia, aged 18, in 1890. Lawrence, in turn, moved to Canada and settled in Edmonton, Alberta. Arthur, however, represents the saddest case. He was drowned on Crosby beach along with fellow Merchant Taylors' boy Norman Kruger. The memorial to their loss is mounted in the clock tower of the school.

After school, in October 1886, Thomas entered HMS *Conway*, a training ship stationed in the Mersey, where he served for two years, leaving in December 1888 and then serving with the Mercantile Marine. He was initially aboard the *Cleomene*, a sailing vessel, from 1889 to 1893 after which he was awarded his Second Mate's certificate. He was advanced to First Mate in 1897 and gained his Master's certificate in 1899.

On 27 January 1902, Thomas's father died. In October of the same year, Thomas gained a commission as sub-lieutenant in the Royal Naval Reserve and the following year married Annabel Foster of New Jersey in St Mary's, Wavertree. Following regulations, he attended training several times a year at HMS *Eagle* after which he was promoted to lieutenant in December 1906 and lieutenant commander in December 1914.

While in the RNR he trained in gunnery and torpedoes at HMS *Cambridge* and *Defiance* and on the outbreak of war was posted to *The Empress of Britain* in August 1914 when she became an armed merchant cruiser patrolling the Atlantic. He remained with her until May 1915 when he was appointed to HMS *Patuca*, another armed merchant cruiser patrolling with 10th Cruiser Squadron on the Northern Patrol. Throughout his time with these ships he was consistently described as a zealous and capable executive and gunnery officer who carried out his duties to the captain's entire satisfaction.

In March 1917 he was given command of HMS *Stephen Furness*. She was employed by the Admiralty as an armed boarding steamer which was used to search neutral ships for contraband. She was returning from Lerwick to

HMS *Stephen Furness*.

Liverpool for repairs when she was torpedoed by *UB 64* at 4.15 p.m. on 13 December 1917 and sank in three minutes with the loss of 100 lives including Thomas Winslow's. He was a week away from his 45th birthday, and had just been awarded the Reserve Decoration, which recognised long service.

Thomas is commemorated on panel 27 of Portsmouth Naval Memorial.

REGINALD JOHN WRATHALL

Private
8447
Inns of Court Officers' Training Corps
MTS 1900–09

Reginald John Wrathall was born on 24 January 1891. His father Henry Lonsdale Wrathall married Mary Alice Metcalfe in 1885. The couple had eight children, of whom only five survived to adulthood.

When Reginald was born, three of these survivors had already been born: Leon Earl in 1886, Constance Mary Lonsdale in 1887 and Blanche Evelyn in 1889. Their father was working as a 'General Produce and Chemical Broker's Salesman' and his family was living at 70 Quorn Street, Liverpool.

Reginald came to Merchant Taylors' as a boarder on 1 May 1900 and a Harrison Scholar having previously attended Elmshurst School, an independent preparatory school in Croydon where he had also been a boarder. The following year, the family was living at 247 Edge Lane, Liverpool.

During his time at Merchant Taylors', he gradually worked his way through his Oxford Local exams reaching a Pass in the Juniors in 1904 and in his Seniors in 1905 and in 1906, the year in which the family moved to Huyton. In 1907 he improved his performance in his Seniors to produce a 3rd Class Honours followed by a 2nd Class in 1908. In 1909 he obtained a Distinction in French, was awarded the Windermere Prize for English Literature and represented the school in the rugby XV in the 1908/09 season. He left the school on 29 July 1909 to attend Liverpool University where he studied engineering and spent time playing for the university rugby XV. While at university he lived at home at 'Frenchwood', Huyton. Unfortunately he failed his final exams and went to work as a cashier in the family firm of Wrathall & Co.

When war broke out, he tried to enlist in the army, was turned down on medical grounds but gained entry into the Inns of Court Officers' Training Corps in London in 1915. In 1917 he married Christine Beecham, daughter of Sir Joseph Beecham, Bart and sister of Sir Thomas Beecham, the conductor. The wedding took place at

St John's church in Hampstead. Reginald was moved to the main Officers' Training Corps unit in Berkhamstead where the recurrence of medical problems brought calls for him to be invalided out of the Officers' Training Corps but he was instead found a billet as assistant armourer for the battalion.

In 1918, he fell foul of the influenza epidemic which swept the country, developed pneumonia and died on 30 October 1918. He was buried on 1 November 1918 in grave 127 of St Bartholomew's churchyard in Roby.

FRANCIS ALAN WRAY

Second Lieutenant
8th Battalion King's (Liverpool Regiment)
MTS 1900–06

Tom and Elizabeth Wray had seven children before they moved to Liverpool, Maggie (born in 1886), Kate (1887), Francis Alan on 17 June 1890, Elsie (1892), Winifred (1894), Grace (1897) and Thomas (1898). The children were all born in Bradford. Tom was also a Yorkshireman, having been born in Knaresbrough in 1857. Elizabeth was from Norfolk.

Between 1898 and 1900, the family moved to Liverpool. In 1900, Francis entered Merchant Taylors'. The 1901 census shows them living at 5 Abbotsford Road, Crosby. Tom was an agent for a fruit broker, continuing the connection with the fruit trade he had had while in Bradford. Margaret seems to be away boarding at Storrs Hall School, Ingleton, while all the other children, including Francis were still at home. Late 1901 saw the birth of Tom and Elizabeth's last child, Wilfrid Austin, who died aged 7 months on 13 June 1902. Francis left Merchant Taylors' in 1906.

In 1911 the family was still living in Abbotsford Road. The eldest daughter, Margaret, had returned home and was working as a cookery teacher. Kate was also a teacher. Francis, aged 20, was a clerk in a broker's office.

On the outbreak of war, Francis enlisted with the King's (Liverpool Regiment) as a private, number 2217 and arrived in France on 21 February 1915. He was commissioned as a second lieutenant in the Liverpool Regiment with effect from 19 December 1916. The 8th (Irish) Battalion of the King's (Liverpool Regiment) at this time formed part of 165th Brigade, 55th (West Lancashire) Division and at the end of July 1917 they were near Wieltje. At 8.30 a.m. on 31 July 1917 they 'went over the top' and were subjected to heavy fire, which eventually caused them to retire. They had lost seven officers and 27 other ranks killed, 200 wounded and 88 missing. The battalion had been reduced to two officers and 160 men. Francis was among those killed/missing.

Francis Alan Wray has no known grave and is commemorated on panels 4 and 6 of the Ypres (Menin Gate) Memorial.

Francis had married Ethel Mary Mosses in early 1917. His 19-year-old brother Thomas was killed in action just a few weeks later on 4 September 1917 while serving with the Royal Flying Corps.

JOHN CROSBY WRIGHT
B ENG

Lieutenant
Royal Garrison Artillery
MTS 1901–10

John's father, Henry Edwin Wright, was born in Scarborough in 1854 and came to Liverpool where, by 1881, he was living in Everton and working as a stevedore. On 9 August 1887, in Glasgow, he married Catherine Chapman, a native of Dumbarton, and by 1891 they had two sons: Edwin George Chapman (born 1888) and Henry Campbell (born 1890).

By 1891, Henry had become a master stevedore employing several men and he and his family were living at 12 Trinity Road, Bootle along with two servants. John Crosby Wright was their third son, born on 3 December 1891.

By 1901, the family had moved and taken up residence at 47 Balliol Road, still in Bootle and John was attending Newlands (Girls') College, Bootle before moving on to Merchant Taylors'.

John entered Merchant Taylors' on 17 December 1901 following his two brothers who both seem to have arrived at the school in 1899. While at the school, he played for the rugby XV between 1908 and 1910 where he played on the wing but was deemed to be 'not fast enough to score much'. He also occasionally played for the 1st XI.

He left school in 1910 and went to Liverpool University to study engineering. He was registered as an engineering student in the 1911 census return, which showed that his family were still living at 47 Balliol Road, Bootle. His brother Edwin had left school in 1906 and by 1911 had become a solicitor's articled clerk while Henry, who left in the same year, had become an assistant stevedore.

While at university, John honed his skills by becoming a sapper in the Royal Fortress Engineers. He graduated with a Bachelor of Engineering degree just prior to the start of the war.

On the outbreak of war, no doubt helped by his practical experience with the RFE, he was quickly granted a commission, being gazetted as second lieutenant with the Royal Garrison Artillery (1st Heavy Battery, West Lancashire Royal Garrison Artillery) with effect from 29 August 1914.

He was promoted to lieutenant on 15 September 1915 and was sent overseas at the beginning of 1916, probably arriving in France on 26 January as the battery (of four 4.7-inch guns) left the 55th Division in December 1915, joining 57th Division and proceeded to France as an independent unit to join 29th Heavy Artillery Brigade.

On 7 April 1917 he was attached as liaison officer to the Canadians with whom he was acting as forward observation officer in an attack on Vimy Ridge. He continued in this capacity until 9 April at which time the telephone line with which he reported his observations was cut. He had with him two telephonists, one wounded, so he elected to crawl into the open himself to make repairs. While returning he was hit by a machine-gun bullet and in spite of medical help in the nearby trench he died shortly afterwards, on 10 April.

Presumably his grave was lost in the subsequent fighting as he is commemorated on bay 1 of the Arras Memorial.

FREDERICK YORKE

Lieutenant
Royal Air Force
MTS 1907–12

Frederick Yorke was the youngest child of Henry Lefroy Yorke and his wife Margaret (formerly Warrington) who were married in 1882 in Liverpool.

Henry was a Wesleyan Methodist minister who moved around from one circuit to another which accounts for his children being born in several locations. His first son, Warrington, was born in Lancaster in 1883 and was followed by Courtenay in Blackpool in 1884; Donald and Roy in Greenock, born 1887 and 1888 respectively; Margaret in Liverpool in 1889; and finally Frederick in Prestwich on 19 May 1894.

In 1901, Frederick, his parents, brothers and sister were living in The Manse, 18 Brighton Road, Rhyl. While he was living in Rhyl, Frederick attended a private school, Epworth College.

Frederick entered Merchant Taylors' on 17 September 1907, being the only member of the family to attend. The governors awarded him a Harrison Scholarship.

In 1908 at the age of 14 he obtained a 1st Class in the Oxford Local Junior exam. The following year he was awarded the Molyneux prize for Junior Divinity and repeated his performance in the Oxford Local Junior exams gaining a distinction in chemistry. In 1911 he was awarded the Davis Prize for Mathematics and in 1912 the Arthur Jackson Memorial Prize for Science, the Tyler Prize for Divinity and the 'Great Crosby' Scholarship.

In addition to his academic talents, Frederick was a sportsman, representing the school at both rugby and cricket in 1911/12. At cricket he headed the list of catchers with 9 and was the team's honorary secretary. In *The School Review's* 'Characters of the XI', it says: '[He] was dogged by misfortune as a batsman throughout the season. Was well worth his place for his fielding alone, brought off many smart catches. He might with advantage to his side have been given more opportunities with the bat.' Being cited as an example of keenness and untiring energy, he was also awarded his rugby colours.

In 1911 the family was living at 16 Wellington Road, Birkenhead. Warrington Yorke, at the age of 27, was the Director of the Liverpool School of Tropical Medicine, the beginning of a distinguished career which would find him appointed a Fellow of the Royal Society in 1932. Courtenay was senior demonstrator of anatomy at Liverpool University, he would become an ear, nose and throat surgeon and a Fellow of the Royal College of Surgeons. Donald was working as a clerk and Roy was a commercial traveller. Margaret, at 21 years of age, was still living at home and unmarried. Frederick was still at school.

Frederick left school on 31 July 1912 and went on to King's College, Cambridge with a science scholarship of £80 per annum.

Originally enlisting in the Cheshire Yeomanry early in the war, Frederick was commissioned as a second lieutenant into the 6th Battalion Cheshire Regiment with effect from 3 March 1915. He went to France on 23 July 1915.

After nearly two years as an officer of the Cheshires, he moved to the Royal Flying Corps, being gazetted 'Flying Officer Observer' with seniority on 5 April 1917. On 1 July 1917 he was promoted to lieutenant while remaining seconded to the RFC.

Frederick Yorke survived the war only to be killed in a flying accident at Ashington on 13 January 1919 while with 36 Squadron. Yorke and Lieutenant Harold Croudace collided while flying in a mist. They were flying Sopwith Pup scouting biplanes close together when the engine of the higher one stopped and it dropped onto the lower one. Both planes spiralled to the ground and the pilots died shortly afterwards.

Frederick is buried in Bishopwearmouth Cemetery in grave 20 CC 2094.

Francis Herbert Zacharias

Second Lieutenant
3rd Battalion attached 1st Battalion South Wales Borderers
MTS 1895–1900

Francis's father, Ernest Robert Zacharias, was German by birth, or more strictly, as he was born in 1839, Prussian. He was born in Danzig, modern-day Gdansk, Poland and emigrated to England some time before 1861 when he settled in London as a commercial clerk. Between 1871 and 1879 he moved from London to the north-west of England where, on 4 July 1879 he married Charlotte Amelia Ashley at Holy Trinity church, Southport. They had five children: John (born 1880), Marie (1882), Frederick (1883), Francis, born on 2 November 1885 in Waterloo, Liverpool, and Helen (1888).

Almost exactly a year after Francis was born, on 3 November 1886, his father became a naturalised British subject.

At the time of his father's naturalisation and in 1891 when the census was taken the family was living at 9 Adelaide Terrace, Waterloo, one of a terrace of Georgian houses which faced the sea and dated from the 1830s. Francis's father was, at this time, employed as a cotton merchant.

Francis joined Merchant Taylors' in 1895 and left in 1900. He does not seem to have been a sportsman of note and his name does not appear in *The School Review.*

After school he entered the cotton trade and the 1901 census shows him working as a 'Clerk and Foreign Correspondent in the raw cotton trade'. The family had by this time moved to 29 Church Road, Waterloo and Francis's father had retired.

In 1909, Francis joined the 6th (Rifle) Battalion King's Liverpool Regiment, previously known as the Liverpool Rifles and helped to recruit a number of Old Boys to the unit. He successfully took part in shooting competitions at Altcar and Bisley.

Domestically, little had changed by 1911; the family was living at the same address and the three youngest children, Frederick, Francis and Helen, were still living at home.

On 3 June 1912, Francis's father died aged 73, still living in Church Road. He seems not to have died a wealthy man, leaving an estate valued at only £5 by 1912 values.

By the outbreak of war in 1914, Francis seems to have risen to the rank of sergeant and went to France with 6th Battalion on 25 February 1915 landing at Le Havre. The battalion then moved to the Ypres area where it formed part of the 15th Brigade, 5th Division and took part in the second battle of Ypres and the attack on Hill 60.

In 1916, Francis married Gladys M. Eastwood, the daughter of William Hastings Eastwood, JP, a cotton merchant of Liverpool and on 2 June 1916, he was commissioned from an officer cadet battalion to be second lieutenant in the South Wales Borderers.

Returning to the front, he joined the battalion on 11 September in the area around Lozenge Wood and Henencourt Wood. Shortly afterwards he was serving as a bombing officer when he was killed in action on 25 September 1916. A fellow officer commented:

> When the enemy was preventing our men from building a barricade, Zacharias rallied his bomb throwers and kept the enemy at bay until the defence was completed. Then, ordering his men to retire, he was himself killed before he could reach the barricade, having covered the retirement of his men – a gallant deed which probably prevented the enemy from penetrating our lines.

His mother Charlotte died soon after, on 21 October 1916. On 23 April 1917, his widow had a baby boy, whom she named Francis James Zacharias. His widow, Gladys died in 1953. His son later qualified MD, FRCP, and died in 2006.

BIBLIOGRAPHY

WAR DIARIES
1st Battalion King's (Liverpool Regiment)
4th Battalion King's [Liverpool Regiment)
5th Battalion King's (Liverpool Regiment)
6th Battalion King's (Liverpool Regiment)
7th Battalion King's (Liverpool Regiment)
10th Battalion King's (Liverpool Regiment)
17th Battalion King's (Liverpool Regiment)
18th Battalion King's (Liverpool Regiment)
19th Battalion King's (Liverpool Regiment)
20th Battalion King's (Liverpool Regiment)
1st Battalion King's Own Scottish Borderers
1st Battalion Royal Warwickshire Regiment
1st Battalion South Wales Borderers
2nd Battalion South Lancashire Regiment
2nd Battalion Sussex Regiment
2nd/6th Battalion Duke of Wellington's (West Riding Regiment)
4th Battalion Royal Fusiliers
4th Battalion Royal Lancaster Regiment
5th Battalion South Lancashire Regiment
7th Battalion South Lancashire Regiment
8th Battalion South Lancashire Regiment
11th Battalion South Lancashire Regiment
12th Battalion Manchester Regiment
13th Battalion East Yorkshire Regiment
39th Machine Gun Battalion
96th Field Company, Royal Engineers

Log book of HMS *Carmania*
Log book of HMS *Arlanza*

BOOKS
Graham Maddox, *Liverpool Pals: 17th, 18th, 19th, 20th (Service) Battalions, The King's (Liverpool Regiment)* (Pen & Sword, 2008)
University of Edinburgh, *Roll of Honour 1914–1919* (Oliver and Boyd, 1921)

NEWSPAPERS AND PERIODICALS
The Crosby Herald
London Gazette
School Review, Merchant Taylors' School, Crosby 1890–1919

WEBSITES
www.ancestry.co.uk
www.cwgc.co.uk
www.1914-1918.net
www.merseysiderollofhonour.co.uk/

ARCHIVES
National Archives, Kew
Library and Archives of Canada
National Archives of Australia

INDEX

3rd Bn 82
King's Royal Rifle Corps:
  9th Bn 166
  16th Bn 57
  23rd Bn 86
  24th Bn 166
King's Shropshire Light Infantry
  200–201
Kingswood School 128
Kirklee 1914–18 Memorial, India 90
Kite Balloon Section 35
Knockaloe internment camp 147
Kut, siege of (1916) 58, 78, 133, 191

Lancashire Fusiliers:
  5th Bn 96, 158
  8th Bn 153
  2/8th Bn 70
Lancashire Hussar Yeomanry 79
Lancaster 76
Lancaster Grammar School 50
Langho 96
Le Cateau Military Cemetery 158
Leicestershire Regiment 75
Lijssenthoek Military Cemetery 79,
  195
Lincoln College, Oxford 105
Litherland 34, 35, 77, 78, 81
Liverpool 42, 44, 58, 59, 71, 91,
  147–48, 163, 166, 197
Liverpool Pals 46, 97, 161
Liverpool University 42, 63, 68, 81,
  108, 126, 147, 189, 203, 205
Locre (Loker) churchyard 182
London Regiment:
  3rd Bn 80
  14th Bn 42
  15th Bn 156–57
  1/18th Bn 138
  19th Bn 181
  28th Bn 77

London University 156
Loos, battle of (1915) 45, 48, 55, 69,
  99, 126, 139, 168, 174, 181, 194
Loos Memorial 55, 109, 139
Loyal North Lancashire Regiment 61
Ludwigshafen 64
Lys, battle of (1918) 20, 47

Machine Gun Corps 67, 99, 120,
  130, 134
  39th Bn 162, 163
Maidan, SS 182
Malvern College 46
Manchester Grammar School 39
Manchester Regiment:
  2/8th Bn 129
  12th Bn 111, 149
  16th Bn 31
Manchester University 39
Marama, SS 33
Marfaux British Cemetery 42
Marina School 179
Marine preparatory school 33
Martinpuich 111
Menin Gate *see* Ypres (Menin Gate)
  Memorial
Menin Road South Military Cemetery
  129
Merchant Taylors' War Memorial 11, *x*
Merchant Taylors' Girls' School 142,
  190
Merton College, Oxford 139
Merville Communal Cemetery 83
Mesopotamia 58, 78, 120, 133, 191,
  iv–v
Messines, battle of (1917) 99, 177,
  181
Middlesex Regiment 67
Military Cross 45, 54, 88, 106, 162–
  63, 164, 168, 181, *vi*
Mill Hill School 145